£18.99

Music for Children and Young People with Complex Needs

Oxford Music Education Series

Series editor: Janet Mills, *Research Fellow, Royal College of Music, London*

The *Oxford Music Education Series* presents concise, readable, and thought-provoking handbooks for all those involved in music education, including teachers, community musicians, researchers, policy-makers, and parents/carers. The series encompasses a wide range of topics and musical styles, and aims to provide 'food for thought' for all those looking to broaden their understanding and further develop their work. Written by acknowledged leaders of education who are passionate about their subject, the books present cutting-edge ideas and aim to stimulate good practice by showing the practical implications of research.

Recent titles in the Oxford Music Education Series

Music for Children and Young People with Complex Needs

Adam Ockelford

MUSIC DEPARTMENT

OXFORD
UNIVERSITY PRESS

OXFORD

UNIVERSITY PRESS

Great Clarendon Street, Oxford OX2 6DP, England
198 Madison Avenue, New York, NY 10016, USA

Oxford University Press is a department of the University of Oxford.
If furthers the University's aim of excellence in research, scholarship,
and education by publishing worldwide in

Oxford New York

Auckland Cape Town Hong Kong Karachi
Kuala Lumpur Madrid Melbourne Mexico City
Nairobi New Delhi Shanghai Taipei Toronto

With offices in

Argentina Austria Brazil Chile Czech Republic France Greece
Guatemala Hungary Italy Japan Poland Portugal Singapore
South Korea Switzerland Thailand Turkey Ukraine Vietnam

Oxford is a registered trade mark of Oxford University Press in the
UK and in certain other countries

British Library Cataloguing-in-Publication Data
Data available

Library of Congress Cataloging-in-Publication Data
Ockelford, Adam, 1959–
  Music for children and young people with complex needs / Adam
Ockelford.
    p. cm. – (Oxford music education series)
  Includes bibliographical references and index.
  ISBN-13: 978–0–19–322301–1
  1. School music–Instruction and study–Great Britain.
  2. Special education–Great Britain.   3. Children with disabilities
  –Music–Instruction and study.   4. Youth with disabilities
  –Music–Instruction and study.   I. Title
  MT17.035 2008
  371.92'80487–dc22   2008003322

10 9 8 7 6 5

Typeset by RefineCatch Limited, Bungay, Suffolk
Printed in Great Britain by Ashford Colour Press Ltd

Dedicated to the memory of Janet Mills, 1954–2007

Foreword

Back in the 1990s, when I first started putting on concerts for children with disabilities with the Orchestra of St John's, I was intrigued by the notion that music could make a real difference to young people with complex needs. Having a son with autism, I knew from personal experience that such children were likely to find the world a confusing, even frightening, place. So what effect would music have?

From the first concert, it was apparent that we were on to something. The pieces we had performed time and again took on a whole new meaning. As we presented our repertoire to groups of new young listeners, wondering how they would react, it was *us* who were moved. We witnessed, first hand, just how powerful an impact music could have on children who usually could not (or would not) engage with others—whose fractured perception of the world seemed to make everyday communication well-nigh impossible.

Our principal cellist was enchanted by the radiant smile that spread across Zoe's face as she reclined motionless in her wheelchair, listening attentively to his solo melody in 'The Swan', as it floated serenely above the instrumental accompaniment. And everyone in the orchestra had to laugh when 8-year-old Tim grabbed the baton and pushed me out the way so that he could conduct the *William Tell* overture—grinning wildly, his whole body pulsing with the beat. What a sense of rhythm! Afterwards, his parents told us that he had never before taken the lead in a social situation, let alone in one as public as this. The music just blew away his inhibitions.

Magical interactions like these between the players and their special audiences continued to occur. The children's vivid—sometimes visceral—reactions to the sheer sound of the orchestra in full flow proved enormously refreshing to us seasoned professional musicians. They made us think about our repertoire, the way we played, and how we could make our performances more spontaneous, more responsive to our young listeners' kaleidoscopic responses to extended patterns in sound. Above all, the children made us want to gain a better understanding of how they 'hear' music—particularly those with complex needs, who are rarely able to express their thoughts and feelings in words. Do these young people perceive what we are playing in broadly the same way as we do, or is music somehow different for them? Do they all react in similar ways, or do they each respond uniquely to music? What can they remember from one concert to another? Can they make progress? How can we use music to help them develop in other areas? And how can we foster the real musical talent that some of them (like Tim) seem to display?

Until now, these questions have remained largely that—queries to which no answers have readily been available. But now, at last, thanks to advances in cognitive science and musicology, solutions are beginning to emerge, and Adam Ockelford captures much of the latest thinking in this book. Crucially, he views both special *needs* and special *abilities* within a common framework, as part of a single continuum of musical achievement—all of which is equally valid, and potentially of equal value. Ockelford contends that by viewing musical development as a series of abilities that build upon one another coherently, it is possible for practitioners to see the way ahead and foster progress wherever possible. His approach is not just theoretical, though, and there are plenty of practical suggestions to enable teachers, therapists, parents, and carers to engage musically with young people, whatever their level of attainment.

And finally, there are some unexpected spin-offs. It becomes clear that by getting to understand what makes children with complex needs 'tick' musically, we can get a firmer grasp of just what 'musicality' means in general. By working out how music makes sense to young people with learning difficulties, we can glean fresh insights into how music is comprehensible to everyone. And by investigating how music stirs the emotions of children in the early stages of development, we can fathom more deeply how music is able to move us all.

John Lubbock
Founder and Conductor of the Orchestra of St John's
Founder, *Music for Autism*

Acknowledgements

I would like to express my gratitude to all those who have been involved in the production of this book, particularly Janet Mills, the Series Editor; Graham Welch, Sally Zimmermann, Evangelos Himonides, and other members of the 'Sounds of Intent' research team; Linda Pring and Derek Paravicini; Kyproulla Markou; and Kristen Thorner, Mary Chandler, and their colleagues at OUP.

About the author

Adam Ockelford has had a lifelong interest in music as a composer, performer, teacher, researcher, and writer. After graduating from the Royal Academy of Music in London in the early 1980s, he took up a post working with children who had special educational needs at Linden Lodge School in Wimbledon. The fact that many of the pupils, despite their disabilities, had exceptional musical abilities, prompted him to develop an interest in music psychology, in particular the central question of how music 'works'. In the 1990s Adam took up the post of Music Education Advisor at the RNIB (Royal National Institute of Blind People), where he subsequently fulfilled a number of roles including, from 2005, Director of Education. At the same time he gained a growing reputation as a researcher and writer through his activity as a part-time Research Fellow at the Institute of Education, London, and in October 2007 he took up the full-time position of Professor of Music at Roehampton University. Here, he continues to work actively with young people who have special musical abilities and needs, and to undertake research with them. Adam is Secretary of the Society for Education, Music and Psychology Research (SEMPRE), which publishes the journal *Psychology of Music*; Chair of Soundabout, an Oxford-based charity that supports music provision for children with complex needs; and founder of The AMBER Trust, which provides music bursaries for blind and partially sighted children.

Contents

Figures

Figs 6.3–6.7 and 6.11 are © Adam Ockelford 1996.

Tables

Music examples

List of abbreviations

AP	absolute pitch
APMT	Association of Professional Music Therapists
ASD	Autistic Spectrum Disorder
BSL	British Sign Language
BSMT	British Society for Music Therapy
CP	cerebral palsy
DCSF	Department for Children, Schools and Families
DfEE	Department for Education and Employment
DfES	Department for Education and Skills
FOCUS	For Our Children's Unique Sight
ICT	Information and Communication Technology
LA	Local Authority
LCA	Leber Congenital Amaurosis
LEA	Local Education Authority
MLD	moderate learning difficulties
MSI	multisensory impairment
ONH	optic nerve hypoplasia
PMLD	profound and multiple learning difficulties
PROMISE	The Provision of Music in Special Education (research initiative)
QCA	Qualifications and Curriculum Authority
RNIB	Royal National Institute of Blind People
ROP	retinopathy of prematurity
SLD	severe learning difficulties
SOD	septo-optic dysplasia
YAMSEN	Yorkshire Association for Music and Special Education Needs

Introduction

Who are the children and young people with 'complex needs'?

The beginning of wisdom, it is said, is to call things by their right names, and certainly, for children and young people who require educational resources over and above those that are typically provided for the majority, being categorized seems to be a fact of life. On what other basis (it is argued) could specialist services be organized to meet the needs of those they serve, effectively and efficiently? Obversely, on an individual level, labels are sometimes viewed as the keys that can unlock entitlement. But (ethical considerations aside) the reality is that many pupils and students do not fit neatly into categories that are constructed according to medical or functional deficit models, and this is particularly true of children and young people whose plurality of special needs interact with each other as they impact on learning and development (cf. Lauchlan and Boyle 2007).

Here, we will follow the pragmatic line that labels of disability or special educational need are a useful servant but a poor master. They are valuable as a reflection of the conceptual shorthand that enables a book such as this to be written and hopefully for it to be of benefit to a broadly based audience, but one should always be mindful of the fact that children and young people need to be judged first and foremost in terms of their individual abilities, requirements, wishes, and propensities. So the label 'complex needs' may provide something of the *context* for planning educational provision but not, ultimately, its *content* for a particular child or young person.

Although the term 'complex needs' is widely and commonly used, it is open to a range of interpretations. In Victoria, Australia, for example, the label is taken to include 'adolescents and adults who may experience various combinations of mental illness, intellectual disability, acquired brain injury, physical disability, behavioural difficulties, social isolation, family dysfunction, and alcohol or other substance abuse'.[1] In Alberta, Canada, children with complex

---

[1] *Responding to People with Multiple and Complex Needs Project: Client Profile Data and Case Studies Report*, State Government of Victoria, 2003.

needs are defined as requiring 'significant extraordinary care due to the severity of their impairment(s) and require services from more than one ministry.[2] Those who require such services may include [those] with multiple impairments, complex mental health and health issues and/or severe behavioural needs.' In the UK, children and young people with complex needs are said to have 'a number of discrete needs—relating to their health, education, welfare, development, home environment ... [that] may be life-long.[3] Different needs tend to interact, exacerbating their impact on the child's development and well-being. Children with higher levels of need are often described as [having] "severe and complex needs" or ... "significant and complex needs"'.

The breadth of these definitions is reflected in the evidence presented to the House of Commons Education and Skills Select Committee's Enquiry into Special Educational Needs (2005–6), where it is evident that different agencies interpret 'complex needs' according to their particular area of concern. So, in employing this term, some groups appear to have in mind those with social, emotional, and behavioural difficulties, for example, whose 'volatility raises issues of health and safety', while others, such as the UK-based disability-focused organizations Scope, Sense, and the RNIB, tend to use the label to refer to children and young people with aggregations of severe, or profound and multiple learning difficulties. It is in this, latter, sense that the term 'complex needs' will be used in this book.

This, of course, begs another question: what is meant by 'severe learning difficulties' ('SLD') and 'profound and multiple learning difficulties' ('PMLD')? Again, there are no agreed definitions, although in undertaking a research project into the provision of music education in special schools in England, the following descriptions were suggested and accepted without demur by the 50 or so schools that participated (Welch, Ockelford, and Zimmermann 2001). First, it was proposed that, in round terms, 'pupils with PMLD have profound global developmental delay, such that cognitive, sensory, physical, emotional and social development are in the very early stages (as in the first 12 months of usual development)', and second that 'pupils with SLD have severe global developmental delay, such that cognitive, sensory, physical, emotional and

---

[2] *Policy Framework for Services for Children and Youth with Special and Complex Needs and their Families*, Alberta Children and Youth Initiative Partners, <http://www.child.gov. ab.ca/acyi/pdf/User-Friendly%20Policy%20Framework.pdf>.

[3] As part of the *Every Child Matters* initiative; details to be found at <http://www.every childmatters.gov.uk/deliveringservices/multiagencyworking/glossary/?asset=glossary& id=22365>.

social development are in the early stages (as in the first 12 to 30 months of usual development)'.

These are the descriptors that will be adopted here, implying that children and young people with complex needs (as defined above in terms of SLD and PMLD) are likely to be functioning well below their chronological age in all areas, although, as we shall see, some have markedly uneven profiles of development.

In terms of numbers, pupils with SLD or PMLD make up only around 0.5 per cent of the school population in England.[4] Here, they are largely educated in special schools—around 29,540 as opposed to 10,970 in mainstream[5]—a ratio of about 3:1.[6]

Music for children and young people with complex needs

Whatever the context in which it occurs—special or mainstream—music education for children and young people with complex needs is still a pedagogical infant. To put this in perspective, in the UK, the statutory entitlement of those with the greatest intellectual disabilities to any form of education is relatively recent, and only started to occur following the Education (Handicapped Children) Act 1970 and the Education (Mentally Handicapped Children) (Scotland) Act 1974. However, in the past four decades or so, the role of the music teacher, as it is generally understood, has not evolved to include the expertise necessary to work in this highly specialized area: as we shall see, this has tended to be the province of music therapists. The problem has been compounded by the lack of nationally recognized courses for music teachers wishing to work with young people with SLD or PMLD, the almost total absence of relevant research, and a dearth of a pertinent literature. Those books that have been written concerning music education for children and young people with disabilities—the more venerable of which being now outmoded in many respects—make little or no reference to those with severe or profound learning difficulties: see, for example, Dobbs (1966), Bailey (1973), Dickinson (1978), Wood (1983/1993), Childs (1996), Streeter (1993/2001), Adamek and Darrow (2005), and Jaquiss and Paterson (2005).

---

[4] DfES data (2006).

[5] Since the categories SLD and PMLD lack nationally agreed definitions, and since other categories (such as autistic spectrum disorder) may include children and young people with learning difficulties, these figures should be treated with some caution.

[6] DfES data (2006).

Aims and structure of the book

It is in this context that the current book was written and is offered to policy makers, planners, and practitioners working in the field of music and learning difficulties, although parents and carers with an interest in the subject may also find material that is of relevance. It is the first volume to be devoted solely to the subject of music education for children and young people with complex needs, and it takes a consciously novel tack. Solutions to the issues that are identified are embedded in a new psycho-musicological theory[7] that seeks to explain how music 'makes sense' to all of us (Ockelford 2005*a*). This stance is adopted in an effort to bring conceptual unity to an area of work that, like many disciplines that are still in the early stages of their evolution, has been characterized by idiosyncratic, piecemeal, and even conflicting approaches— among which, for sure, are some of individual value. Accordingly, the two main aims of *Music for Children and Young People with Complex Needs* are, first, to offer a coherent model that can be used to underpin education *in* music and education *through* music for this group of young people, and, second, to use this model to contextualize practical advice for teachers, teaching assistants, and others.

The book is divided into four parts. Part I, 'Issues', sets out three of the greatest challenges in the field: the patchy nature of music-educational provision for children and young people with complex needs; the confusion over the role of 'teachers' and 'therapists', and, consequently, what constitutes 'education' and 'therapy' for this group; and difficulties with the framework of music education for those with severe or profound learning difficulties that was published by the Qualifications and Curriculum Authority (QCA) in 2001. Although this framework has an English purview, there is no evidence elsewhere of a coherent, evidence-based music curriculum appropriate to the potential levels of attainment and progress of pupils with SLD or PMLD. Hence the observations that are made have wider applicability.

Part II, 'A New Model', presents the theory of musical understanding that will be used to inform the potential solutions and discussions of these that follow. The theory grapples with the question of just how music 'works': of how it is that abstract patterns in sound are able to convey meaning, and what the characteristics of that meaning are. It has three important implications for *Music for Children and Young People with Complex Needs*. First, that the unrelenting (though typically subconscious) search for different manifestations of repetition and variation must be fundamental to music cognition. Second, the

---

[7] That is, one that uses psychological information and ideas in a musicological context.

pursuit of this form of pattern-recognition must be embedded in music development. Third, promoting this necessary aspect of musical thinking should be central to curricula that seek to nurture the advancement of musical abilities.

Part III, 'Addressing Special Musical Needs', offers a model of musical development for children and young people with SLD and PMLD, and shows how this can be used as a basis for curriculum planning and delivery, and to assess attainment and progress, both for musical activities and other areas of engagement in which music is a permeating strand. This section explains how those in the early stages of development can represent and communicate about music, and convey their musical preferences.

Part IV, 'Identifying and fostering special musical abilities', examines the issue found across the learning disability spectrum of uneven profiles of development, in which one facet or more of musicality evolves markedly beyond other skills or domains of knowledge. Occasionally, several narrow peaks of ability (such as auditory processing, memory, and motor skills) arise together and are fused through exceptional motivation, resulting in the emergence of a so-called 'musical savant'. Young people with capacities such as these present particular challenges to teachers and the educational systems within which they operate, and this section includes accounts of a number of tried and tested pedagogical strategies.

Hence (inevitably) *Music for Children and Young People with Complex Needs* covers a range of topics embedded in a variety of disciplines, including special educational needs, music, music education, music therapy, musicology, and developmental and cognitive psychology. These are likely to correspond idiosyncratically to different readers' areas of particular interest and expertise, and two strategies are adopted to minimize the potentially negative impact that this may have. First, all specialist language and concepts are explained in footnotes, with extensive references to other literature and relevant websites. Second, as well as being tied in to the overall narrative thread of the book, each chapter is designed to stand alone. So, teachers faced for the first time with the responsibility of educating a musical savant may wish to concentrate their attention on Part IV, for example, whereas a therapist seeking to support those with profound and multiple learning difficulties may find Part III of most relevance.

Finally, it is hoped that the book will be of interest not only to those working with and children and young people with complex needs, but to *all* those engaged in music education. This is because although an understanding of those with special needs should be informed by the way that the majority of children and young people develop, it is equally clear that there are lessons for us all from those whose abilities or disabilities are at the extremes.

PART I

ISSUES

Chapter 1

Promises, promises

Introduction

In 1992, the Royal National Institute of Blind People (RNIB)[1] set up a Music Education Advisory Service to support visually impaired children and young people, including those with other disabilities, their families, the practitioners who work with them, and policy makers. In 1998, the data from the first five years of the service's operation were reviewed informally, and analysis of the hundreds of contacts that had been made indicated the existence of a widespread belief that music has a special value for children and young people with learning difficulties—both as a unique medium of self-expression, and as a means of promoting wider learning, development, and well-being. However, there was no information nationally as to what music provision was made for these young people, although it was clear that there were two main forms of professional input: music therapy and music education.

RNIB's wide-ranging connections with special schools across the country suggested that the provision of music therapy varied considerably: some establishments had none at all, whereas others used it to complement or even substitute for the music-educational curriculum. However, it was unclear how these models were distributed across the hundreds of schools in the UK that were thought to make provision for pupils with learning difficulties.

In terms of music education, it appeared that provision was patchy too. In some schools, there was appropriate input from a teacher with a background in music, who coordinated the involvement of other staff, together ensuring that music functioned as a coherent strand in the wider curriculum. In others, there appeared to be little engagement in musical activities. This anecdotal view was subsequently supported by Ofsted's[2] review of Special Education, 1994–8, which was published in 1999. This noted that in a third of the inspections of special schools, secure units, and pupil referral units, insufficient

---

[1] The RNIB is the UK's leading charity for people with sight loss—see <http://www.rnib.org.uk>.

[2] Ofsted is the official body for inspecting schools in England—see <http://www.ofsted.gov.uk>.

music lessons were seen to provide secure judgements of pupils' progress, or that music was not taught. Where it was possible to make a judgement, progress was satisfactory or better in only just over half of schools. The implication of these figures is that only one third of special schools were observed to have effective music education provision.

Ofsted found that, across the curriculum, teachers' lack of subject knowledge reduced the overall quality of teaching in almost half of special schools, with insufficient subject-specific in-service training taking place. Moreover, there were often difficulties in recruiting staff with a background in music—especially in secondary and all-age schools. Almost half of schools were reported to have insufficient specialist accommodation for music, which limited the range of pupils' experiences and the standards that they could attain. These findings existed despite the entitlement of all pupils in England to music education as part of the National Curriculum at Key Stages 1, 2, and 3.[3]

Aim and objectives of the PROMISE[4] research

It was evident that, if music provision for pupils with learning difficulties—and particularly those with complex needs—were to be improved, a necessary preliminary stage was to gather detailed and reliable information as to what was happening in schools. It was with this broad aim in mind that the 'PROMISE' research project was set up: a joint initiative between the Institute of Education, University of London,[5] and the RNIB (Welch, Ockelford, and Zimmermann 2001; Ockelford, Welch, and Zimmermann 2002). In relation to the music provision offered by schools for children and young people with SLD and PMLD, the objectives were to:

+ identify examples of practice that were considered to be of value;

+ determine any significant areas of concern;

+ understand better the range of formal and informal opportunities for music within schools and their wider communities;

---

[3] In England, the National Curriculum is divided into four stages: Key Stage 1—5 to 7 years old; Key Stage 2—7 to 11 years old; Key Stage 3—11 to 14 years old; Key Stage 4—14 to 16 years old. For further information see, for example, <http://www.teachernet.gov.uk/teachinginengland>.

[4] The 'PRovision Of Music In Special Education'.

[5] The Institute of Education, University of London, undertakes research, teacher training, higher degrees, and consultancy in education and education-related areas of social science—see <http://ioewebserver.ioe.ac.uk/ioe>.

- gain insights into levels of teacher expertise and their professional development;
- learn more about the nature of the resources available; and
- clarify and review the nature of the distinction that may be made between education *in* music and education *through* music, as well as between music *therapy* and music *education.*

Although the work was to be undertaken in England, the research team believed that the findings would have wider relevance, since there was nothing in RNIB's experience or the literature to suggest that provision was significantly more advanced elsewhere.

Approach

The research was undertaken in three phases. In Phase 1, a sample of 10 per cent of schools was randomly selected from those identified on behalf of the then Department for Education and Employment (DfEE)[6] as catering for pupils with SLD (375 schools), PMLD (18) or MSI (multisensory impairment) (4) in England—a total of 397. These schools were sent a questionnaire, designed to gather data that would allow the research team to clarify key issues concerning the nature and purpose of the music provision that was made for their pupils. Phase 2 involved visiting a small number of schools that had responded to the questionnaire in order to explore their responses in more detail, observe timetabled activities for music, and follow one or two pupils throughout the school day. The latter element was intended to enable the researchers to gain an impression of what the complete musical experience of the young people at school may be like, through noting all of a pupil's encounters with music. In Phase 3, a revised questionnaire was distributed to all 397 schools.

In total, 52 schools (13 per cent) responded either to the first questionnaire or the second or to both. Forty-six (88 per cent) of these were maintained by their Local Education Authority (LEA) and the remainder were non-maintained or independent. Of the 52 schools, 50 were designated as catering for pupils with SLD, one was classified as making provision for pupils with PMLD, and one for those with MSI. However, on analysing the data, it quickly became apparent that the designation of the schools often did not necessarily reflect the nature of their intake accurately. Nor could it have done, since there were no nationally agreed definitions of the terms 'SLD' and 'PMLD'. Hence an

---

[6] The nearest equivalent currently being the 'DCFS'—the UK government's 'Department for Children, Schools and Families'—see <http://www.dcfs.gov.uk>.

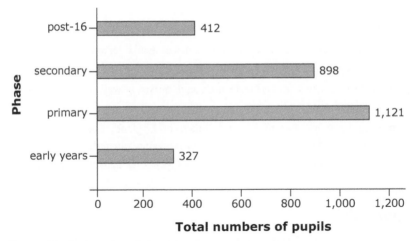

Fig. 1.1 Distribution of pupils by phase

early task in the project was to ascribe meanings to these labels, based on the researchers' own experience (see p. 2 above). In the event, these definitions were accepted without question by the schools that participated.

Of the 52 schools, 43 provided information about the age ranges of their 2,578 pupils (a little under 10 per cent of the total estimated to be in special schools today; cf. p. 3). Fig. 1.1 shows the distribution by phase. The majority of pupils (2,109 or 73 per cent) were of statutory school age (5–16 years). Around half the 43 schools (21 or 49 per cent) were 'all age' (from the Early Years to Post-16), and only two were single phase—something which, as we shall see, has implications for the breadth of expertise demanded of music teachers.

Additional Information from Ofsted Reports, 2000–5

To supplement and update the findings of the original PROMISE research, information has subsequently been distilled from the music sections of 50 Ofsted reports on special schools that make provision for pupils with SLD, PMLD, or both, and this is included, where relevant, below. These reports were carried out under Section 10 of the School Inspections Act 1996 in the period 2000–5, and each relates to a school in a different LEA[7] region, selected at random from across England.

---

[7] That is, 'Local Education Authority', now replaced by 'LA's ('Local Authorities').

In summary, the findings of these reports are as follows. Insufficient evidence had been obtained in nine cases (18 per cent) to enable inspectors to make an overall judgement. In the remainder of the schools, music provision was deemed to be unsatisfactory in only one instance. Hence it can be inferred that 80 per cent of music education offered to pupils with SLD or PMLD was known to be satisfactory or better. Although the comparison is not an exact one, this appears to represent a considerable improvement upon the position which Ofsted reported in the 1990s. However, this assumption should be treated with caution for two reasons. First, in only 40 per cent of the 2000–5 reports was music provision said to have improved to a degree that the inspectors regarded as 'satisfactory' or better. Second, many of the observations that are cited in the reports—that are used as evidence to inform the overall judgements of teaching and learning that are made—are often so bland ('In lessons pupils have the opportunity to perform by singing or playing instruments'), lacking in any form of wider comparator ('PMLD pupils respond well to music'), or downright nonsensical ('pupils learnt rhythm, tempo, pitch and instruments') that the validity of the findings must be in doubt. These concerns notwithstanding, other elements of the reports—those pertaining to resources, for example (that do not rely on specialist music-educational knowledge)—do appear to be more securely based on credible evidence, and it is largely from these that inferences will be drawn in what follows.

Key findings from PROMISE
The music curriculum

Almost all schools reported that they based their music lessons on the National Curriculum (for 5- to 14-year-olds) across each age phase, including the Early Years group (for which the National Curriculum was not then intended).[8] This

---

[8] The National Curriculum is mentioned on only eight occasions (in 16 per cent) of the 50 Ofsted reports (2000–5), and from the commentaries, which frequently verge on the vacuous, it is simply not possible to gain an overall impression of the music curricula that the schools were following. Take, for example, the following commentary, which, following the first sentence, manages to achieve complete freedom of musical content. 'Teachers provide pupils with many opportunities to listen to music, sing and play instruments. These opportunities match pupils' capabilities well and therefore all pupils are able to achieve well and make good progress in acquiring new skills and understanding. The subject curriculum is well structured and organized by an effective subject co-ordinator. There has been good improvement since the last inspection. Teachers' very good management of pupils and their classroom organization result in well planned and structured activities that pupils thoroughly enjoy. Therefore, with the significant input of education and care officers, who work very well with teachers, pupils are enabled to participate in all

was supplemented in most cases by schemes of work produced by the school itself. Of the schools with Early Years pupils, 40 per cent reported the use of Baseline assessment[9]—'creative development'. Over half extended this to classes beyond the Early Years. Twenty per cent of schools reported using 'Equals'[10] documents, which at the time included a creative development scheme of work. A few schools used schemes of work produced either by their own or another LEA. For post-16 students, two schools used the ASDAN[11] Creative Development scheme and one school used the Certificate of Achievement: Music.

Schools were asked whether the National Curriculum for Music was useful to them or not. Of the 21 that responded, nearly two out of three stated that it was, while one in five said that it was not, and the remainder commented on both positive and negative aspects. One school felt that the National Curriculum could be regarded as a good general framework that provided progression that 'takes us beyond just sing-along and play-along percussion sessions' but is 'not detailed or broken down enough for us'. Similarly, another school expressed the desire for a more detailed curriculum relevant to special needs to be produced that incorporated particular links to the more therapeutic uses of music. Since the PROMISE research was undertaken, the Qualifications and Curriculum Authority (QCA)[12] has produced the P-scale for music, which aims to show how access to the National Curriculum

---

activities. For instance, a class of Year 9 pupils with severe learning difficulties were able to respond to symbol/text cards that showed instructions such as "stop", "go", "quickly", and "quietly" because of their focused attention and the prompts of all staff.' Ironically, it is only when the inspector indicates how much music supports pupils' personal development (in the second half of this section of the report) that specific musical references start to appear. In the 50 reports as a whole, analysis indicates that accounts of purely *musical* activities—which are not present in every report—account for only 26 per cent of the texts.

[9] Baseline assessment was the statutory form of assessment in reception classes in England until 2002.

[10] 'Equals' is a national charity that is committed to improving the lives of children and young people with learning difficulties and disabilities through supporting high-quality education. Its mission is to promote, share, and reflect best practice in learning and teaching through collaborative working with practitioners and professionals at national, regional, and local level. See <http://www.equals.co.uk/home/index.asp>.

[11] ASDAN is an approved awarding body offering programmes and qualifications to develop key skills and life skills. See <http://www.asdan.co.uk>.

[12] The QCA is a non-departmental government body that seeks to regulate, develop, and modernize the curriculum, assessments, examinations, and qualifications in England—see <http://www.qca.org.uk>.

preceding Level 1 is possible. However, as we shall see in Chapter 3, it is arguable the extent to which this scheme fulfils its objectives.

In the view of music coordinators, the most successful activities in Early Years classrooms utilized action songs and involved the children playing simple instruments.[13] Similar activities were mentioned at Key Stages 1 and 2, with the addition of other types of instrument, including some tuned percussion. Coordinators referred to the introduction of keyboards at Key Stages 3 and 4, with more references to composing and performing activities, as well as mention of 'popular' and 'world' music for listening. It is of interest to note that most respondents provided detailed answers to the Early Years phase questions, while many repeated their initial responses with one or two additional features for age phases further up the school.

With regard to curriculum content, the following types of music were mentioned: pieces with a strong beat, pieces with repetition, chants, pieces with simple tunes, nursery rhymes, songs with names in, songs about animals, rounds, pop, jazz, and non-western styles. The musical techniques employed included performing, composing, and improvising.

Two head teachers commented on the lack of space for music on the timetable, with one believing that the increased emphasis on literacy and numeracy meant that less time was spent on music than had previously been the case. This view was echoed in one of the sample of 50 Ofsted reports (2000–5), where the school was reported to be 'compensating with an increase in the amount of music and singing in assembly and by bringing in outside performers such as a brass quintet and the band "Rock to Baroque"'.

In summary, at the time of the PROMISE research project and subsequently (based on the evidence of Ofsted reports), there appears to have been no common music curriculum in place for pupils with SLD and PMLD, references to the framework theoretically offered by the National Curriculum notwithstanding. Indeed, it seems that, nationally, music education provision for young people with complex needs has been characterized by diversity and idiosyncrasy. In some cases, approaches that have been developed in the context of Early Years appear to have been extended to later phases—on account, no doubt, of pupils' limited levels of functional development. However, as we shall see, extending the curriculum in this way risks failing to provide material that is appropriately challenging or age appropriate.

---

[13] Somewhat at odds with the comment above, that the National Curriculum 'takes us beyond just sing-along and play-along percussion sessions'!

Resources

With regard to accommodation, just under half the schools reported having a discrete music room. Two-thirds had multisensory rooms (in which sound and music activities took place) or other areas containing musical equipment.

Untuned percussion instruments typically formed the staple of schools' music-making resources, although autoharps, guitars, 'whirlies',[14] hand-chimes, and 'pentatonic percussion'[15] were also mentioned.[16] Small instruments like these were usually stored partly in a dedicated area and partly in individual classrooms. Unsurprisingly, then, a number of teachers reported that they spent considerable amounts of time moving instruments from one place to another. This was summed up in the remarks of one: 'After twenty years of carrying instruments around schools, I am resigned to doing it forever! I just get on with it. It is part of the job.' Over half the schools had a piano, with twelve having more than one, and a number of schools mentioned the use of keyboards in class music lessons with secondary-aged pupils. Only one school reported having no keyboard of any type.[17]

The main forms of music technology used across the school day were what are best described as 'domestic' sound reproduction systems—namely CD and tape players.[18] Most classrooms were said to have some means of playing recorded music, though five schools stated that they had no stereo system at all. The quality of the audio equipment that was observed during visits to schools in Phase 2 of the PROMISE research was variable, and its utilization was not always well thought through, with speakers often placed too far away from pupils to make it easy for them to concentrate on the music that was being played. Schools' collections of CDs and audio cassettes typically reflected a broad range of musical styles, including 'world', popular, and classical music, tracks specifically intended for multisensory work and children's tapes (such as nursery rhymes and 'educational' music recordings).

---

[14] The whirly is a corrugated plastic tube that produces pure tones when it is twirled around.

[15] Pentatonic percussion derives from the pedagogical ideas of Carl Orff—see <http://www.orff.de>.

[16] Only 38 of the 50 Ofsted reports made any reference to musical instruments. In these, percussion was mentioned in 36 cases (95 per cent), wind instruments of different types were noted four times (13 per cent), the guitar four times (11 per cent), strings once, and the piano once (3 per cent). 'Junk' instruments were alluded to twice (5 per cent).

[17] Eight schools (21 per cent) of the 38 in which instruments were mentioned by Ofsted were reported to have keyboards.

[18] CDs and CD players were referred to eight times (16 per cent) in the 50 Ofsted reports (2000–5) and there were five references to tapes (10 per cent).

At the time of the PROMISE research, there were two main systems available for converting movement to sound by means of an ultrasonic beam, which served as a switch (or a series of switches) to control a MIDI system. These were 'Soundbeam'[19] and 'MIDIcreator'.[20] Although around 80 per cent of schools reported having beam equipment of some kind, only 14 per cent of this figure (a little over 11 per cent of the total) stated that they had used a beam with a pupil or pupils in the week of the sound and music audit that they were asked to complete. There were few comments as to the perceived value of these systems to pupils, though one school considered Soundbeam to be particularly helpful as an activity through which pupils with PMLD could provide evidence of their understanding and abilities. The head teacher wrote: 'Soundbeam has made a great difference to mobility, concentration [and] understanding of cause and effect.'[21]

Some schools stated that they used electromechanical switches to enable pupils to turn music on or off.[22] Some used karaoke machines, particularly with older students. Some had equipment for stimulating pupils in a number of sensory domains, such as 'bubble tubes', which were typically located in multisensory rooms. In one school the head teacher was the main operator—'unfortunately infrequently'—of a sampler and multi-track recording system with 'MIDIgrid',[23] which he used with post-16 students. Another school reported having a 'Soundbox',[24] a pitch-linked touch-screen, MIDIcreator, a radio microphone and a sound processor.[25] A further school had a sound-editing suite, while others mentioned using sound programmes from the internet and computer programmes to facilitate composition.[26]

---

[19] Soundbeam is a 'distance to MIDI' device that converts physical movements into sound by using information from interruptions of ultrasonic pulses—see <http://www.soundbeam.co.uk>.

[20] Produced by the York Electronics Centre at the University of York, MIDIcreator can detect a wide range of body movements using sensors and switches and uses these to control sounds—see <http://www.midicreator.com>.

[21] The Soundbeam was mentioned in two of the 50 Ofsted reports (4 per cent).

[22] Switches were mentioned in two of the 50 Ofsted reports (4 per cent).

[23] A programme produced by the York Electronics Centre that enables users to explore, compose, and perform music—see <http://www.midigrid.com>.

[24] Soundbox is a portable platform that contains loudspeakers mounted beneath resonant cavities which enable the vibrations of sound and music to be experienced physically—see <http://www.soundbeam.co.uk/vibroacoustic>.

[25] The 50 Ofsted reports referred to the use of microphones in four schools (8 per cent).

[26] ICT was referenced three times in the 50 Ofsted reports (6 per cent).

A notable feature of the schools visited by the research team was the range of sound-making toys, which typically played nursery rhymes or made animal noises, although none was mentioned in the questionnaire returns, even in the detailed sound audits that were submitted.[27]

In terms of the resources that teachers used for curriculum planning and delivery, the most popular were children's songbooks—including music written specifically for pupils with special needs (such as Nordoff-Robbins Music Therapy[28] songbooks) and those produced with the mainstream in mind.[29] Other resources used included Longhorn (1988), Peters and Wills (1995), Childs (1996), Ockelford (1996a; 1998a) and the publications of Soundabout[30] and YHAMSE.[31] Schemes of work from five LEAs were mentioned, and the *British Journal of Music Therapy* was alluded to as a potentially valuable source of general reference materials.

Local Authority provision of instrumental teaching varied, as it did in mainstream schools.[32] One school had free instrumental lessons, while another required a £10 contribution per pupil.

In summary, the PROMISE research and subsequent Ofsted reports suggest that the resources available for the music education of many children and young people with SLD and PMLD are limited in a number of respects—a deficiency that must inevitably constrain the range of school-based musical experiences that are available to this cohort of pupils. For example, the prevalence of untuned percussion instruments can only reinforce the conceptualization of much of the music curriculum within an Early Years framework, while the domination of 'domestic' music technology mitigates against pupils' active musical participation.

---

[27] No mention was made of sound-making toys in the Ofsted reports.

[28] An independent provider of music therapy services in the UK—see <http://www.nordoff-robbins.org.uk>.

[29] The 50 Ofsted reports made no reference to musical resources that were used in curriculum delivery.

[30] Soundabout is an Oxford-based charity that helps children and adults who have complex disabilities develop their ability to communicate and interact with the world around them through music and sound—see <http://www.soundabout.org.uk>.

[31] Now known as YAMSEN—the Yorkshire Association for Music and Special Education Needs; see <http://www.yamsen.org.uk>.

[32] See Ofsted's report into the *Provision of Music in Services in 15 Local Education Authorities* (2004), which found that specialist tuition was available in 73 per cent of primary, 86 per cent of secondary, and 35 per cent of special schools.

Table 1.1 The four most-cited occasions or activities where teachers (other than music teachers) used music in the wider curriculum

Occasion or activity	Frequency/type of music
Greeting times	*All schools reported using greeting songs—most frequently with younger children and those with the most complex needs*
	Gathering-together songs; social songs including names; assembly songs; festival songs
Transition times	*All schools reported using songs as cues for other activities*
	Songs to reinforce activity that has taken place; songs for departing
Movement sessions (including swimming and mobility)	*92% of schools reported using music in movement work of one kind or another*
	Pieces with an appropriate tempo and dynamics
Multisensory activities	*83% of schools reported using music as part of multisensory activities*
	Music that provides a fitting 'background'

Music in the wider curriculum

Music coordinators were asked to give examples of where other teachers used music. The top four are shown in Table 1.1.

In addition, literacy activities were enhanced by songs that told a story and songs about the days of the week; in numeracy, teachers used counting songs; humanities lessons benefited from songs about the weather, and music from the past and from different cultures; and in many lessons, different types of music were played in the background to set particular moods. Those working in Conductive Education[33] made particular use of repetitive rhymes, and therapists (other than music therapists) used music in their work too, notably speech and language therapists (mentioned by 66 per cent of music coordinators, $n=15$), physiotherapists (acknowledged by 53 per cent), and aromatherapists (20 per cent). Finally, having pupils select their favourite songs

---

[33] Conductive Education aims to teach children and adults with physical disabilities such as cerebral palsy, dyspraxia, multiple sclerosis, Parkinson's Disease, stroke, and head injury how to overcome their movement problems to lead more independent, dignified, and fulfilled lives—see <http://www.conductive-education.org.uk>.

and pieces of recorded music was considered to be an effective way of encouraging and enabling them to make choices.[34]

To get an impression of just how much music permeated activities throughout the children's time at school, staff were asked to identify where and when music was used on a specific day during the week in which they completed the questionnaire. Fifty-nine per cent of respondents reported using recorded music as a background to other activity at some point during the day; 52 per cent stated that they had heard live music-making of some kind; 49 per cent said that they had used recorded music in part of a lesson to enhance or support other learning; 41 per cent of staff disclosed that they had sung or had heard someone else singing one-to-one with pupils; 40 per cent revealed that they had used musical equipment in some primarily non-musical activity; and 10 per cent had heard live music made by pupils during break times. Additionally, staff reported having heard music in assembly and on videos, having sung grace at lunchtime, and practised songs for the school play. One school detailed having used music in the entrance hall as pupils arrived.

It is worth noting that the days chosen for this analysis by participating schools were in the latter part of the summer term when it was not unusual for special events to be taking place, or rehearsals to be underway for end-of-term concerts and productions. Hence there may have been more opportunities for music-making than usual. One school, for example, was holding a 'Music and Sensory Fun Week', while another was employing a professional arts company to work with a class using music technology. In another school, a senior class was producing its own radio programme with a DJ and sing-along artists.

The research team visited a school for pupils with cerebral palsy, where the physiotherapy that was reported to lie at the heart of all children's programmes was said to be supported by music throughout the school day. This claim was borne out by the researchers' own observations. The head physiotherapist was seen in action with two classes, before being interviewed. She was asked how and why she used music to such a great extent. Her response was that, in her opinion:

- the rhythmic structure in rhymes and songs stimulated and helped to inform movement;
- the children *enjoyed* moving to music and responded well to it, with their faces regularly lighting up;

---

[34] In the 50 Ofsted reports (2000–5), references to education *through* music are made in all but one of those that mention musical activity at all (47 out of 48, or 98 per cent). In total, 16 per cent of the text is devoted to music and the wider curriculum (37 per cent of that devoted to accounts of musical activity of any type).

- synchronized movements were encouraged by the use of set songs in the pool, for example, 'Feel the water' to the tune of *Frère Jacques* and a Glenn Miller track for floating supine, while 'I'm singing in my special chair' accompanied children in the hoist;
- the children were able to anticipate what was coming next through the use of songs that were linked to the forthcoming activity;
- most of the children at the school had ears that worked better than their eyes (with the exception of two pupils who had severe hearing loss); and
- *staff* enjoyed music as well as the children.

In summary, the physiotherapist said that she could not imagine a session without music.

Through the questionnaire, the researchers sought to ascertain the *type* of music that was used to support other activity across the phases of education, and the following summary is drawn from the 36 responses that were received.

In Early Years work, 'Top of the Pops' tapes and children's party CDs were used to foster motor skills and body awareness, Vivaldi's 'Summer' and Bjork's 'Oh so quiet' were played in a multisensory room and an Enya CD in hydrotherapy.

In Key Stages 1 and 2, nursery rhymes and children's songs were used in movement work, 'mood music' tapes were played in multisensory areas and special education tapes were utilized to support physiotherapy. In addition, mention was made of staff creating special compilation tapes 'in house'. 'Contemporary pop' (performed by groups such as All Saints) and 'old pop' (Pink Floyd) were played for dance and at break times. In contrast, one school reported using Classic FM's 'Hall of Fame' CDs during breaks.

In Key Stages 3 and 4, one school said that they used live songs to prompt movement during physiotherapy, but all other examples were of recorded music. Educational tapes were used to support mathematics and English lessons. Relaxation CDs were played in multisensory rooms and during massage sessions. Specific classical CDs were often mentioned in this age phase, with one school playing Mozart at break times and others using classical music in language, drama, and multisensory work. References were made to 'Hobgoblin' music in country dancing, ABBA's *Money, Money, Money* in numeracy sessions, Bart's *Food, Glorious Food* to indicate that lunch was approaching, and Davy Crockett for a news session.

In the Post-16 phase, fewer references were made to music and the wider curriculum, with only one mention made of music being employed with a whole class—an 'interactive music with guitar session'. Eight examples of the kinds of music used during the day were supplied, with two reporting Boyzone and one Steps being played at break time, while another Post-16 group made use of Enya for relaxation. One class explored <www.peoplesound.com> in an ICT session.

The use of 'background' music was a recurring theme in the questionnaire responses, and the researchers investigated this further during their visits to schools. Here, the reality was that the background music used in classrooms tended to merge with the general ambient sounds that were being made by staff talking, sound-making toys, children vocalizing, computer programmes, and furniture being moved. The styles of 'background' music that the researchers heard were very varied, and included movements from Vivaldi's *Four Seasons*, 'world' music, classical flute and piano pieces (chosen because one of the pupils responded well to bird-like sounds), relaxation tracks, a 'Winnie the Pooh' tape, and contemporary South African pop. Occasionally, the researchers noticed pupils reacting to the opening of a new piece, and sometimes a member of staff would interact with individual pupils by moving with them or vocalizing to the music close to them. Pieces were often stopped midway through, though.

Head teachers were asked what they considered the value of music in the wider curriculum to be. Their views may be summarized as follows.

- *Language and communication development:* 'improved eye contact'; 'increased vocalisation'; 'developing expressive and receptive language'; 'singing along with signing using BSL'.[35]

- *Behavioural, emotional, and social development:* 'showing pleasure during musical activities'; 'for reflection times'; 'encourages facial expressions'; 'gives pupils a means to make choices'; 'inclusion and participation'; 'learning to mix through shared musical activity'; 'waiting your turn, sharing, being quiet, noisy'; 'building and demonstrating confidence to play an instrument to an audience'; 'prestige of playing drum kit, using a microphone, full-sized synthesizer, bass guitar'; 'builds self-esteem'; 'awareness of style and culture through listening to music'.

- *Sensory and cognitive development:* 'improved attention'; 'Soundbeam has made a great difference to concentration and understanding of cause and effect'; 'learning starts and ends of activities through using a song'; 'music gives structure and routine to an activity'; 'learning discrimination, sequencing, closure and completion'; 'developing numeracy'.

---

[35] That is, British Sign Language—the main form of sign language for deaf people used in the UK.

◆ *Physical development*: 'encourages intentional movement'; 'head control'; 'hand function'; 'increased looking, reaching, grasping'; 'increased movement, more controlled movement'; 'learning motor skills, body awareness, laterality, coordination'; 'balance'; 'Soundbeam has made a great difference to mobility'.

As these comments indicate, head teachers were very positive about the benefits of music in promoting broader learning and development.

In summary, the PROMISE research and the subsequent accounts of Ofsted suggest that the use of music as a medium for the delivery of the wider curriculum—as an agent to enhance learning throughout the school day—is highly valued and widespread in special schools making provision for pupils with SLD and PMLD. However, there are no indications that music is systematically conceptualized in this role, nor that education *through* music is coherently linked to music education per se. Yet commonsense suggests that, for pupils whose perception of the world is likely to be fragmented and confusing, a joined-up approach could only benefit learning and development.

External links

Almost all schools reported working with outside music organizations on one-off or short-term projects. During the summer term, 2000, 20 schools listed 59 events or projects that had been led by outside musicians or artists. The majority of these entailed pupils participating actively in music-making, although some were traditional concerts with performers playing to a pupil audience.[36]

In the majority of projects, musicians came to schools, rather than children and young people going out to arts venues. Most outside events involved a number of schools, and were often held in prestigious venues such as cathedrals. The year of the survey (2000) prompted many large-scale Millennium functions, such as JC2000[37] city festivals. One school described how 'all pupils in the school are taking part in a Millennium celebration at the Bridgewater Hall in Manchester with a number of local schools. The event is based on the "Hopes and Dreams" musical and our school's contribution is a song composed by one of our year six pupils and performed by her and other pupils on stage at the Hall.'

---

[36] Funding for projects was usually provided by the schools themselves, sometimes by the LEA and occasionally by the organization providing the specialist input. Other sources of funding were local businesses and clubs, and parents.

[37] A UK-wide initiative which encouraged schools to mark the Christian significance of the Millennium through the performing arts. Over 18,000 schools participated.

'Live Music Now!'[38] was the organization most frequently mentioned as having provided concerts and workshops over many years, both at schools and external venues, using music in a wide range of different styles. Through this connection, the band Graffiti had recently played at one school, for example, while a classical harpist had entertained children in another. A few schools, which were located close to concert halls with resident ensembles, had established regular patterns of contact with them. For instance, a small independent establishment near the Fairfield Halls in Croydon reported regular visits from members of the London Mozart Players, who performed for pupils and allowed them to explore the instruments that they brought along.

Non-western music was a feature of many of the outside links. There was an emphasis on rhythm, with examples of African drumming, percussion with African-Caribbean roots and a Maori Stick Group working with a whole school. Broader arts work also featured frequently, with illustrated storytelling and pan-art productions,[39] such those by Oily Cart.[40] One school, where the head teacher was a musician, created a multimedia extravaganza entitled 'In the Black' using the services of a professional dance teacher and a specially commissioned music score—the performance being set against a backdrop of slides about the Black Country. Another school were having a 'music week' at the time the researchers visited. All pupils and staff were involved, mainly in half-day sessions, which ranged from an instrument-making workshop (a valuable exercise since the school possessed very few instruments), a tabla class, a 'Spice Girls' party, a brass group concert from the LEA Music Service, and a community vocal workshop. Most of the artists involved in such events did not specialize in working with children and young people with special needs.

School staff were asked what they considered the educational benefits of these special musical activities to be. Their many comments included the belief that such events:

- provided pupils with the opportunity to hear *live* music of a high quality, which was perceived to have a particularly strong effect on pupils with PMLD;
- fostered pupils' musicality, including listening skills and rhythmic abilities;

---

[38] Live Music Now! pays young professional musicians to play for needy groups, including children in special schools—see <http://www.livemusicnow.org>.

[39] Sometimes elements of Personal, Social, and Health Education, such as drug awareness, were addressed through artistic productions.

[40] A group that specializes in multisensory, interactive productions for the very young and young people with complex disabilities—see <http://www.oilycart.org.uk>.

- nurtured their development in *extra*-musical domains, such as language, socialization, and movement;
- offered them new, stimulating, multisensory experiences and promoted multi-cultural awareness; and, above all,
- brought pupils enjoyment and gave them a sense of excitement.

The staff at one school said that they thought the impact of special musical events on children with learning difficulties was potentially the same as for anyone else, adding that 'music is life-enhancing'. Another noted that most 'respond extraordinarily to sound'; they 'can't get enough.'

Many schools reported longer-term external commitments to music too, which tended to be less exotic in nature than the one-off projects. Examples of musicians coming into school included having a local vicar with his guitar in one instance and a Salvation Army band in another (to provide music in assemblies), and employing local people to play for music and movement sessions.

Staff were also asked how many pupils took part in musical activities outside school. In the Early Years, six children attended external schemes of one form or another, including one who participated in sessions run by Scope,[41] where music was used to support other activities. At Key Stages 1 and 2, seven children were involved in out-of-school musical ventures, a figure which rose to 24 at Key Stages 3 and 4. These included several who attended Scouts or Guides, one who was a member of a meditation group that used music, one who went along to listen to her sister's recorder class, one who received singing lessons provided by the LEA music service, and four who attended a youth club. In the Post-16 phase, it was noted that two students went to a local music centre for composing using IT, one had drum lessons out of school, and one school sent what were described as 'musically able students' to an Education Action Zone[42] music club.

In summary, it appears that, in some schools at least, there are strong links with the wider musical community, and a good deal of activity is taking place that is reckoned by those involved to have much intrinsic merit for the pupils concerned, despite few of the staff having any special training to work with

---

[41] Scope is a national disability organization in England and Wales whose focus is people with cerebral palsy—see <http://www.scope.org.uk>.

[42] 'Education Action Zones' ('EAZs') were created by the Schools Standards and Framework Act (1998) with the aim of raising educational standards in challenging areas through establishing new partnerships involving business, parents, local authorities, schools, and their communities. These were subsequently transformed into 'Excellence in Cities Action Zones ('EiCAZs')—see <http://www.standards.dfes.gov.uk/sie/eic/eicactionzones>.

young people with special needs. Moreover, external links seem to have arisen *opportunistically* rather than *strategically*, and there is no evidence, either in the PROMISE research or the 50 Ofsted reports (2000–5), that any attempts have been made to relate special events to day-to-day music curricula.

Gauging attainment and progress *in* music and across the curriculum *through* music

Many responses to the questionnaires did not distinguish between attainment and progress in music. Often, after completion of the section headed 'attainment' ('A'), the corresponding section for 'progress' ('B') just received the response 'see section 'A' '.

Schools were asked about the kinds of attainment targets that were recorded on individual pupil's learning plans in the different age phases. Examples of these follow.

In the Early Years, specific targets included 'facial responses, vocalizations, body movements', 'will turn to a sound', 'awareness of starting and stopping', 'can distinguish between high and low sounds', 'will play bells in imitation', 'playing independently during song (on drum)', '[copying] rhythm independently'. Generally speaking, identifying sounds, imitating sounds, and moving to sounds were deemed to be significant indicators of attainment. A few comments referred to emotional responses to music, including becoming calm to 'relaxing' music.

In Key Stages 1 and 2, the examples given related mainly to pupils' responses to action songs, such as knocking down the bottles in the right places in the song 'Ten Green Bottles'. Other comments referred to responding to the vibrations of a gong by moving towards it and playing instruments with varying degrees of independence.

In Key Stages 3 and 4, the comments on attainment were divided into those featuring *musical elements*, such as 'able to keep the beat', '[can copy] simple rhythm' and '[can] identify . . . the higher note'; *playing of percussion instruments*, such as '[uses] tambourine to play along with song'; *communicating about music*, such as signing 'music' to indicate the wish for a CD, and playing to 'a visual cue'; and *moving in response to music*, such as '[will respond] to the number song . . . beginning by turning head and smiling' and 'will still to listen'.

In the Post-16 phase, comments about attainment were rare. One school mentioned that they kept a record of performances in concerts and participation in outside trips. Another school commented on musical elements relating to more general communication targets.

In one of the schools visited by the researchers, a checklist for each pupil was observed being prepared for adult helpers to complete during the music lesson. The results were later used to stimulate discussion and to inform report-writing. As an example, a few of the elements listed on one pupil's sheet were: 'to take turns at making a sound with an adult', 'to find a matching instrument to one heard out of sight', 'to establish a steady beat', and 'to copy a rhythm pattern up to a specific number of beats'.

Music coordinators reported that they formally assessed progress in areas other than music (primarily in language development) during music sessions, and they were asked about the general progress that they saw in their pupils through the use of music. Their observations, which are very similar to those made by head teachers in relation to music and the wider curriculum, are set out below. It is of interest to note that these are far more numerous, rich, and varied than the attainment targets pertaining (or said to pertain) specifically to music listed above.

- *Language and communication development*: 'increased engagement shown by eye contact'; 'beginnings of vocalizing'; 'smiling and vocalizing at changes in volume, pace and rhythm'; 'listening to others more'; 'making sounds in response to the sounds of others'; 'creating a dialogue with another person'; 'verbalization'; 'learning and recalling of words or sounds'; 'language and concept development'; 'choosing activities through singing or using sound cues'.

- *Behavioural, emotional, and social development*: 'ceasing ritualistic activities to attend to sound or music'; 'extending self-awareness'; 'showing enjoyment'; 'obvious signs of pleasure'; 'sense of pride'; 'relax to appropriately chosen music'; 'awareness of themselves and other people'; 'sitting and working as part of a group'; 'participation whatever their ability'; 'sharing of experiences'; 'children who will not join in other subjects will join in music voluntarily'; 'following simple instructions'.

- *Sensory and cognitive development*: 'awareness of consequences and meaning of sounds in the environment'; 'increased concentration span'; 'more sustained responses'; 'extending memory and sequencing abilities'; 'awareness of routine'; 'counting'; 'increased desire to experiment with sound'.

- *Physical development*: 'relaxing'; 'settling'; 'stretching'; 'increased movement'; 'making big body movements'; 'more controlled movement'; 'fine motor skills'; 'showing hand/eye coordination'; 'showing left/right balance'.

One teacher cautioned against assuming that abilities developed in the context of music would necessarily generalize to other domains: 'There have been significant improvements in speech in a small number of pupils. Also general concentration levels have increased in others, though often only in music—the ability does not always transfer to the general learning situation.'

In summary, it appears that music coordinators find it easier to conceptualize *extra*-musical outcomes to musical activity with pupils with SLD and PMLD than purely *musical* attainment and progress. This anomaly is echoed in the numerous and wide-ranging comments made by head teachers in relation to music's perceived wider benefits (cited above) and in the percentage of text that Ofsted music reports devote to the description and analysis of extra-musical (as opposed to musical) activity (cf. footnote 8, page 13).

Music therapy

The provision of music therapy varied across the schools in the PROMISE sample. It was provided on site by 36 per cent of schools,[43] while 19 per cent were aware of some pupils receiving music therapy outside. Reference to music therapy was sometimes—although by no means always—made on Statements of Special Educational Needs. Two schools reported offering music therapy to all their pupils, although in one of these schools an untrained music therapist was responsible for the sessions. In the other 17 schools providing music therapy, the number of pupils receiving this service was quite small, with six schools making provision for between 1 and 5 pupils; four schools, between 6 and 10; five schools, between 11 and 15; and one school, between 16 and 20. On average, this equates to around 5 per cent of pupils receiving music therapy in the schools that provided it, and only about 2 per cent of the SLD/PMLD population of children and young people as a whole. The average time allocated to music therapy every week was seven hours per school. All the therapists worked with individual pupils, with some undertaking additional work with up to four children or young people at a time, and three taking larger groups. Without exception, music therapists reported that they had a suitable space for sessions, although one worked in a room without a piano.

As far as the musical content of the sessions is concerned, one therapist used improvised music exclusively, five improvised most of the time, and two improvised and used established repertoire in equal measure. As to the style of this repertoire, half the therapists reported using nursery rhymes; two also used folksongs; two, pieces that they had composed; one, pop songs; and one, classical pieces. Only one therapist used recorded music in sessions, although this was reported to be a rarity, since 'the children—especially those with PMLD—have a lot of recorded music played to them anyway'. One therapist

---

[43] Music therapy was mentioned in six (12 per cent) of the 50 Ofsted reports (2000–5).

wrote: 'The value of space/pausing in music is crucial, whether improvised or in a planned structure. The children must have enough time to respond and when they do, the therapist adapts her music to their responses, the music created is then a joint/shared experience. The therapist is not playing to the children, but inviting them to create music with her.' Another noted that sessions gave children and young people the opportunities to do things that were not encouraged in other areas of school life such 'dancing, screaming, singing loudly, hitting (a drum rather than the face)'.

All music therapists said that they used untuned percussion in their sessions and all but one used tuned percussion too. Most used pianos; half used guitars. One therapist mentioned wind instruments—the recorder and the oboe. As an example, during one school visit, a video recording was made available to the researchers of a one-to-one music therapy session. The therapist provided a diatonic ostinato[44] with melodic fragments on the piano, to which the child at different times vocalized and played untuned percussion and the piano.

With regard to technology, one therapist reported *always* using microphones and electronic keyboard, one *sometimes* used touch-pad drums and a musical mat, two *rarely* used technology of any type and four *never* did. Half the therapists regularly recorded sessions in audio format and occasionally on video.

Music therapists were asked how they gauged progress. They gave detailed responses that were largely centred on communication—for example, 'eye contact', 'vocalization', 'language development', 'ability to express emotions through playing', 'awareness of others', and 'turn-taking'. They also mentioned 'increasing confidence', 'enjoyment', 'increased attention span', and 'anticipation of sessions'. It is worth noting that these criteria are in many cases identical to those used by head teachers and music coordinators to assess general progress *through* music (see pp. 22 and 27 above).

Other school staff were asked what they considered to be the benefits of music therapy. A number were identified, including various aspects of communication ('developing eye contact', 'non-verbal ... communication', 'increasing vocalization and pre-verbal skills', 'developing interpersonal expressive communication', and 'turn-taking') and personal growth ('development of listening and attention', 'increased awareness of self', 'confidence building', 'gaining freedom and independence', and 'making choices'). Again, these closely resemble music coordinators' and head teachers' comments made in relation to music *education* and progress in other areas.

---

[44] That is, a repeated series of notes that used only the notes of the major or minor scale.

All therapists stated that they contributed to school reports for parents, and the great majority had input to pupils' Annual Reviews. It was usual for music therapists to discuss children's progress with other professionals. Examples given were speech and language therapists, an art psychotherapist, an occupational therapist, clinical and educational psychologists, paediatricians, social workers, and care staff. Some music therapists discussed their cases with other music therapy colleagues. The frequency of meetings with music coordinators was variable—indeed, one music therapist reported never having met the music coordinator at the school where she worked—and little more than half the music coordinators involved said that they had access to the notes that music therapists made on their pupils.

In summary, despite the belief that music therapy may be beneficial for children and young people with SLD and PMLD, it appears that only a small proportion have access to this provision. The activities that go to make up music therapy sessions with pupils who have learning difficulties apparently display a similar eclectic mix to those undertaken in the name of music education—based largely on the personal beliefs and expertise of the practitioner concerned—and many of the perceived benefits of music therapy for pupils with SLD or PMLD appear to be very similar to those ascribed to music education. Yet there is no evidence that music-therapeutic activity or outcomes are typically used to inform other experiential or developmental programmes that involve music, or vice versa. Rather, for the few children who receive music therapy, it appears to be another strand of musical experience, running at best in parallel with others.

Pupils with a particular interest in music or a flair for performing

As part of the PROMISE research, school staff were asked to describe any pupils who showed a particular interest in music or a noticeable flair for performing. Thirty-one pupils[45] (around 10 per cent) were identified by those who responded to this section of the questionnaire. Staff comments—at times suggestive of developmental hierarchies of skills—can be summarized as follows.

- *Listening and responding*: 'loves to listen to all music'; 'enjoys live music'; 'stills when first listening to a piece and smiles if likes it'; 'responds to others' playing'; 'wide-eyed and smiling'; 'good facial expression'; 'more alert'; 'behaviour calms when music comes on'; 'changes whole body

---

[45] By phase, the breakdown of pupils was as follows: Early Years (4); Key Stages 1 and 2 (9); Key Stages 3 and 4 (13); Post-16 (4); phase not given (1).

language when music is on'; 'spontaneous movement'; 'lots of body movement'; 'moves to match mood of music'; 'constant verbal demand for music
or for favoured CD'.

♦ *Singing and playing*: 'whistling'; 'vocalizing'; 'sings and encourages others to
sing'; 'singing full songs'; 'able to learn new songs quickly and sing them at
a later date'; 'sings songs after one hearing'; 'rocks in time to music he likes';
'keen to play'; 'can tap out the rhythm of a song'; 'good rhythmic ability';
'good on drums'; 'repetition of short musical phrases'; 'able to pick out a
tune by ear on the keyboard'; 'plays tunes on the piano and self-corrects if
plays a wrong note'; 'quick to pick out tunes'; 'loves to compose at the keyboard'; 'learning recorder'; 'learnt a brass instrument quickly'; 'knowledge
of chords'; 'guitar playing to accompany folksongs'; 'playing the violin'.

In summary, extrapolating the figure of 10 per cent to the national population of pupils with SLD and PMLD would mean that there are currently
around 4,000 children and young people with complex needs who have noteworthy musical interests or abilities. However, given that most music coordinators working in special schools do not have specialist training, there must be
a high risk that some pupils' musical potential goes unrecognized. This conclusion is supported anecdotally by findings from the RNIB Music Advisory
Service, who are regularly contacted by parents and teachers seeking support
for young people, sometimes in their teens, whose musicality has only recently
been recognized. Yet it is almost certain that their musical potential was present much earlier (cf. p. 216), and, had staff at the time been alive to the possibility, intervention in Key Stage 1 or before could have had a far greater
longer-term impact (see Ockelford, Pring, Welch, and Treffert 2006). The
issues of identifying and working with children and young people who have
exceptional musical abilities is taken up in Chapters 8 and 10.

Examples from the visits to schools by the research team

During the research team's visits to three schools, Sally Zimmermann, the
RNIB Music Advisor, made detailed observations of some music sessions.
These are reproduced here in order to give a sense of what musical activities in
schools with children with complex needs are like.[46]

Example 1
A music lesson was observed in the hall. There were 11 pupils present, with a teacher
and two classroom assistants who were working with three individual children. Of
these, one was profoundly deaf and the other two did not speak during the session.

---

[46] See Welch, Ockelford, and Zimmermann 2001 (the PROMISE report): 25–8.

Initially, the whole group sat in a semicircle and listened to a piece of music. Some were able to name it and could identify the composer. Several pupils were also able to pick out the style of music and the instruments used when presented with a choice of flash-cards. The class then played musical instruments. Some pupils read their notes from sheets on which the appropriate letter names had been printed. One pupil had the rhythm written out in stave notation.

In another music session at the same school there were eight pupils. Three were functioning at a non-verbal level, of whom one received unobtrusive medical care during the lesson. In addition to the music teacher, three classroom assistants were present. A piece of recorded music was played, and some pupils recognized the instruments that they could hear. These pupils subsequently sang reasonably fluently with clear words. Three were able to pitch a rising fifth, unaccompanied, consistently and accurately. One of the pupils who could not speak was asked to choose one of two instruments that were offered successively, by smiling at the appropriate time. The pupil did not react to a fellow pupil or a classroom assistant's efforts to elicit a response, but did eventually smile for the music teacher. The pupil then hit his chosen instrument a few times independently with a beater that was supplied by the classroom assistant, before nudging it off his tray. Another of the pupils who was non-verbal grinned and vocalized while bells were played close to her. The pupil who appeared to be least developmentally advanced had an instrument played against her leg, which she moved in time to the music, and smiled.

A feature of the music lessons in this school, where the pupils displayed a wide range of abilities, was the manner in which the most able copied the teacher's approach and sought to involve some of their peers who were less able to participate. For example, without being prompted, one pupil gently tapped out the pulse of a piece on another's arm.

Example 2

In the second school that was visited, music was used throughout the day despite the fact that the music co-ordinator had recently left. The timetable was divided into general activities (rather than subjects), such as 'individual playtime', 'circle time' and 'communication session'. In one of the classes observed, two pupils out of eight were absent. One was ambulant. Two were frail and slept for much of the day. Two appeared to have some verbal comprehension, although only one verbalized in response. One showed an understanding of visual gesture and sequence. Two staff were with the pupils for the majority of the time, while other adults came and worked with the children on specific activities.

Musically, some sound-makers (such as chimes) were hung from frames that the children could knock from their prone, supported positions. Several pupils played with sound-making toys, which produced pre-recorded tunes, and which were placed within reach. At different times, some pupils tapped out rhythms on toys and the surfaces to which they had access, and some vocalized. Occasionally, an adult would join in with a child's sound-making and, sometimes, when a pattern emerged with the most physically able, turn-taking was established.

In the three whole-group sessions that were observed during the day, teachers exaggerated music and speech patterns using longer durations and a greater pitch range than normal. Most of the class responded by attending visually and tracking actions following the sound cues. From time to time, some of the children would respond with their own sounds too. It was noticeable that pupils were more likely to turn towards sounds when they were combined with a visual stimulus (such as a shimmering cymbal).

A striking feature of the class was the lack of sounds heard from beyond the room and the absence of casual conversation between staff. It appeared that the adults only spoke when it was essential—and then quietly. On the whole, the children were able to make little noise with the objects they were given as they had very limited strength. At one stage, the child who was ambulant explored the contrasting sounds that could be made on different floor surfaces (carpet and lino), and evidently preferred the noisier area!

Circle time was led by the teacher with very little intervention on the part of the other staff; rather they were there to offer physical support to the pupils. Using expansive gestures, the teacher sang all the songs—familiar tunes whose words had been customized. Some pupils' names were sung and some were spoken. During the 'hello' song, one pupil whistled back at his verse, another pupil lifted her head and the girl who could speak helped to count out 'one, two, three' in the correct place. Later, this pupil copied much of the teacher's singing, mainly using a 'bah' sound. In a further song, two of the other pupils sang back after the teacher. The pupil who had whistled kept to the beat of a song quite accurately, tapping his hands or feet on the carpet. He maintained the pulse for a while after the music had stopped. A member of staff attached bells to a girl's wrist. This appeared to perk her up, and she played the bells on her own after the session was over. Some of the children appeared to anticipate what was coming next.

Example 3

The third school was having a whole week of musical activities. Among these was a concert from a local brass quintet, which was held in the school hall. All sixty pupils attended, as well as one class from a nearby mainstream primary school. The brass group started by playing outside the hall, then continued to perform as they marched in. Most pupils who could move freely (around ten were in wheelchairs) turned to face the sound and tracked the musicians' progress to the front of the hall. Some pupils clapped along with the music, but few could keep to the steady beat. A number of the adults tapped out rhythms on the pupils' hands, arms and legs, encouraging them to join in. To assist them in this, some staff sat opposite their pupils rather than beside them. The children were fairly noisy throughout, and applauded at the end of pieces and whenever the group had a rest! The group played one Beatles number that appeared to be well known to the pupils. This resulted in the most vocalization with at least ten pupils singing along.

Three pupils were observed in particular during the concert. The oldest was in a wheelchair and did not speak, though he did appear to understand some straightforward verbal instructions. He had very limited motor control and moved his head continuously. He was wearing arm and leg braces. He smiled at the low notes on the tuba as it came past him, and moved his head more during a faster verse. Later on, he smiled again—this time apparently in response to a descending chromatic scale on the trumpet, though he did not subsequently show any reaction to a glissando on the trombone. He smiled once more when the trumpet produced sounds using the mute, and then again at the 'Pink Panther' theme. Two adults relayed the music to him by 'playing' on his hands, and he turned towards whichever adult was doing this and giggled.

The second pupil was younger and was in a buggy. He appeared to have no verbal understanding, though he had good motor control and played repetitive games with a jigsaw and a piece of railway track (and then the researcher's pen). He showed no signs of listening to the music at all—though he did not disturb anyone else.

A third pupil was the most obviously engaged in the whole event. At the demonstration of blowing a raspberry to get a sound through a brass instrument's mouthpiece, he called out 'bees'. Then he shouted 'Star Wars' after the band had played a few notes of this theme.

What do these observations tell us? And to what extent do they support the findings from the PROMISE research and the analysis of the 50 Ofsted reports (2000–5)?

First, Zimmermann's impressions indicate a considerable range of abilities and needs among those who were educated in special schools that catered for pupils with learning difficulties at the time of the PROMISE research—a diversity that is likely to become more common as the move to greater genericism in special schools gathers pace (Byers 2003). Clearly, such variety poses teachers considerable challenges, and makes it all the more important to have a clearly defined music curriculum for those with the greatest levels of disability, lest activities that are planned with the majority of pupils in mind are unsuitable for those profound needs, for whom tokenistic accommodation is made during lessons.[47] It is evident that the children's musical experiences varied considerably from school to school—supporting the notion that, the existence of the National Curriculum framework notwithstanding, at the time of the PROMISE study, there was indeed no common music-educational approach being used for pupils with SLD and PMLD—a state of affairs that the 50 Ofsted reports suggest has not changed in the intervening years.

Second, Zimmermann's classroom observations lend weight to the concerns over resources raised by the PROMISE and Ofsted research—particularly in relation to the limited utilization of technology that would promote active engagement with music. Yet it is widely known that by using appropriate

---

[47] One gets a sense of musical activities for pupils with PMLD being something of an afterthought through the commentaries in a number of the 50 Ofsted reports. Indeed, the very nature of the commentaries reinforces this discrimination by typically describing other pupils' achievements first and treating these quasi-normatively, in the context of which the efforts of those with PMLD are set. For example, 'Pupils make good progress in the primary department so by Year 6, they are confident using percussion instruments, and take pleasure in shaking a set of small bells to the rhythm of the song. Those with more profound and complex needs turn their heads towards sound, such as a triangle, and play instruments with assistance.'

switching devices linked through a MIDI system, a range of movements can be made to trigger sounds, offering some pupils an otherwise unrealizable degree of emancipation from their physical constraints.

Third, Zimmermann's notes reinforce the belief that music education is being used as a medium to support wider learning and development, as well as being offered as a subject area in its own right. Links with the wider musical community were observed in action too. However, in common with the PROMISE research and the review of Ofsted reports, there was no evidence of these three areas being connected in any systematic way—of them adding up to anything more than the sum of their parts.

Conclusion

The data gathered from the PROMISE research project and the 50 Ofsted reports (2000–5) indicate that there is a widespread recognition of the potential significance of music in the lives of pupils with SLD and PMLD and of its power to assist in many areas of their learning and development. While the research was undertaken in England, anecdotal evidence gathered by the RNIB and comments in the (very scarce) literature on the subject suggest that the findings summarized here may well have an international relevance. In summary: while, in a few schools, there is evidence of structured music provision for different age groups, with fruitful links to the wider musical community, the general impression is one of relatively isolated professional activity in music, with schools taking an essentially pragmatic and eclectic approach in the absence of a nationally agreed framework, informed by empirical data, that sets out the musical development of children and young people with complex needs. Chapter 5 takes the first steps towards making good this shortfall.

Chapter 2

All in the mind?

Introduction

The PROMISE research, whose findings were summarized in Chapter 1, indicates that the activities that go to make up music therapy sessions and music lessons with children and young people who have learning difficulties are often much the same, and display a similarly heterogeneous mix, based largely on the personal beliefs and expertise of individual practitioners. It also suggests that many of the perceived benefits of music therapy and music education for pupils with SLD or PMLD are identical. Yet no evidence was found of the outcomes of either music-therapeutic or music-educational interventions being used to inform planning or practice in the other domain. Rather, for the small percentage of children and young people who are in receipt of music therapy, it appears that this merely forms another strand in the complex network of day-to-day music-educational experiences, between which there is no discernible coherence.

Music therapy and music education— definitions and issues

The conceptual confusion found in PROMISE was echoed in the subsequent research into the musicality of children and young people with septo-optic dysplasia or retinopathy of prematurity, and the music provision that is made for them, that will be reported in Chapter 8. As we shall see, some descriptions of the music *therapy* that is being offered seem to indicate that in reality music *education* is taking place. For example, a $7\frac{1}{2}$-year-old visually impaired autistic girl 'works with her music therapist on learning the piano and also a variety of instruments'.

This comment supports anecdotal evidence indicating that the prevalent view among those working in the field (as well as lay people) is that music *therapy* is the appropriate term to use for formal musical activities undertaken with children and young people with disabilities (Ockelford 2000). Certainly, the music-therapeutic literature describes a broad range of activities and their potential benefits to young people with learning difficulties. For instance,

Nordoff and Robbins reflect on how some of their young clients learnt 'new activities, new words, new music' and became more responsive to other people (1971: 123), how a young girl began to develop speech through music therapy (pp. 30–1), and how music even helped an autistic boy to develop independence skills (p. 105). In similar vein, Postacchini, Borghesi, Flucher, Guida, Mancini, Nocentini, Rubin, and Santoni (1993) describe how music therapy sessions with a 5-year-old girl who had what they term 'severe infantile regression' were considered to improve, among other things, her movement and use of vision, and assist her in moving from pre-symbolic to symbolic communication. Among the reasons that Bunt sets out for undertaking music therapy with a 9-year-old boy with learning difficulties are 'to help develop auditory awareness and memory' and 'to help develop his ability to share' (1994: 105). Similarly, Schwalkwijk (1994: 79 ff.) discusses the potential role of music therapy in the stimulation of motor and cognitive skills.

But do these accounts accord with definitions of music therapy offered by therapists themselves? Bruscia (1987: 47), for example, asserts that 'Music therapy is a systematic process of intervention wherein the therapist helps the client to achieve health, using musical experiences and the relationships that develop through them as dynamic forces of change'. Bunt (1994: 8), in referring to this definition and others, concludes that 'Music therapy is the use of organised sounds and music within an evolving relationship between client and therapist to support and encourage physical, mental, social and emotional well-being'. When these aims are compared with the descriptions of the music-therapeutic activities cited above, it is evident that some therapists working with children and young people with learning difficulties have strayed from fostering 'well-being' through music into what may reasonably be considered areas of education—promoting learning and development, for example— where, as the PROMISE research indicated and, as we shall see in Chapter 6, music can fulfil a range of functions. Indeed, the leaflet *Music Therapy in the Education Service* (published by the Association of Professional Music Therapists in 1992), is quite explicit about the role that music therapists can assume when working in the domain of education, where therapy is held to be a valuable means of facilitating access to the music curriculum (p. 1). A further example of the conceptual confusion evident even within the music-therapeutic community is the fact that Elaine Streeter's monograph *Making Music with the Young Child with Special Needs* (1993) is categorized by the British Society for Music Therapy as a 'music therapy book' (BSMT 1998: 21), and by the APMT as a book about 'music in special education' (as *opposed* to music therapy) (1992: 32).

Why is it that therapists should have become involved in educational activity? Contributory factors include the fact that those working in music education at all levels have been comparatively inactive in the field of special needs: taking on pupils with learning difficulties is not something that the majority of teachers have in the past seen as part of their role. Although this is changing with the increasing inclusion of children and young people with disabilities in mainstream schools, the majority of those with SLD and PMLD are likely to continue to be educated in special schools for some time to come where, as the PROMISE research indicates, few pupils are taught by music specialists. Moreover, as we saw in the Introduction (p. 31), relatively little has been written on music education for children and young people with disabilities, and most of the texts that do exist were published largely before the education of those with severe or profound learning difficulties had seriously got underway. Finally, while there are a number of nationally recognized music therapy courses in the UK, there is currently no comparable training in music education available for those who wish to work with children and young people with SLD or PMLD.

Previously, I proposed that music education for children and young people with severe, or profound and multiple disabilities should be considered as having two distinct strands, reflecting what was believed to be common practice in schools and which the PROMISE and Ofsted-derived research have subsequently confirmed (Ockelford 1998*b*; 2000). These are (a) activities that are undertaken primarily for their intrinsic musical value (education *in* music), and (b) those whose main function is to promote wider learning and development (education *through* music).

With regard to education *in* music, in England, the aims and objectives for all pupils are described in detail in the National Curriculum under the following four programmes of study:

- Listening and applying knowledge and understanding.
- Controlling sounds through singing and playing—performing skills.
- Creating and developing musical ideas—composing skills.
- Responding and reviewing—appraising skills.

While this fourfold conceptual framework is a reflection of thinking in a particular country at a particular time (2007), and one can argue about its relevance to pupils with SLD and PMLD (see Chapter 5), the philosophical position is clear: it is believed that pupils with learning difficulties are *entitled* to an appropriate music education, just as their able-bodied peers are. For all children and young people, irrespective of abilities or needs, music is there to enhance the quality of life, potentially providing a medium of self-expression and communication with others. For a few so-called 'savants', as will become apparent in Chapter 10, *irrespective* of disability, music provides an opportunity for exceptional attainment.

However, savants are the exception rather than the rule. For the great majority of children and young people with SLD and PMLD, who are functionally very young, music may not yet be a discrete phenomenon. As we shall see (p. 51), it may not be perceived as a distinct strand amid a welter of other sensory stimuli, and may not even be distinguished from other forms of auditory input, such as speech and everyday noises. This has the implication that, since music tends to be part of larger experiences, these can be turned to advantage by using music consistently to help *structure* those experiences. And since making music is dependent on a number of attributes in addition to the perceptual skills directly associated with the processing of sound, musical activity can promote a wide range of learning and development. For example, performance, at any level, may well enhance fine motor control and coordination, while playing or listening engage cognitive skills such as concentration and memory.

Clearly, there is considerable overlap between the activities that constitute education in and through music and those that constitute music therapy, as described above in the practical accounts of music therapists. Hence, it is reasonable to ask whether education is an inevitable part of the therapeutic process for children and young people with SLD or PMLD. Is it ever possible to engage in music therapy with this group without, at least to an extent, indulging in educational activity too? At the most basic level, how could a young person benefit from therapy without some pre-existing skills and understanding (presumably acquired through education, formal or informal)? And is it not reasonable—and indeed desirable—to assume that, in many young people, skills and understanding will develop in the course of therapy sessions? Surely, the greater their technical proficiency, the more effectively children and young people will be able to express themselves in music, and the more likely they will be able to attain, albeit transiently, Bunt's state of 'well-being'? Conversely, it seems unimaginable that a child or young person could make educational progress unless he or she had a feeling of well-being, at least in part. And it would appear inconceivable that a teacher could work effectively with pupils with severe or profound learning difficulties without relating to them closely. Hence, is there not inevitably a therapeutic component in education too?

Towards a new model

Perhaps, ultimately, it is a matter of where the priorities of the therapist or teacher lie. As the Association of Professional Music Therapists (1992: 39) states: 'Children will often acquire certain musical skills in the course of a music therapy programme, such as sensitivity to pitch, rhythmic control, awareness of form, manipulative control, etc. These skills, whilst constituting an important part of the therapy programme, are likely to be secondary to pre-determined therapeutic objectives.' That is, it appears that the two disciplines may not be distinguishable so much by the nature of the activity that is under-taken as by their underlying aims and intentions. As Bruhn (2000) puts it: the difference between music therapy and music education lies in the way that music is used in the two disciplines, whereby in therapy, music is considered to be the *means* through which goals are achieved, whereas in education, it is held to be the *purpose*.[1]

Hence a model can be conceived as shown in Fig. 2.1. This model shows how both music therapy and music education promote 'well-being', but that this is a more important feature of therapy, whereas music education has more to do with 'development' (of skills, knowledge, and understanding); and that therapy has more client-centred, 'internally' determined goals, whereas effective music education usually balances 'internally' and 'externally' driven aspirations.[2]

This last point is supported by Kyproulla Markou's research into where the boundaries lie of music therapy and education for children and young people

---

[1] Cf. Robertson (2000), who addresses the conceptual problem by proposing the creation of a new discrete category called 'educational music therapy', which, in his terms, exists between 'clinical music therapy' and 'music education', which itself is distinct from 'music profession'. Robertson considers that this fourfold taxonomy reflects Laing's notion that the educational and therapeutic dimensions of art are complementary. Robertson's four categories are characterized as follows. 'Clinical music therapy' is concerned with the needs of clients that pertain to basic functioning and survival in life. The focus of 'educational music therapy' is on aspects such as personal and interpersonal growth, sub-conscious learning through music, and informing the aesthetic response of those with special educational needs. Similarly, music education recognizes the importance of the aesthetic response and aspects of learning through music. Music education, however, is associated more with the mainstream sector. It concerns itself with curricular issues such as the development of artistic and learning skills. Robertson's final category—'music profession'—pertains to the formulation of careers in music, with their reliance on training to facilitate the acquisition of skills.

[2] As Fig. 2.1 shows, both therapy and education are considered to be distinct from 'train-ing'—included here for conceptual clarity—which is solely concerned with the acquisi-tion of externally determined skills.

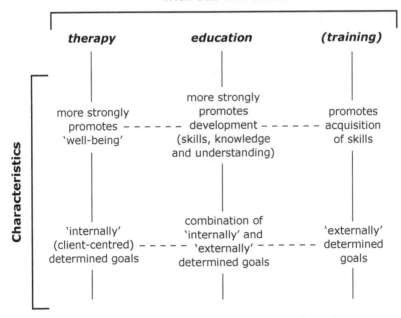

Music provision for children and young people with SLD or PMLD

Fig. 2.1 The characteristics of music education, therapy (and training) for children and young people with complex needs

with severe, or profound and multiple learning difficulties.[3] Among the questions she asked an equal sample of teachers and therapists working in the field ($N = 96$) was 'To what extent does the child play a part in guiding your sessions/lessons? The permitted range of responses was from '1 = not at all' to '10 = completely' set out on a Likert scale. The results are shown in Fig. 2.2. These suggest that, as populations, teachers and therapists do indeed differ in the emphasis they claim to put on child-centredness, with teachers, as the model in Fig. 2.1 suggests, on average perceiving themselves as being slightly more child-centred than not, but with a spread of responses across the entire spectrum ($M = 6.23$, $SD = 2.37$),[4] and therapists believing themselves to be almost entirely child-centred in their work ($M = 7.90$, $SD = 1.70$).[5] These perceptions tie in with the declared content of the music lessons and therapy sessions, with

---

[3] Undertaken as a doctoral student at Roehampton University.

[4] M is the 'mean'—the sum of the data divided by the sample size. SD is the 'standard deviation'—a measure of the range of variation from the mean.

[5] Independent samples t-test yields $t(96) = -3.95$, $p < 0.001$.

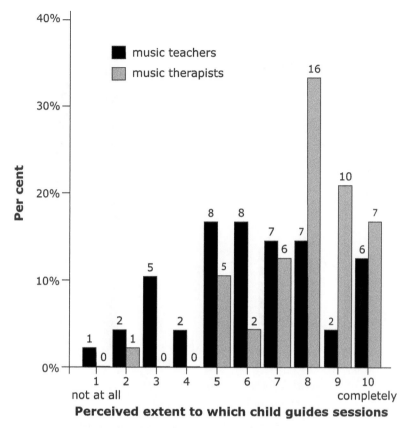

Fig. 2.2 The extent to which children are thought by therapists and teachers to guide sessions

the majority of teachers and therapists claiming to use both improvised *and* pre-composed songs and instrumental music; 13 teachers using *only* pre-composed instrumental music and 12, *only* pre-composed songs; and 14 therapists using *only* improvised instrumental music and 11, *only* improvised songs (see Fig. 2.3).[6]

However, the matter is by no means straightforward, since people's perceptions of what they do and the reality may be at odds. Consider, for example, Margaret Corke's 'Interactive Music' approach (2002), which claims to start 'from the learner's frame of reference' despite (apparently) having 'a set structure starting and finishing with hello and goodbye songs' (p. 6). Clearly, the

---

[6] The differences between the two groups are significant both for songs χ^2 (2, $N = 98$) = 20.31, $p < 0.001$ and instrumental music χ^2 (1, $N = 98$) = 24.27, $p < 0.001$.

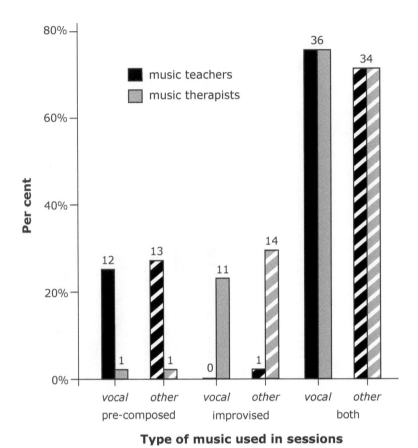

Fig. 2.3 The proportions of improvised and pre-composed vocal and instrumental music that teachers and therapists claim to use

issue of just where the locus of control lies is a key one for both therapists and teachers, and a method for gauging this through musical analysis is presented in Chapter 9.

Conclusion

Evidently, despite some of the rhetoric, there is a good deal of overlap in the content of music lessons and music therapy sessions for children and young people with SLD and PMLD. While this is not in itself a bad thing, since both disciplines have much to offer those with disabilities, the conceptual confusion that exists means that there is a danger of duplication and, worse still, that this will not be managed coherently. Hence a teacher and therapist may well be engaging in similar activities with a particular pupil/client, but with quite

different expectations of him or her. It is hoped that, merely by raising awareness of the issue, publications such as this will encourage more effective inter-
disciplinary working. However, more than this, it is hoped that the
music-developmental framework set out in Chapter 5 and the model of using
music to promote the wider development detailed in Chapter 6 may come to
serve as a common scaffold for all work in the field, whether undertaken by
teachers, therapists, community musicians, or others. And the system for
measuring musical influence set out in Chapter 9 gives an example of the tools
that may be developed to align judgements of attainment and progress that are
made from differing professional perspectives.

Chapter 3

Levels of uncertainty

Introduction

In 2001, the QCA published a set of guidelines, *Planning, teaching and assessing the curriculum for pupils with learning difficulties*, in a belated attempt to support teachers and others who were striving to meet the needs of children and young people deemed to be functioning 'below' Level 1 of the National Curriculum—for whom these materials as originally conceived had little applicability or required substantial modification, despite the original claims of 'entitlement for all'. The QCA's 2001 publication comprises separate guidelines for each curriculum area, including one for music. In common with the others, the music document contains 'Performance Descriptions', which outline early learning and attainment in eight levels, from 'P1' to 'P8', although the first three levels, corresponding to those with profound needs, are each subdivided into two: P1(i) and P1(ii), P2(i) and P2(ii), and P3(i) and P3(ii). These six descriptors are common across the whole curriculum, with different subject-focused examples added to illustrate some of the ways in which, it is suggested, staff may be able to identify attainment in different subject contexts. From level P4 to P8, the document states that 'it is possible to describe pupils' performance in a way that indicates the emergence of skills, knowledge and understanding in music'—and examples are provided of how this can be achieved. It is claimed that teachers can use the 11 Performance Descriptions to decide which best fits a pupil over a period of time and in different contexts, and so track his or her 'linear progress' towards attainment at Level 1 of the National Curriculum.

But is this claim sustainable? It will be argued that it is not, and that in reality there are a number of serious issues with the 'P-Levels' (as they became known in the field). These difficulties are outlined below. It is important that they are identified, acknowledged, and understood, to inform the process of charting an alternative route (in Chapter 5).

The 'P-Levels'—Issues

The first issue is the basis on which the P-Levels were developed: it remains unclear what evidence was used to underpin their construction, although they are said to 'draw on effective practice across a range of schools'. But in the absence of a demonstrable, systematically derived, empirical foundation, one is left with an abiding sense of the anecdotal. In relation to music, for example, the following is an exhaustive list of the examples given for levels P1 to P3, in the order in which they occur.[1]

startles at sudden noise
becomes still in a concert hall
becomes excited at repeated patterns of sounds
turns towards unfamiliar sounds
looks for the source of music
is encouraged to stroke the strings of a guitar
relaxes during certain pieces of music but not others
recognizes a favourite song
repeatedly presses the keys of an electronic keyboard instrument
taps piano keys gently and with more vigour
listens intently when moving across and through a sound beam
anticipates a loud sound at a particular point in a piece of music
taps, strokes, rubs or shakes an instrument to produce various effects

One wonders how these examples can possibly be thought to be representative when there is no mention (for example) of vocalization or vocal interaction—widely considered to be the bedrock of early music-making and musical communication (see, for instance, H. Papoušek 1996; Trevarthen 2002).[2]

Then, conceptually, the P-Levels suffer from the major disadvantage of starting with what is essentially an arbitrary cultural construct (the division of children's learning into subject areas) and working 'backwards' to the earliest stages of development—which, of course, Nature did not design with the National Curriculum in mind. Inevitably, there is a fault line where children's personal evolutionary paths coming 'upwards' meet the tracks of the National Curriculum extrapolated 'downwards'—a discontinuity that seems to be recognized implicitly with the move to subject-focused descriptors at Level 4. But is this, in any case, the appropriate tack to take? It relies on at least two assumptions: first, that a pupil with PMLD who is functioning globally at a 'typical'

---

[1] Some examples, which do not in reality pertain to achievement in music (such as 'leading an adult to the CD player'), are omitted.

[2] The extent to which it is reasonable to 'read across' from 'typical' early musical development to the evolution of musicality in children and young people with SLD or PMLD is an important issue that is taken up in the chapters that follow.

12-month level is developmentally ready to learn in discrete subject areas; and second, that this state of readiness occurs at the same point in different educational domains.

Are these assumptions reasonable? At what stage, for example, does music become a distinct strand in human thinking? The answer is not straightforward. For instance, it appears that, even before birth, babies can become familiar with certain pieces or passages of music, as well as the tone of their mother's voice and the language she speaks. To all or any of these classes of sound, the unborn child may develop a particular sensitivity, which may subsequently influence his or her auditory preferences *post partum* (Lecanuet 1996). Hence it may be that among those pupils with even the most profound learning difficulties, there are some who will be responsive to particular pieces of music, suggesting the presence of some form of discrete cognitive processing. Then, according to Trehub (1990), by the age of five or six months, infants can discriminate between different melodic patterns according to the way in which the notes relate to one another—detecting violations in contour[3] while appreciating the isomorphic nature of transposition,[4] for example. Hence the infant's representation of melodies is *abstract*, with contour playing a critical role. Again, the implication is that pupils with PMLD who are functioning globally at a sixth-month level may be able to process certain forms of musical structure (an issue discussed at some length in the chapters that follow).

In other respects, though, the development of musical perception and thinking appears to be inextricably intertwined with that in other domains—particularly language. For example, M. Papoušek (1996: 90) notes that 'from early on, parents and infants share a "prelinguistic alphabet" or code in the form of musical elements that both infant-directed speech and infant vocal sounds have in common'. So, preverbal communication 'may represent a common ontogenetic avenue along which two highly structured and exclusively human capacities develop': speech and singing (1996: 104). Similarly, Fassbender (1996: 80) observes that, to begin with, 'perceptions of speech and music seem to arise from the same basis, but they may take different developmental courses when meaning becomes attached to specific acoustical information in the social interaction of intuitive parenting'. And this early connection between language and music apparently has longer-term developmental consequences since, according to M. Papoušek (1996: 90), the 'proportion of reciprocal vocal matching and maternal imitation during mother–infant interactions before 6 months of age predicts the rate of infant lexical imitation at

---

[3] The pattern of 'ups' and 'downs' in a melody.

[4] Moving a group of pitches as a whole up or down in pitch.

15 months of age'. This suggests that teachers and therapists working with those with profound developmental delay, as well as valuing pupils' vocal communication as a natural and valid form of expression in its own right, should also conceptualize it as a precursor both to speech and to singing.

How, then, can early auditory development usefully be modelled for those working with children and young people with complex needs? A functional approach seems most appropriate, resulting in a model with at least two strands, pertaining to the main channels of communication through sound— language and music. The research cited above shows that these have a complex interrelationship, initially with common features, increasingly supplemented with unique characteristics, and finally dividing into conceptually distinguishable domains (in the period following the first 12 months of 'typical' development). To this view we need to add the perspective of ecological acoustics developed by William Gaver (1993), who suggests that as well as 'musical listening', which focuses on *perceptual qualities* such as pitch and loudness, there is also 'everyday listening' which is concerned with attending to *events* such as a dog barking or a car driving by. Hence a tripartite model is suggested along the lines shown in Fig. 3.1.

Of course, in real life, things are not as neat and tidy as this, and as well as occurring discretely, the three types of sound function may well be mixed up together:

Think of a child in a supermarket, for example, who is being assailed simultaneously by background music (ultimately intended to encourage shoppers to spend more), his father discussing the price of baked beans with a friend, and the clatter of tins on the shelf. Then, two sound functions may consciously be combined, as in songs, for example (the fusion of music and speech), or a single sound may serve a dual or even triple function, as is the case with clock chimes, for instance (comprising musical, everyday sounds which also convey symbolic meaning). (Ockelford, 2005*b*: 51)

Learning to make sense of all these different types of auditory input—developing different ways of processing sounds according to their context and function—usually occurs without specially thought-through intervention on the part of parents or carers. However, pupils with complex needs may well find it much more difficult to make sense of things in auditory terms, and much of the world around will remain a confusing place for them well into childhood and beyond. So it is essential that their educational programmes acknowledge this challenge, and accord music its own, unique place in the curriculum as well as using it to enhance wider programmes of learning (see Chapter 6).

These, then, are some of the broader issues around the P-Levels for Music. However, they also raise a number of specific concerns. These are best illustrated by allocating the material presented in the Performance Descriptions to

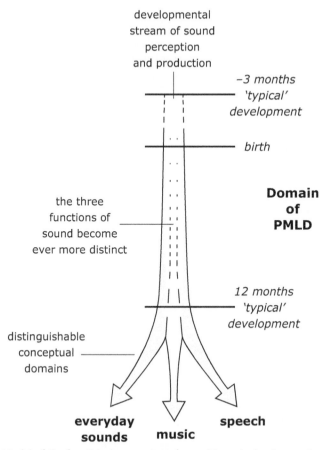

Fig. 3.1 Model of the functional processing of sound in early development

one of three domains: 'listening, reacting, and responding', 'causing, creating, and controlling' (alone or with others), and 'reflecting on/communicating about music'.[5] Here, the analysis is restricted to Levels P1–P3 (corresponding to the curriculum for pupils with PMLD) (see Table 3.1).

Recasting the Performance Descriptions for music in this format reveals a number of problems with their structure and content. First, and most obviously, there are *gaps*. Whatever happened to causing, creating, or controlling

---

[5] These domains represent a simplification and consolidation of the four aspects of music identified in the National Curriculum programmes of study ('Listening, and applying knowledge and understanding', 'Controlling sounds through singing and playing—performing skills', 'Creating and developing musical ideas—composing skills', and 'Responding and reviewing—appraising skills').

Table 3.1 Analysis of P-Levels 1–3 for music

Level	Listening, reacting, and responding	Causing, creating, and controlling (alone or with others)	Reflecting on and communicating about music
P1(i)	Pupils encounter activities and experiences. They may be passive or resistant. They may show simple reflex responses, *for example, startling at sudden noises or movements.*	Any participation is fully prompted.	
P1(ii)	Pupils show emerging awareness of activities and experiences. They may have periods when they appear alert and ready to focus their attention on certain people, events, objects or parts of objects, *for example, becoming still in a concert hall.* They may give intermittent reactions, *for example, sometimes becoming excited at repeated patterns of sounds.*		
P2(i)	Pupils begin to respond consistently to familiar people, events, and objects. They react to new activities and experiences, *for example, turning towards unfamiliar sounds.* They begin to show interest in people, events, and objects, *for example, looking for the source of music*	They accept and engage in coactive exploration, *for example, being encouraged to stroke the strings of a guitar.*	
P2(ii)	They recognize familiar people, events, and objects, *for example, a favourite song.*	Pupils begin to be proactive in their interactions. They perform actions, often by trial and improvement, and they remember learned responses over short periods of time, *for example, repeatedly pressing the keys of an electronic keyboard instrument.* They cooperate with shared exploration and supported participation, *for example, holding an ocean drum.*	They communicate consistent preferences and affective responses, *for example, relaxing during certain pieces of music but not others.*

Continued

Table 3.1 Cont.

Level	Listening, reacting, and responding	Causing, creating, and controlling (alone or with others)	Reflecting on and communicating about music
P3(i)	They sustain concentration for short periods.	They participate in shared activities with less support.	Pupils begin to communicate intentionally.
	They observe the results of their own actions with interest, *for example, listening intently when moving across and through a sound beam.*	They explore materials in increasingly complex ways, *for example, tapping piano keys gently and with more vigour.*	They seek attention through eye contact, gesture or action.
			They request events or activities, *for example, leading an adult to the CD player.*
	They remember learned responses over more extended periods. . .	*. . . For example, recalling movements associated with a particular song from week to week.*	
P3(ii)	They can remember learned responses over increasing periods of time and may anticipate known events, *for example, a loud sound at a particular point in a piece of music.*	They actively explore objects and events for extended periods, *for example, tapping stroking, rubbing or shaking an instrument to produce various effects.*	Pupils use emerging conventional communication.
			They greet known people and may initiate interactions and activities, *for example, performing an action such as clapping hands to initiate a particular song.*
			They may respond to options and choices with actions or gestures, *for example, choosing a shaker in a rhythm band activity.*
			They apply potential solutions systematically to problems, *for example, indicating by eye contact or gesture the pupil whose turn it is to play in a 'call and response' activity.*

sound at P1(ii), for example—at a time when pupils are apparently showing an 'emerging awareness of activities and experiences'? Second, the descriptors are often ambiguous. For example, P3(i) states 'They participate in shared activities with less support'. Less than what? What kind of support? As a result, it is sometimes unclear how levels are meant to be distinguished from one another. For example, P2(i) states '[Pupils] accept and engage in coactive exploration, *for example, being encouraged to stroke the strings of a guitar*' while at level P2(ii) 'They cooperate with shared exploration and supported participation, *for example, holding an ocean drum*'. But would it not be reasonable to assume that being supported to stroke the strings of a guitar is a more advanced activity than being assisted in holding an ocean drum? Then again, at level P3(i) 'They remember responses over more extended periods', while at P3(ii) 'They can remember learned responses over increasing periods'. How could teachers reasonably be expected to evaluate pupils' attainment using non-specific criteria such as these?

Sometimes, problems appear to arise because of the difficulty in trying make music conform to the general developmental path that Levels P1–P3 seek to map out. For example, at P3(ii) 'They apply potential solutions systematically to problems, *for example, indicating by eye contact or gesture the pupil whose turn it is to play in a 'call and response' activity*. Moreover, the example given here only tenuously pertains to attainment in music. Others have nothing to do with music at all—for example, P3(ii), 'They greet known people'.

Conclusion

In summary, it appears that music perception begins as one aspect of general auditory processing that gradually becomes more distinct during the first year of life, although cognitive links with other categories of sound always remain. Hence, it is reasonable to assert that those functioning at an early developmental level *should* have a music curriculum that, while founded in general auditory perception, soon becomes discrete, in acknowledgement of the unique evolutionary path that music cognition takes in the mind. For sure, once it is securely established, this curriculum will be of value to those who wish to use music to promote wider learning and development. But the two things should not be conflated.

However, this is precisely what the P-Levels for music do: confusing musical and extra-musical issues, and ultimately being clear about neither. Above all, it is faulty in conception, setting out from social constructs rather than music perception and cognition: from an understanding of how human beings come to understand music. And it is to this most basic of questions—how it is that music makes sense—that we next turn our attention.

PART II

A NEW MODEL

Chapter 4

Making sense of music making sense

Introduction

Most of us engage with music in one way or another, consciously or unwittingly, every day of our lives. Indeed, recent research has reinforced the anecdotal view that music permeates much of what we do: according to Sloboda, O'Neill, and Ivaldi (2001), 'non-musicians' reported hearing music on 44 per cent of occasions that were chosen at random during waking hours over the period of a week. Yet listening to music as a main activity accounted for a small minority (2 per cent) of these episodes. The other occurrences of music were variously categorized by the researchers as 'time fillers' (such as waiting), 'personal—being' (for example, waking up), 'personal—maintenance' (for instance, washing, getting dressed, cooking, eating at home, and doing housework), 'personal—travelling' (including driving and walking), 'leisure—passive' (such as watching TV, relaxing, and reading for pleasure), 'leisure—active' (for example, games, sport, socializing, and eating out), 'work—self' (for instance, writing, using the computer, and reading for study) and 'work—other' (including planning for meetings).

A comparable study involving children and young people with complex needs has yet to be undertaken, although given music's reported permeation of activities throughout the school day reported in Chapter 1, it is probable that the proportion of time in which music is present in pupils' environments is at least as great as it is for adults in everyday life. This assumption is supported by Ockelford (2000), who, following a series of visits to special schools, identified the areas of activity where music was likely to be experienced, as shown in Table 4.1.

At the heart of Sloboda, O'Neill, and Ivaldi's finding lies the fact that for 'ordinary' people, music makes sense and has the power to communicate directly on an emotional level, quite without the need for special knowledge or skills. For example:

Harry, a retired accountant, driving through the city traffic, fiddles absently with the tuning on the car radio. A station is located, there's a moment's silence, and then a piece

Table 4.1 Observed areas of musical engagement of children and young people with complex needs

Activity	For whom?	Where?	Provided by	Organized by
General music education	Class (children and young people with SLD or PMLD)	School	Class teacher; music coordinator	Music coordinator
Music to promote wider learning and development	Individuals or groups (with SLD or PMLD)	Largely in school; possibly at home	Class teacher; teaching assistant; physiotherapist; speech and language therapist; other	Any lead professional
Specialist instrumental or singing tuition	Individuals (with SLD)	School; home; other	Specialist music teacher	Music coordinator; parents
Music therapy	Individuals or groups (with SLD or PMLD)	School; music therapy centre	Music therapist	Music coordinator; parents
Taking part in special musical events	Individuals or groups (with SLD or PMLD)	School; community	*For example,* education section of professional group	School; parents; voluntary agency
Listening to live music (attendance at concerts, etc.)	Individuals or groups (with SLD or PMLD)	School; community; concert venues; etc.	Performers (amateur or professional)	School; parents; voluntary agency
Listening to recorded music for leisure	Individuals or groups (with SLD or PMLD)	Largely at home (possibly in school)	Performers (amateur or professional)	Parents; carers; others
Incidental musical experiences	**Individuals (with SLD or PMLD)**	**Anywhere (and almost everywhere)**	**Various**	**No one**

of piano music starts up. Harry is struck by its immediacy, elegance, and what strikes him as a wistful beauty. He suspects the piece may be by his favourite composer, Mozart. For him, the music of Mozart is incomparable, and he can usually pick it out from other compositions from the Classical period—despite having had no formal music education. (Ockelford 2005*c*)

Similarly, the PROMISE research identified the widely held belief that music is of value to pupils with complex needs (both in its own right and as an agent for promoting wider learning and development) apparently deriving from the unspoken assumption that music 'works' for pupils with special needs as it does for most other people. But is this actually the case?

To answer this question requires an understanding of how music 'works' in general terms; of how it is, just through exposure, that music 'makes sense', that it *means* something; that, just by listening, it offers a coherent aesthetic experience. And it is to this issue that we first turn our attention.

Musical meaning

Although, as we noted in the previous chapter, music typically occurs along-side or integrated with other modes of artistic or cultural endeavour, such as language (in the case of song) or movement (in the case of dance) it can, nonetheless, function effectively in its own right. For example, in the west, cer-tain styles of music are deemed to be valid artistically and to have meaning purely as abstract patterns in sound, which are not connected to anything else. And it is with 'absolute' music that our investigation will kick off.

First, however, to provide a context, we take a preliminary detour into the realm of language-based art-forms, which have an evident source of meaning construction since they communicate about an external 'reality'. According to T. S. Eliot (1920/1997; 1933), literature communicates on an aesthetic level in three ways: through an *objective correlative*—a 'set of objects, a situation, a chain of events which shall be the formula of that *particular* emotion'; through the *manner* of representation (including, for example, the use of metaphor); and through the sound qualities and structure of the language itself. Hence, meaning in a literary work arises from its semantic, syntactic, and sonic ele-ments working together 'in an evocative fusion of content, structure and sound' (Ockelford 2005*d*: 84). This thinking may be represented as shown in Fig. 4.1.

But 'pure' music has no external referents—no 'objective correlatives', to use Eliot's term (Fig. 4.2). So where does music derive its meaning from?

Logically, it must stem from the fabric of music itself—from the sounds and the relationships between them that make up pieces. It is my contention that each of these sonic elements potentially bears affect, causing or enabling an

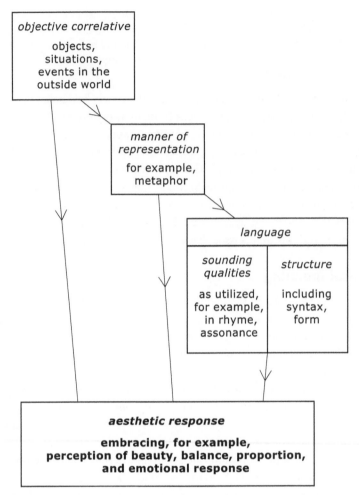

Fig. 4.1 Aesthetic response to language (after T. S. Eliot)

emotional response (cf. Johnson-Laird and Oatley 1992: 20; Sparshott 1994: 28). There appear to be two main sources of such responses: 'expressive non-verbal vocalizations' and 'music-specific' qualities of sound.

'Expressive nonverbal vocalizations' comprise the cues used to express emotions vocally in nonverbal communication and speech (Juslin, Friberg, and Bresin 2001–2). They are present cross-culturally (Scherer, Banse, and Wallbott 2001), suggesting a common phylogenetic[1] derivation from 'nonverbal affect

---

[1] That is, through evolution of a species.

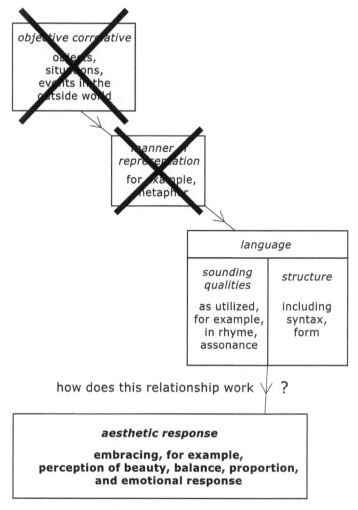

Fig. 4.2 Music has no 'objective correlative' or 'manner of representation'

vocalizations' (Scherer 1991) and apparently embedded ontogenetically[2] in early maternal/infant vocal interaction (Malloch 1999–2000; Trehub and Nakata, 2001–2)—see p. 49 above. It seems that these cues can be transferred in a general way to music, and music-psychological research over the last 70 years or so has shown that features such as register, tempo, and dynamic level do relate with some consistency to particular emotional states (Gabrielsson and Lindström 2001). For example, passages in a high register can feel exciting

---

[2] Through the development of an individual.

(Watson 1942) or exhibit potency (Scherer and Oshinsky 1977), whereas series of low notes are more likely to promote solemnity or to be perceived as serious (Watson 1942). A fast tempo will tend to induce feelings of excitement (Thompson and Robitaille 1992), in contrast to slow tempi that may connote tranquility (Gundlach 1935) or even peace (Balkwill and Thompson 1999). Loud dynamic levels are held to be exciting (Watson 1942), triumphant (Gundlach 1935) or to represent gaiety (Nielzén and Cesarec 1982), while quiet sounds have been found to express fear, tenderness or grief (Juslin 1997). Conversely, as Leonard Meyer asserts, 'one cannot imagine sadness being portrayed by a fast forte tune played in a high register, or a playful child being depicted by a solemnity of trombones' (Meyer 2001).

However, while these basic properties of sound appear to be necessary in determining musical expression (London 2001–2), they are not sufficient to evoke a response that is inherently musical. Indeed, *any* succession of sounds may induce a primitive emotional reaction according to the disposition of what Meyer (2001: 342) terms their 'statistical parameters' (which he takes to include register, dynamic level, speed, and continuity). So what are the ingredients needed to arouse a specifically musical response?

One factor is the very nature of the sounds that are used in most styles and genres: they have intrinsically musical characteristics that, like those identified above pertaining to vocalization, have the capacity to induce consistent emotional responses, within and sometimes between cultures. For example, in the west and elsewhere, music typically utilizes a framework of relative pitches with close connections to the harmonic series. These are used idiosyncratically, with context-dependent frequencies of occurrence and transition patterns, together yielding the sensation of 'tonality'[3] (Krumhansl 1997; Peretz, Gagnon, and Bouchard 1998). Such frameworks can accommodate different *modalities*, each potentially bearing distinct emotional connotations. In Indian music, for example, the concept of the 'raga' is based on the idea that particular patterns of notes are able to evoke heightened states of emotion (Jariazbhoy 1971), while in the western tradition of the last four centuries or so, the 'major mode' is typically associated with happiness, for example, and the 'minor mode' with sadness (Hevner 1936; Crowder 1985).

While the reactions that individual or small groups of sounds can engender are important in setting the 'auditory scene' of music, as they stand, they do not add up to a coherent musical response, merely amounting to a series of separate sensations pertaining to a sequence of discrete events. So how are

---

[3] The sense that individual pitches fulfil different functions in relation to one another, according to their position within a diatonic scale.

these distinct, abstract responses bound together into a unified aesthetic experience—to create meaning that unfolds over time—during the course of listening to a piece of music?

Consider verbal language once more. Eliot's 'objective correlative' is likely to be a series of events, actions, feelings, or thoughts that are in some way reckoned to be *logically related*, each contingent upon one of the others or more through relationships of causation or other forms of dependency. These are represented through a linguistic narrative, which underpins readers' or listeners' coherent aesthetic response over time (see Fig. 4.3).

How does a comparable sense of coherence and unity come about in music, when it cannot borrow a sense of contingency from the external world? In the absence of an objective correlative, musical events can refer only to *themselves* (Selincourt 1920/1958). Self-evidently, one sound does not *cause* another one to happen (it is performers who do that), but one can *imply* another (Meyer 1989: 84 ff.) through a sense of *derivation*. That is, one musical event can be felt to stem from another, and it is my contention that this occurs through *imitation*. If one fragment or feature of music echoes another, then it owes the nature of its existence to its model. And just as certain perceptual qualities of sound are felt to derive from one another, so too, it is hypothesized, are the emotional responses to each. Hence over time a metaphorical (musical) narrative can be built up through abstract patterns of sound (see Fig. 4.4). This hypothesis lies at the heart of 'zygonic theory' (Ockelford 1991, 1999, 2002*b*, 2004, 2005*a*, 2005*d*, 2006*a*), which predicts that if music makes sense through

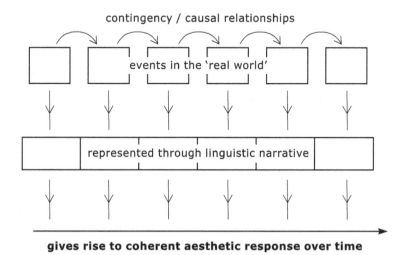

Fig. 4.3 The linguistic narrative reflecting external events, ideas, and feelings

events in the 'real world'

'implicative' relationships

musical narrative

gives rise to coherent aesthetic response over time

Fig. 4.4 The musical narrative need make no external reference

a feeling of derivation (which stems from imitation), then repetition in music should be pervasive. And it is.[4]

The easiest place to hear the theory in action is in musical 'canons', which are explicitly structured through repetition—one musical line consciously being made to copy another. Ex. 4.1 shows, for example, the opening of 'Et in unum Dominum' from the Mass in B minor, where Bach uses the derivation of the alto part from the soprano within a unified musical framework as a symbol of the Father *begetting* (not creating) the Son, which, according to Christian dogma (and Bach, by all accounts, was a devout believer), subsequently coexisted as parts of the same spiritual entity.

Irrespective of the symbolism, it is easy to appreciate how each note in the alto voice, ensuing shortly after an identical event sung by the soprano, sounds irresistibly to the musical ear as though it derives from it. In the mind, each

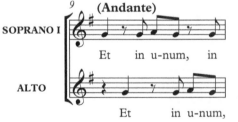

Ex. 4.1 The opening of 'Et in unum' from Bach's Mass in B minor (BWV 232); *Symbolum Nicenum*, No. 3

---

[4] Something that is widely recognized in the musicological literature. See, for example: Réti (1951); Zuckerkandl (1956); Meyer (1956; 1967; 1973); Chávez (1961); Ruwet (1966/87); Forte (1973); Rahn (1980); Lerdahl and Jackendoff (1983); Lewin (1987); Nattiez (1990); and Morris (1995).

pair of notes appears to be connected via a mental 'bridge' that spans the two perceived sounds. Each of these may be termed a 'zygonic relationship' or 'zygon' (after the Greek word for 'yoke', meaning the union of two similar things). In order to make analysis and understanding easier, it is sometimes helpful to represent these cognitive connections visually, and, at its simplest, this can be achieved through an arrow with a superimposed 'Z' (Ex. 4.2).

The solid-looking nature of these links should not be taken to mean that zygonic relationships have any material substance—they are *hypothetical constructs*: conceptual shorthand for a range of logically equivalent cognitive processes that we may reasonably suppose occur during listeners' engagement with music. This supposition is reasonable since if one were to attempt to create 'music' with no repetition whatsoever, then there would be no sense of contingency between the fragments of sound that were presented, and the 'music' would make no sense at all.[5] There would be 'nothing but a haphazard succession of irregularly varying pitches which, differing widely in duration and time of attack, would describe wildly irregular rhythms, unpredictable in loudness, coloured by a bewildering confusion of timbres and proceeding indiscriminately from random locations potentially spaced the world apart' (Ockelford 1999: 1).

In fact, musicological research using zygonic theory has shown that every aspect of music is supersaturated with repetition in a way that goes far beyond the motivic and thematic replications and variations that traditional music analysis seeks to identify. Take, for example, the piece that Harry (the retired accountant) heard on his car radio (see pp. 57 and 59). His supposition was correct—it was by Mozart—the first movement of his Piano Sonata K333 (Ex. 4.3).

To the ear familiar with western classical music, nothing could sound more natural, more unpretentious—and less like a multidimensional matrix of meticulously crafted logical connections in sound. Yet zygonic analysis has shown that there are actually over 40 types of structural imitation in this movement operating at any given time (Ockelford 1999: 704 ff.), connecting

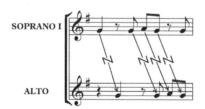

Ex. 4.2 Zygonic relationships symbolizing the sense of derivation of one note from another

---

[5] See, for example, Eschman's critique of Hába, who had claimed to have written melodies in a style devoid of repetition (1945/1968: 19 ff.).

Ex. 4.3 The opening of Mozart's Piano Sonata K333

individual pitches, the intervals between them, and their relative probabilities of occurrence; harmonies, harmonic transitions, forms of dissonance, and the manner in which these are resolved; keys, modulations, and longer-term tonal structures; the durations of notes, their inter-onset intervals,[6] metre, rhythms, phrase-lengths, and lengths of sections; textures, melodies, the connections between them, and overall form. Compromise the structure in any one of these dimensions and the musical fabric as a whole would no longer hang together coherently. Of course, that is not to say that Mozart gave any of this a moment's conscious thought as he composed K333. For him, by all accounts, creating music was as natural and effortless as speaking.[7] But just as producing and understanding cogent and expressive verbal language makes huge demands on cognitive processing (of which speakers and listeners are typically wholly unaware), so too does generating and attending to music. Unless he had had an intuitive grasp of the underlying transition probabilities between notes in relation to pitch and perceived time that hearing K333 stimulated him to recall from other, similar pieces he had heard in the past, how else could Harry have concluded that the piece was by Mozart? Unless he had been able to process the moment-to-moment connections between events, how else would the music have sounded coherent? And, as Ockelford (2005*a*: 35 ff.) shows, the source of its 'elegance' and 'wistful beauty' lay entirely in Harry's capacity to process complex, abstract patterns of sound.

Yet, by his own admission, Harry had had no formal music education, and never performed music beyond, as a child, singing in assembly at school and, subsequently, joining in with the hymns in church every Sunday—hardly the level of sophistication of K333. So mere *exposure* was enough for him to acquire advanced music-processing skills (as it is for most people). How does this work, though, for children and young people with complex needs? Indeed,

---

[6] The lengths of time between the beginnings of (typically successive) notes.

[7] See also the accounts of musical savants in Chapter 10, for some of whom engaging with music appears to be *easier* than using verbal language.

is it the same for them? Is being exposed to music sufficient for them to learn as Harry had done, or are they never likely to acquire his music-cognitive abilities?

Virtually the only evidence that was able to shed light on this issue prior to the current Sounds of Intent study[8] lay within the growing corpus of research literature pertaining to the development of musicality in infants, and relevant findings are set out below. It should be acknowledged, however, that adopting this strategy makes two important assumptions: first, that the individual music-developmental paths taken by those with SLD or PMLD have sufficient in common to be regarded as a single conceptual entity, and, second, that this evolutionary route is broadly in line with the 'typical' musical development that occurs for the majority in the early stages of life. Both these assertions will be tested in Chapter 5.

Returning, for the moment, to early musical development, it is axiomatic that the musical significance of the *repetition* of sounds can only be appreciated within the context of understanding their potential *variation*, and it appears that this capacity is usually in place shortly after birth, evidenced both by listening:

Infants in the first postpartum months are able to detect and discriminate small differences in frequency, amplitude, and the harmonic spectrum ... They are able to process time-related information and to differentiate sounds in terms of duration, pause length, tempo and relative timing in rhythmic sequences. (M. Papoušek 1996: 89)

and by vocal production:

Recent accounts of prelinguistic stages of vocal development from a number of laboratories ... converge on a differentiation of six stages of vocal production: phonation (0–1 months); melodic modulation and primitive articulation in cooing (2–3 months); exploratory vocal play (4–6 months) ... Infants alternately produce squealing and growling sounds, screams and whispers, brief staccato-like noises, and drawn-out vowel-like sounds with extensive frequency modulation, which occasionally expand across one or two octaves. (M. Papoušek 1996: 103 and 104)

In parallel with this recognition and production of variety within and between sounds, repetition—brought about initially through humans' built-in propensity to imitate others (see, for example, Meltzoff and Prinz 2002)— soon comes to play a part in early sound-making. 'Careful auditory and acoustic analyses of preverbal communication at 2, 3, 5 and 7 months demonstrate that 34–53 percent of infant vocal sounds are part of reciprocal matching sequences, framed by mothers' modelling and/or matching utterances'

---

[8] Described in Chapter 5.

(M. Papoušek 1996: 97). Moreover, it appears that infants below five months of age are capable of imitating pitches (Kessen, Levine, and Wendrich 1979), pitch contours (Kuhl and Meltzoff 1982), and vowel-like harmonic resonances (Legerstee 1990).

In music, similarity and difference in sound work *together* to create in listeners a sense of movement and repose, of initiation and closure, and to enable them to perceive trends and hierarchies. At a fundamental level, repetition binds variety together through the principles of *Gestalt* perception (Ockelford 2002*b*). This capacity features early in musical development. For example, Fassbender (1996) observed that infants as young as two to five-and-a-half months of age organize rapid tone sequences perceptually on the basis of proximity and similarity.

The integrated recognition of sameness and difference is important too in the discrimination of melodic patterns. For example, Trehub (1990) notes that infants can distinguish between different tunes on the basis of relational information at the age of five to six months—sensitively detecting violations of contours but *not* transpositions or contour-preserving transformations.

Babies integrate repetition and variety in their vocal production too. For instance, between four and six months 'The impression of playful creative exploration arises from observations of infants' persistent motivation to reproduce sounds discovered by chance, and to repeat and modify their vocal products with overt signs of effort, eagerness, and joy' (M. Papoušek 1996: 104 and 105). Later, from seven to eleven months, the notion of repeating and varying *groups* of sounds as the basic units of proto-musical structure appears: 'canonical babbling involves production of regular-beat rhythms with superimposed melodies, short musical patterns or phrases that soon become the core units for a new level of vocal practising and play' (M. Papoušek 1996: 106).

Gradually, groups of sounds may be linked through repetition or transposition to form chains, and the first self-sufficient improvised pieces emerge.

Between the ages of one to two years . . . a typically spontaneous infant song consists of repetitions of one brief melodic phrase at different pitch centres. (Welch 2006: 318)

They are unlike adult songs, however, because they lack a framework of stable pitches (a scale) and use a very limited set of contours in one song. (Dowling 1982: 416 and 417)

At the same time, complete songs emerge as discrete conceptual objects, implying the cognition of repetition *between* performances. Dowling (1982) writes: 'During their second year children begin to recognize certain melodies as stable entities in their environments. My daughter at 18 months would run to the TV set when she heard the "Sesame Street" theme come on but not for other melodies.'

From the age of $2\frac{1}{2}$, 'pot pourri' songs may appear (Moog 1968/1976: 115), which borrow (and may transform) features and fragments from others—standard songs that are assimilated into the child's own spontaneous song schemes (Hargreaves 1986: 73).[9]

Finally, around the age of 5, two major advances typically occur. First, children develop the capacity to abstract an underlying pulse from the surface rhythm of songs (meaning that he or she performs 'in time' to a regular beat). Second, they acquire 'tonal stability', with the clear projection of a key centre across all the phrases of a piece (Hargreaves 1986: 76 and 77).[10] These abilities imply an cognizance of repetition at a deeper structural level in the 'background' organization of music.

So much for the development of the music-processing abilities that appear to underpin the cognition of musical structure according to the principle that one sound can be derived from another through imitation (and therefore repetition). However, the way in which the mind grapples with abstract patterns of sound—a facet of cognitive processing that arguably lies at the heart of the musical experience—is profoundly affected by individual abilities, attitudes, interests, the interaction with others who are present, and the broader cultural context in which the artistic endeavour occurs. The nature and extent of these other factors is admirably captured by the contributors to Patrik Juslin and John Sloboda's book *Music and Emotion: Theory and Research* (2001). Here an overview of items of potential relevance to young people with complex needs is offered.

At a physical level, the environmental context—the nature of the location in which the music is heard—is critical to the experience of listeners. As Berlioz puts it, in his *Grand traité d'instrumentation et d'orchestration modernes*, op. 10:

The place occupied by musicians, their disposal on a horizontal plane or an inclined plane, in an enclosed space with three sides, or in the very centre of a room, with reverberators formed by hard bodies fit for sending back the sound, or soft bodies which absorb and interrupt the vibrations, and more or less near to the performers, are all of great importance. (1855/1858: 240)

To the physical nature of the space in which music is heard should be added the effect of social expectations associated with different venues. Hence, to

---

[9] See also Mang (2005), who notes that self-generated songs may be seen as 'referent-guided improvisation' using source materials derived from learned songs.

[10] The notion of 'tonality'—of pitches fulfilling different roles in relation to one another according to frequency of occurrence and transition probabilities—is present cross-culturally (cf. n. 3).

initiated listeners, Mendelssohn's *Wedding March* would, no doubt, seem as incongruous in Ronnie Scott's as Charlie Parker's *Anthropology* would sound in Canterbury Cathedral. Then, listeners may well be affected by the demeanour of the performers and by the reactions of others who are present, through empathy and 'emotional contagion', for example (Scherer and Zentner 2001: 370).

Turning to 'internal' matters, there are attitudinal factors, such as values, beliefs, preferences and propensities, and the listener's prevailing mood, which will provide the affective backdrop against which any emotions aroused by a piece will be superimposed as 'phasic perturbations' (Davidson 1994: 52); we have all experienced how a favourite piece may be unappealing or even irritating on certain occasions. Musical abilities are important too. A listener such as Derek Paravicini (see p. 215), who can apparently hear each of the notes that the instruments in a large ensemble are playing, will presumably have a different aesthetic experience from the majority of listeners, for whom orchestral chords (for example) provide a homogeneous harmonic and timbral effect.

The nature of a listener's knowledge of music may well have a substantial impact too, and there may be affective experiences associated with previous hearings of the piece in question. As John Booth Davies (1978: 69) wryly remarks:

The classic example of this is perhaps the 'Darling, they're playing our tune' phenomenon. The lady from whose mouth this apocryphal saying is supposed to have emanated has acquired a specific emotional response to a specific tune simply because she heard it at a time when some other pleasurable business was taking place, at some time in the past. . . . Even the most unmusical people usually have an associative response of this type to at least one or two tunes. (A man might therefore justifiably feel some alarm if his unmusical wife suddenly develops an apparently spontaneous liking for a new tune.)

However, as Davies notes, not all melodies will do the job equally well.

Tunes of the DTPOT (*Darling, They're Playing Our Tune*) type are usually drawn from the ranks of 'Songs for swinging lovers' or something similar, where the words and the mood of the music are somehow appropriate to the events with which they become associated. This, of course, begs another question, since moods are properties of people and not of music. None the less, people who use the overture 'William Tell' or 'The ride of the Valkyries' as a DTPOT tune are definitely in a minority.

Davies attributes this to the probability that 'people learn as a cultural norm that certain types of music are conventionally used in particular situations'. However, that leaves unexplained how certain associations arise in the first place, and to understand that, it is my contention that one needs to consider intra-musical factors of the type suggested by zygonic theory.

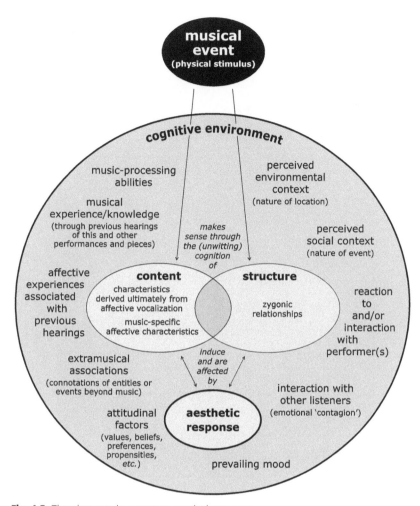

Fig. 4.5 The elements in a mature musical response

Conclusion

Taking all these factors into account, a complete model of a mature response to music is likely to contain the elements shown in Fig. 4.5. Here, the important question is whether this conceptualization helps us to understand the musical responses of young people with SLD or PMLD. To what extent is the model applicable to them? Do children with complex needs follow the same music-developmental path as the majority of people—albeit, perhaps, at a slower rate and possibly never travelling as far—or are their lines of musical development fundamentally different in certain respects? It is to this issue that the next chapter is devoted.

PART III

ADDRESSING SPECIAL MUSICAL NEEDS

Chapter 5

Sounds of Intent

Introduction

Chapter 4 sketched out two lines of thought that are likely to have a bearing on the way that the musical development of children and young people with SLD or PMLD is modelled. The first was a theory of how music makes sense and is able to communicate at an emotional and aesthetic level, and the second was an account of how musicality 'typically' evolves, which was derived from a range of empirical work in the field of psychology. Self-evidently, though, at the heart of any attempt to model the musical development of those with complex needs should lie direct evidence gathered from observing the children and young people themselves.

It was with this aim in mind that, following the completion of the PROMISE survey, a new research team was set up by the Institute of Education, University of London and RNIB, involving a group of practitioners who were active in the field—both specialists and non-specialists in music—to participate in what became known as the 'Sounds of Intent' project. The prospect of gathering sufficient evidence to map musical development across the domains of PMLD and SLD was a daunting one, and so it was decided to focus initially on pupils with profound needs. The team analysed video recordings of their own and one another's pupils in detail and undertook direct observation in each other's classrooms. The children's responses, actions, and interactions were carefully noted, and attempts were made to gauge which could reasonably be considered to be representative of musical attainment or progress. A number of short examples follow.[1]

Observations

1. Abigail sits motionless in her chair. Her teacher approaches and plays a cymbal with a soft beater, gently at first, and then more loudly, in front of her and then near to each ear. Abigail does not appear to react.

---

[1] Pseudonyms are used throughout. Note that the accounts set out in Chapter 1 provide further evidence.

2. Rosina is lying in the 'Little Room',[2] vocalizing in an almost constant drone. Occasionally a sudden movement of her right arm knocks her hand against a bell. Each time, she smiles and her vocalizing briefly turns into a laugh.

3. Mark's music therapy session begins—as ever—with the 'hello' song. And as ever, he makes no discernible response.

4. Ben startles and then smiles when someone drops a tray of cutlery in the dining room.

5. Taybah brushes her left hand against the strings of guitar that someone is holding near to her. There is a pause and then she raises her hand and brushes the strings again, and then for a third time.

6. Yakov usually makes a rasping sound as he breathes. He seems to be unaware of what he is doing, and the rasping persists, irrespective of external stimulation. His class teacher has tried to see whether Yakov can be made aware of his sounds by making them louder (using a microphone, amplifier and speakers), but so far this approach has met with no response.

7. Grant's teacher notices that he often turns his head towards her when she sings to him, but she has never noticed him turn towards other sounds.

8. Wendy giggles when people repeat patterns of syllables to her such as 'ma ma ma ma ma', 'da da da da da ', or 'ba ba ba ba ba'.

9. Jamie's short, sharp vocalizations are interpreted by his teachers and carers to mean that he wants someone to vocalize back to him.

10. Khira gets very excited when she hears the regular beat on the school's drum machine.

11. Ubanwa loves 'call and response' games and joins in by making his own sounds.

12. Carol copies simple patterns of vocalization—imitating the ups and downs of her speech and language therapist's voice.

13. Samantha waves her hand more and more vigorously through an ultrasonic beam, creating an ever wider range of swirling sounds.

14. Nathan often vocalizes in response to vocal sounds that are made close to him, although he doesn't seem to copy what he hears.

15. Zabrina loves the sound of the bell tree and when it stops she rocks in her chair which staff interpret as a gesture for 'more'.

16. Damario has been able to make a wide range of vocal sounds ever since he started school, but recently he has begun to make more melodious vowel sounds, which he repeats in short sequences.

17. Lottie hums distinct patterns of notes and repeats them. Her favourite sounds rather like a playground chant, and she repeats it from one day to the next, though not always starting on the same note, her music teacher notices (see Ex. 5.1).

18. Freya cries whenever she hears the 'goodbye' song. It only takes the first two or three notes to be played on the keyboard, and she experiences a strong emotional reaction.

---

[2] A small, largely enclosed area, originally designed by Lilli Nielsen, which may be placed over a prone child's head and upper torso, and in which potentially sound-making objects and toys are suspended, so that movements the child makes (whether accidentally or deliberately) are likely to create a range of sounds with a good deal of acoustic feedback. At the same time, auditory clutter from the outside is minimized. For further information, see <http://www.lilliworks.com/products.htm>.

Ex. 5.1 Lottie's playground chant

19. Hirsch enjoys copying simple rhythms on an untuned percussion instrument. Now he's started making his own rhythms up too, and he flaps his hands with delight when someone else copies what he's doing.
20. Ellen just laughs and laughs when people imitate her vocalizations.
21. Vaughan vocalizes to get his therapist to make a sound—it doesn't matter what, he just seems to relish having a vocal response.
22. Imogen always gets excited in the middle of the 'slowly/quickly' song—anticipating the sudden change of pace.
23. Oliver scratches the tambourine, making a range of sounds. Whenever he plays near the rim and the bells jingle, he smiles.
24. Qiang's eye movements intensify when he hears the big band play.
25. Xavier distinctly tries to copy high notes and low notes in vocal interaction sessions.
26. Peter has learnt to associate his teacher's jangly bracelet, which she always wears, with *her*: for him, it is an important part of her identity.

Towards a model of musical development in the domain of PMLD

It quickly became evident to the Sounds of Intent research team, in the light of examples such as these, that it would be difficult (if not impossible) to conceptualize musical development unidimensionally since, for instance, a child's capacity for attending to sounds may well have outstripped his or her ability to produce them. Hence, at least two dimensions would be required: 'listening and responding', for which the single term 'reactive' was adopted, and 'causing, creating, and controlling', for which the label 'proactive' was used. In relation to the examples given above, 1, 2, 4, 7, 8, 10, 15, 18, 22, 23, 24, and 26 could be considered to be entirely or predominantly 'reactive' and 2, 5, 6, 13, 16, 17, and 23 'proactive'.[3] However, that left a further group of observations (as in examples 3, 9, 11, 12, 14, 19, 20, 21, and 25 above) in which listening to sounds and making them occurred in the context of participation with others, and it was decided that this concept too merited the status of a separate dimension, which became known as 'interactive'.

A series of attempts were made to place examples such as those given (and a good many others) along each of the three dimensions—reactive, proactive,

---

[3] Some observations, such as 23, pertained to two dimensions.

and interactive—based on the notion of contingency (that is, by seeking to identify each stage as a necessary precursor or possible successor to another or others). For example, it is clear that an awareness of sound (as in example 2) must precede a differentiated response (as in example 7), which in turn must precede the capacity to anticipate change (example 22). As potential sequences like this emerged, they were mapped onto what is known of 'typical' early musical development as a way of benchmarking what was being proposed (though the generation of new models of progression was not constrained by this prior knowledge, since it was not known just how relevant 'typical' development was to the way in which the musicality of children with complex needs evolves). It was inevitable that this iterative approach to modelling should have been adopted, since the evidence available largely comprised snapshots of *different* children at various stages of development, rather than longitudinal data on the *same* children as they matured, which would have offered greater certainty as to the nature of developmental change. Taking a more heuristic tack, though, was deemed valid as a preliminary step for two reasons: first, since it was not yet known what the appropriate data to collect would be; and second, since meaningful longitudinal studies of children with PMLD would be likely to last for several years at least. However, it was felt that once an initial model had been developed, this could subsequently be used to inform longer-term empirical work—as well as being informed by it.

The project team decided first to try to identify the key stages in the recognition and understanding of musical structure that young people with profound and multiple difficulties were likely to follow. Using the iterative process described above, five broad levels of attainment were established:

(a) *No awareness of sound* (corresponding in 'typical' development to that found four to five months prior to birth and earlier—see Lecanuet 1996: 13; example 1).

(b) *A developing awareness of sound (including musical sound)* (corresponding in 'typical' development to that found four to three months before birth and later—see Lecanuet 1996: 24, 'fetuses beyond 28–30 weeks of gestation reliably react to external sounds ... displaying either startle responses or with either heart-rate accelerations or decelerations'; examples 2, 4, 15, 24, and 26).

(c) *A developing awareness of the* variety *of sounds that are possible* (corresponding in 'typical' development to that found at least as early as in the first few months after birth—see M. Papoušek 1996: 89 cited on p. 67; examples 7 and 23).

(d) *A developing awareness of simple patterns of sound brought about through repetition, whereby sounds seem to form coherent clusters or streams* ('*groups*') (corresponding in 'typical' development to that found at two-and-a-half to five months after birth—see Fassbender 1996, cited on p. 68; examples 8 and 10).

(e) *A developing awareness that groups of sounds may themselves be repeated or varied, and thereby have a sense of connectedness, forming short pieces* (corresponding in 'typical' development to that found from the age of 7 to 11 months—see M. Papoušek 1996: 106; examples 18 and 22).

As far as their emotional or aesthetic response to music is concerned, it seemed that children and young people with PMLD react to music largely as a consequence of the basic qualities of its constituent sounds—high/low, loud/soft, quick/slow, and so on—(see examples 2, 23, 24, and 26) in much the same way as children who are chronologically in the first few months of life: reactions that, as we have seen, may stem ultimately from maternal vocalization (pp. 60 and 61). The case studies also showed that some pupils with PMLD respond to music as it stimulates memories of affective experiences with which it had previously been associated (as in example 18; cf. p. 70). However, it seemed that, as pupils' awareness of how sound is structured in music develops (as in (d) and (e) above), their capacity to respond to it may evolve too. So, for example, some young people with PMLD may come to savour repetition of one form or another (see examples 8 and 19), and develop the capacity to anticipate changes in pitch, loudness, tone colour, or tempo, based on their knowledge of previous hearings of a short piece—relishing the feeling that having their expectations fulfilled can bring (example 22). Zygonic theory suggests that these responses and the processing abilities that underpin them represent important steps on the road to being able to make sense of music as most mature listeners do (see pp. 65 ff).

So much for the 'reactive' strand in young peoples' musical development. Next, the Sounds of Intent team turned its attention to pupils' *proactive* efforts at creating, causing, and controlling sounds. At this point, there were potentially two sets of contingencies to be considered: one within the proactive strand itself, and one between the reactive and proactive strands. For example, it was evident that the capacity to make sounds deliberately (as in example 5) would necessarily precede the ability to produce a range of different sounds intentionally (example 13), which in turn would come before the faculty of reproducing regular patterns of notes with consistency (example 17). At the same time, though, it was clear that while a developing awareness of auditory input could come on stream at the same time as intentional efforts to produce sound (as example 2 suggests), the former was more likely to precede the latter developmentally. And it seemed inconceivable that intentionality in sound production could occur before the development of an awareness of sound.

That is to say, it appeared that stages in the proactive strand could never *precede* equivalent reactive stages.

With all these issues in mind, the following broad levels of attainment were identified:

(a) *The unwitting production or control of sound* (typically corresponding from any time following the early stages in foetal development when movement becomes possible; examples 2 and 6).

(b) *The intentional production or control of sound* (typically occurring at least from birth; example 5).

(c) *The intentional production of a* variety *of sounds* (corresponding in 'typical' development to that found from four to six months after birth—see M. Papoušek 1996: 103 and 104 cited on p. 67; examples 13 and 23).

(d) *The intentional production of simple patterns through repetition* (corresponding in 'typical' development to that found from four to six months after birth—see M. Papoušek 1996: pp. 104 and 105 cited on p. 68; example 16).

(e) *The repetition of short groups of sounds, which may incorporate recognizable fragments or features of music* (corresponding in 'typical' development to that found between seven and 11 months—M. Papoušek 1996: 106 cited on p. 68; example 17).

Finally, the Sounds of Intent research team considered the 'interactive' strand in the musical development of those with PMLD. Because this drew on elements from the pre-existing reactive and proactive strands, a number of constraints were already in place. For example, imitation of the contour of another person's vocalizations (as in example 12) could only occur alongside or after the ability to recognize differences in sound and produce a variety of sounds intentionally (example 23). In the context of contingencies such as these, observations of pupils and a knowledge of what occurs in 'typical' development, the team distinguished the following levels of attainment:

(a) *Chance interactions* (occurring in 'typical' development from birth; example 3).

(b) *Sound-making in response to an external stimulus or to stimulate a response or both* (occurring in 'typical' development from birth; examples 9 and 14).

(c) *Turn-taking without imitation* (occurring in 'typical' development from two months onwards—see M. Papoušek 1996: 97 cited on pp. 67 and 68; examples 11 and 21).

(d) *Turn-taking with imitation* (occurring in 'typical' development from two months onwards; see M. Papoušek 1996: 97 and 98 cited on pp. 67 and 68; examples 20 and 25).

(e) *Turn-taking with imitation of groups of sounds* (occurring in 'typical' development from 12 months onwards or before—see M. Papoušek 1996: 106; examples 12 and 19).

Representing the sequences of development visually

Having set out these potential sequences of development in three key domains of musical activity, the next issue with which the research team had to grapple was how to display the information visually in a way that would reinforce a feeling of growth, evolving intentionality, and agency—of moving out from a limited sense of self into the more extensive environment of others—that was not implicitly judgemental. Somehow, the conventional lists and tables, which start at the top of the page and move with an inexorable linearity to the bottom, were felt to reinforce the notion that the differing levels of attainment they register are not all equally commendable: that there is only one worthy educational goal, that of progress from one level to the next. Yet the reality is, depending on the nature of their medical condition and its functional implications, that some pupils with PMLD will change, developing new skills and abilities, knowledge, and understanding; some will stay much the same, retaining what they have; while the capacities of others will wane, irrespective of the external input they are given. But, depending on a pupil's personal circumstances, each state may be equally valid. It is the quality of the educational experience in enabling potential to be maximized that the Sounds of Intent research team felt was the important thing.

With this in mind, a number of representational schemes were proposed. First, all sense of hierarchy was removed by placing the attainment statements in discrete metaphorical 'bubbles' on the page, which, within the three broad domains of musical reactivity, proactivity, and interactivity, were conceptually free to float, as it were, on their own, unconnected to each other. For sure, this escaped the tyranny of value-laden lists and matrices, but the painstakingly worked-out relationships between categories and levels of attainment were lost too, and with them, much of the potential pedagogical merit of the scheme. So, an attempt was made to capture what were felt to be the most important contingent relationships between different attainment statements in what rapidly became an intricate network of lines. However, this was felt to be excessively complex and, like the bubbles, it failed to portray the notion of growth—of expanding from a small inner core of self to a wider world of other. One way of depicting this expansion was through a series of concentric circles, and it was this design that came to form the basis of the scheme that was piloted by the Sounds of Intent group.

The three domains of engagement with music ('reactive', 'proactive', and 'interactive') were each represented by a 120° sector. Although the five developmental stages within each domain were aligned across sectors, they were not connected, to make it easier to conceive (as the research team suspected might often be the case) that profiles of attainment could be non-uniform. Each segment had a descriptor, which aimed to encapsulate a particular level of experience or ability, that was short but intended to be meaningful to music specialists and non-specialists alike. These descriptors were not meant to be self-sufficient, but were supposed to serve as 'hooks' to draw teachers, therapists, and carers to fuller accounts that were to be developed in due course. At this stage, it was felt that the most important thing was to get the global structure of the model right: the detail that lay beneath could be filled out in due course, through further periods of observation. After some discussion of the precise wording to be used in each segment, the framework shown in Fig. 5.1 was deemed fit to be used for more formal testing in the field. For ease of reference, the segments in the reactive domain were labelled, from the centre, R.1, R.2, R.3, R.4, and R.5; those in the proactive domain, P.1, P.2, P.3, P.4, and P.5; and those in the interactive domain, I.1, I.2, I.3, I.4, and I.5.

It is important to recognize that, like all models of this type, the framework is a gross conceptual simplification of a highly complex area of human activity: it could only function as a model by being selective and summative. Graphically, too, the manner of representation inevitably simplifies things. For example, there is no suggestion that the boundaries between adjacent segments are in reality clear-cut, as they appear in Fig. 5.2; for sure, they are fuzzy. Indeed, experience suggests that it is often at the *edges* of notional categories such as these—when it is not immediately obvious, for example, whether a pupil has accomplished a particular skill or not—that real insights into his or her functioning are often to be had.

There is also a danger that once a model such as this is fixed in print (albeit with the rider that it constitutes only a preliminary attempt to portray children's development), rather than being the servant of further observation, it comes to constrain it. Inevitably, teachers, therapists, and caregivers start to see and hear children in terms of the categories that are presented—to fit their pupils and clients into the available boxes—rather than regarding them with an open mind. Hence, potentially important information may be distorted or even ignored. Nonetheless, without some structure, some system, some overarching set of beliefs, everything becomes ad hoc (as the PROMISE research outlined in Chapter 1 indicates that it is at present), and coherent progress on a larger scale is not possible. And it is worth remembering that a theory need not be correct to be useful.[4]

---

[4] See, for example, <http://plato.stanford.edu/entries/physics-experiment/app5.html>.

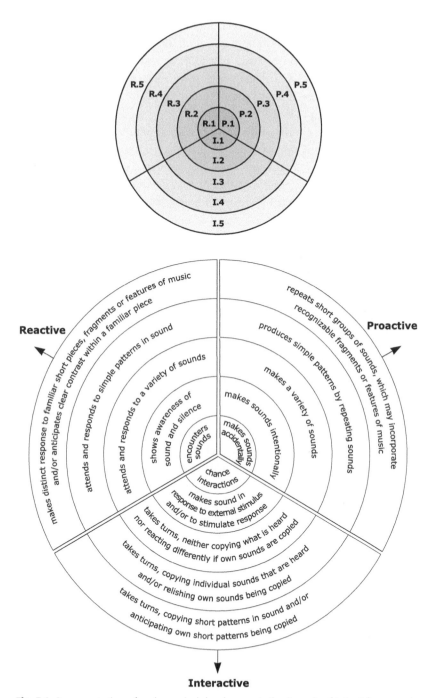

Fig. 5.1 Representation of early musical development: the Sounds of Intent framework, version 1

As well as offering a broad curricular outline to inform the development of schemes of work and other sorts of planning, the research team considered that the framework could be used as a tool for assessment, recording, and organizing resources. To facilitate this, an interactive version was created, which users could access using touch-screen technology on a 'tablet' PC,[5] and data-gathering began in earnest.

Five special schools in the south-east of England were invited to participate in this next stage of the project, based on their previously expressed interest in the Sounds of Intent research, and a series of visits over two terms were made to each of the schools in order to gather observational data.

Altogether, during the spring and summer terms (January to July) 2006, the framework was used to guide the observation of 68 pupils' engagement with music. All had PMLD, and, in total, 630 separate observations were made. The ages of the participants ranged from 4 years, 7 months, to 19 years, 1 month, with a mean of 13 years, 1 month. There was a slight bias towards boys and young men in the sample (males 59 per cent, females 41 per cent). There was little difference between the numbers of observations recorded for each of the three sectors, with reactive = 217, proactive = 208, and interactive = 205 (see Fig. 5.2).

It was found that, in each domain, there is a tendency for the observational data to exhibit a bias towards the lower to mid range (that is, levels 2–3 of the 5-level scales), with 'interactive' observations tending to be skewed more towards levels 1 and 2. There is a strong correlation between the reactive and proactive patterns of observations,[6] but a much weaker correlation between the reactive and interactive patterns,[7] and between the proactive and interactive.[8]

The data indicate that the vast majority of pupils (518 out of 630, or 82 per cent) were identified as having some sense of personal agency in musical and other sound-making activity, such as 'makes sound in response to an external stimulus' (I.2) and 'makes sounds intentionally' (P.2). However, there were relatively few observations in the most advanced levels of each segment (levels 4 and 5).

A comparison between the five schools indicates that there is a relatively high degree of similarity in the pattern of the observations for each location.[9]

---

[5] A slate-shaped mobile computer.

[6] $r = 0.927, p < 0.05$.

[7] $r = 0.458$, non-significant.

[8] $r = 0.673$, non-significant.

[9] Kendall's Coefficient of Concordance (W) for reactive = 0.737, proactive = 0.755, interactive = 0.800; each $p < 0.05$.

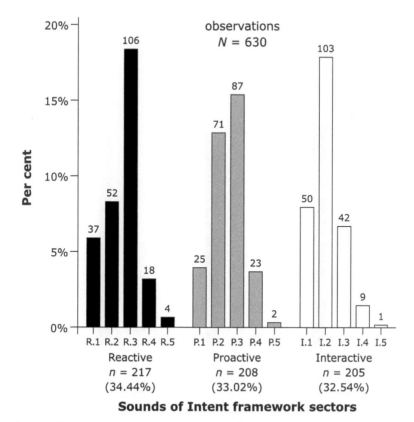

Fig. 5.2 Observations of pupils pertaining to the Sounds of Intent framework

This finding implies that a common approach was adopted in the application of the framework and process of observation across the five school sites (something that was endorsed by the research team's reviews of sample videoed observations) and that the schools have similar patterns of reactive, proactive, and interactive observational data.

With regard to the pattern of observations in relation to the gender of the participants, there is a significant correlation in the data between scores across the 15 segments for the sexes,[10] although the observational ratings for the female participants are consistently higher than those of the males in each of the three sectors (see Fig. 5.3).

Work was also undertaken to ascertain whether the framework was potentially useful in mapping any musical development in individuals with PMLD that may occur over time. To this end, visits to one school generated ten

[10] $r = 0.979, p < 0.001$.

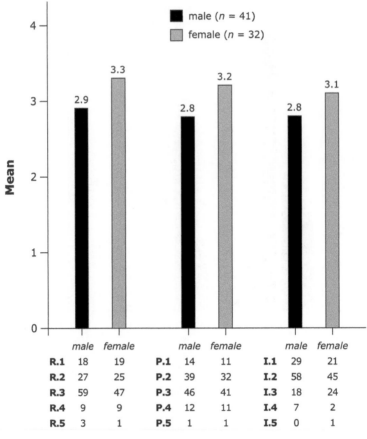

Sounds of Intent framework segments

Fig. 5.3 The distribution of observations pertaining to male and female pupils

successive weeks of observational data pertaining to seven pupils (with only a few individual absences) over a term. Of the seven participants, four were exhibiting more advanced musical behaviour in the final week compared to their first session, one had made no change and two were rated at slightly lower levels (see Table 5.1).

While these few data are, of course, statistically inconclusive, they do show how the framework could be used to indicate individual change. To test this notion further in respect of *groups* of children and young people, an analysis was undertaken of participants' observed levels of attainment on the framework in relation to their age. This revealed a weak relationship[11] between age

_____

[11] $r = 0.289$, $p = 0.018$.

Table 5.1 The change in observations over time

Pupil	Week 1				Week 2				Change
	R	P	I	**Total**	R	P	I	**Total**	
A	3	3	3	**9**	3	3	2	**8**	**−1**
B	2	2	1	**5**	2	2	1	**5**	**0**
C	1	2	1	**4**	3	3	2	**8**	**+4**
D	3	3	2	**8**	3	4	3	**10**	**+2**
E	3	3	2	**8**	3	3	3	**9**	**+1**
F	3	2	2	**7**	3	3	2	**8**	**+1**
G	2	2	1	**5**	1	1	1	**3**	**−2**

and level, with older participants tending to be more highly rated (see Fig. 5.4). Notwithstanding this trend, it was also evident that there was a wide range of individual variation, with some young participants being much more highly rated than their older peers. Nonetheless, the Sounds of Intent framework appeared to offer, for the first time, a grounded and empirically verifiable means of measuring musical progress in pupils with profound learning difficulties.

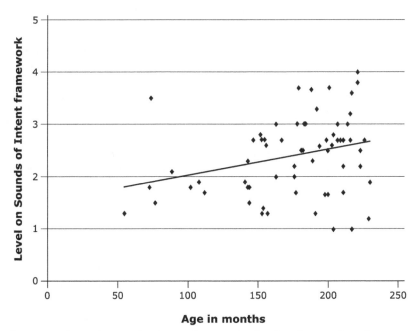

Fig. 5.4 Levels on the Sounds of Intent framework related to the age of pupils

A model of musical development in the domains of PMLD and SLD

In the course of evaluating the framework, four main issues emerged that suggested ways in which it could be improved and extended. The first was that more detail was required behind each of the 'headlines' in order to give practitioners a better understanding of just what each level of attainment meant, and to make it easier to gauge small steps of progress or to acknowledge 'lateral' development (through a child's broadening experience, for example). The second issue was that the dissimilarity in the profile of observations in the interactive domain and those in the reactive and proactive sectors should be corrected. In particular, practitioners in the research group wondered whether 'turn-taking' was placed too early in the developmental sequence. The third issue appeared in the form of case studies that indicated that some pupils with PMLD may be functioning musically at a more advanced level than that of their global development. The fourth and final issue was that the framework should be expanded to encompass the abilities and experiences of pupils with SLD, whose musicality (as we shall see in Chapter 10) may be highly developed by any standards.

In parallel with the observations that were made in the five participant schools to test the framework, further evidence was gathered of pupils' engagement with music, including those with PMLD *and* SLD. The following examples are broadly representative of the new data that were amassed.[12]

27. William's rocking increases markedly as the Japanese taiko drumming gets faster and faster.
28. Milán is lead singer in a pop group at school, whose members all have learning difficulties. With the help of their music teacher, the group are getting better at following him as he slows down before the return of each chorus for expressive effect.
29. Ashley's parents have tried playing her just about every kind of music, and have taken her to all sorts of performances, from traditional church choirs to big band jazz, but as yet she has shown no reaction.
30. Hackett gets a buzz out of playing the drum, starting with a slow beat and getting faster and faster.
31. Yuma likes it when her teaching assistants play 'catch' with short vocal phrases, each time changing slightly what the last person sang.
32. Dennis will respond to musical sounds that are made near him by vocalizing, and he is now sustaining his concentration on this task for longer periods of time.
33. Vic can choose which activity he would like to do next by shaking the bells (for music) or squeezing a horn (for 'ride the bike').
34. Faisal has severe learning difficulties and hemiplegia. He plays the keyboard with his left hand only, learning material by ear quite quickly. He has recently joined the

---

[12] Again, pseudonyms are used.

school's band, and has found a role for himself playing the bass parts. Now he not only picks up on what the left hand of the other keyboard player is doing, but he has started to improvise around the harmonies too.

35. Penny has come to realize that the gong in her classroom means 'lunchtime' when it is sounded.

36. Gabrielle does not appear to relate to others' sound-making and, in an effort to gain her attention, her co-workers model interactions for her, one taking her part vocally in the 'good morning' routine, for example.

37. Emily makes up songs with short phrases that sound connected—and when her teacher listened carefully to a recording that she had made of Emily's singing, she noticed that one phrase often started more or less where the other one left off.

38. Jamil has severe learning difficulties but he has sophisticated musical tastes. He likes the vocal music of the Baroque period—especially Bach and Handel—but much prefers a purity and lightness of vocal tone with little vibrato.

39. Tanya likes improvising responses on the keyboard to the melodic openings that her teacher makes up—and she's now learnt to 'hear' the same structures in many themes by Haydn and Mozart.

40. Quincy knows that when his music teacher plays the last verse of *Molly Malone* in the minor key it signifies sadness.

41. Noriko loves the little runs on the panpipes in Papageno's Birdcatcher's song from *The Magic Flute.*

42. Sabina plays her cello with a Suzuki group, and is much better now at performing in time and in tune with the other children.

43. Osman enjoys singing the bass-line in his school choir, and has memorized around 50 pieces that they have sung over the last few years.

44. Brett went to an African performing arts workshop, and he was really engaged as the short bursts of music were echoed back and forth between groups.

45. Ruth is a good singer, used to performing in public, although she has severe learning difficulties. She can learn new songs just by listening to her teacher (who is not a singer) run through them, and as she gets to know a piece, she intuitively adds expression as she feels appropriate, showing that she has an underlying sense of the structure and content of the music. Later, when she listens to other people singing the songs she knows, she clearly prefers some performances to others. Her teacher believes this shows that she has a mature engagement with pieces in mid-twentieth-century popular style.

46. Lacey uses a switch to operate a drum synthesizer, and she is showing an increasing ability to control the sounds that are made.

47. Ushma improvises short groups of notes on the recorder using the five pitches for which she knows the fingerings (D, E, G, A, B).

48. Liz can tap out a regular beat at different speeds on a range of hand-held percussion instruments.

49. Zachary loves to compose using the computer, which he can do with someone to help him control the software. He has been creating pieces to accompany the school play, and has now put together a dozen excerpts which convey a range of different moods.

50. Tabitha can't speak, but she can hum short phrases to communicate her preference for certain activities. See, for example, Ex. 5.2.

51. Udo is fascinated with the ever-changing sonorities produced by the didgeridoo.

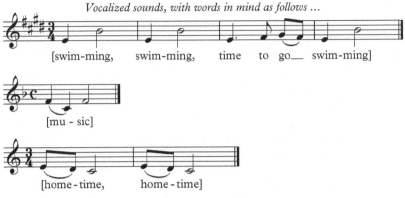

Vocalized sounds, with words in mind as follows …

[swim-ming,   swim-ming,   time   to   go___ swim-ming]

[mu - sic]

[home - time,   home - time]

Ex. 5.2 Tabitha's hummed phrases help her to communicate

52. Ciara, who is a good vocalist despite having severe learning difficulties, is learning how to convey a range of different emotions in her singing through using techniques such as *rubato*, consciously employing a wider range of dynamics, and producing darker and lighter sounds.

53. Aletia experiences a strong emotional reaction when she hears 'This Little Light of Mine' ever since it was played at her classmate's funeral.

54. Xiang has at lasted started to respond to her teacher singing as well as her mum.

55. Valerie has a good deal of involuntary movement in her arms, and her music therapist has tried to give her a sense of cause and effect by using an ultrasonic beam, which she links to a variety of electronic sounds. To date, Valerie has shown no signs of awareness that she is controlling the sounds, however.

56. Diane makes short melodic patterns—usually going up three or four notes—using single syllables such as 'dah' or 'me'.

57. Heidi's speech and language therapist tries to interpret her vocalizations in the context of early communication, producing similar sounds in return.

58. Chas really enjoys playing the bongos in his college band—maintaining a regular beat even when the music gets quite syncopated, and not afraid to add his own ideas too.

59. Eamon is always listening to pop music, but he has his clear favourites to which he returns time and again.

60. Iona appears to have no voluntary movement, and her therapist lifts her arm up and down in the ultrasonic beam to generate flute-like sounds from the computer.

61. Faith used to be able to play only a few nursery rhymes on the keyboard, mostly with the right hand, but now she can manage whole pop songs, with a simple bass-line all the way through.

62. Oscar has learnt to sing much more in time and in tune over the last year, his music teacher notices.

63. Xena waits for the 'tick, tocks' in *My Grandfather's Clock* and grins with excitement when the moment comes. Very occasionally she joins in.

64. George loves it when his one-to-one support worker claps short rhythmic patterns to him.

65. Imran's piano technique has improved dramatically over the past year since his new teacher taught him scales and arpeggios in every key, and he can now perform his repertoire of early jazz much more fluently.

66. Janet, with severe learning difficulties, has developed the confidence to introduce new material on her saxophone in the school's jazz quartet, and is thrilled when the other players pick up on what she is doing.
67. Yolanda can sing most of *Twinkle, Twinkle Little Star* when prompted at the beginning of each phrase.
68. Keith can improvise in a simple style over a number of pop songs on the keyboard.
69. Stephen plays the clarinet in the local wind band, and intuitively picks up on the changes in dynamics and tempi that they make.
70. Mehul performs expressively on his guitar, whether he's playing folk music, blues, or country and western. He's happy playing on his own or with others, and he enjoys going to concerts to hear music in these different styles played live too. If he had to choose, his preference would always be for folk music, though.
71. Zeeshan laughs and rocks when he hears his teacher imitating Tom's vocal sounds.
72. Neha copies elements of the short phrases her music therapist sings, particularly picking up vocally on the highest or lowest notes, or the first or last in a group.
73. Patrick's music therapist tries interacting with him in a number of different environments—the music room, the multisensory room, and the hall—to see if the different acoustics will encourage him to engage with her and respond.
74. Rachel enjoys 'give and take' sessions with her piano teacher using two keyboards. She can copy the short rhythms that her teacher makes up and gets most of the pitches right too.
75. Wallace can make up pieces that have a distinct 'beginning', 'middle', and an 'end'.
76. Brian always plays the bell-tree in music sessions (he becomes distressed if attempts are made to encourage him to play other instruments)—for him, at this stage, it is an integral part of the experience.
77. Karen thinks it's great fun when her music therapist copies the number of beats that she makes on the tambourine.
78. Qabil's day at school is organized so that key activities have sounds that precede them as auditory cues—shaking the bell-tree means 'it's time for music', for example, banging the gong means 'lunchtime', and a horn means 'ride the bike'. Similarly, his key worker always wears the same jangly bracelet, and his classroom is identifiable by the windchimes at the door. At the moment, Qabil does not react to any of the sounds, and there's no evidence that he understands any of the connections that are being presented to him—but staff persist in the hope that offering Qabil a structured learning environment will eventually pay off.

To analyse these and other comparable data, a similar approach was adopted to that used before. The first step was to place the observations within the three domains that were now established: reactive, proactive, and interactive. The results are shown in Table 5.2.[13]

Before seeking to integrate these new observations into the three developmental sequences that had previously been proposed, the second step was to ascertain what modifications to framework could be made that would resolve the issues that had been identified in relation to the interactive domain (the view that turn-taking seemed to occur too early) and the fact that the levels of

---

[13] Note that some observations occur in two domains.

Table 5.2 The distribution of observations 27–78 in the reactive, proactive, and interactive domains

Domain	Relevant observations	*n*
Reactive	27, 29, 31, 35, 38, 39, 40, 41, 44, 45, 51, 53, 54, 59, 63, 64, 70, 71, 78	19
Proactive	30, 33, 37, 39, 42, 45, 46, 47, 48, 49, 50, 52, 55, 56, 60, 61, 62, 63, 65, 67, 68, 70, 75, 76	24
Interactive	28, 32, 34, 36, 42, 43, 54, 57, 58, 66, 69, 70, 72, 73, 74, 77	16

interactive observations that were made did not entirely correspond with those made in the reactive and proactive sectors. The difficulties arose particularly around levels 2 and 3, and one proposed solution was to integrate these at the 'headline' level. This would not compromise the developmental sequences that had been established, and it was felt that any loss of detail could be recaptured in the sub-categories of attainment that were yet to be developed. Hence it was suggested that, in the reactive domain, 'shows awareness of sound and silence' and 'attends and responds to a variety of sounds' should become 'shows emerging awareness of sound'; in the proactive domain, 'makes sounds intentionally' and 'makes a variety of sounds' should become 'causes, creates or controls sounds intentionally';[14] and in the interactive domain 'makes sound in response to external stimulus and/or to stimulate response' and 'takes turns, neither copying what is heard nor reacting differently if own sounds are copied' should become, more straightforwardly, 'interacts with another or others using sound'.

Quantitatively, this change meant that the 630 observations made in five schools during the first half of 2006 (see Fig. 5.3) would be re-profiled as shown in Table 5.3.

Statistically, there is now a very strong correlation between the reactive and proactive profiles of observations,[15] with a slightly weaker, but nonetheless strong correlation between the reactive and interactive profiles,[16] and between the proactive and interactive.[17]

---

[14] Also a more accurate reflection of what may be occurring, since, for example, through using a switch, a pupil may not be making sounds but causing them, and, by using an ultrasonic beam, he or she may be causing sounds or controlling them (see Ockelford 1996*b*: 11).

[15] $r = 0.995$, $p < 0.01$.

[16] $r = 0.989$, $p < 0.05$.

[17] $r = 0.969$, $p < 0.05$.

Table 5.3 The effect of combining levels 2 and 3

Domain	Level				
	1	2 + 3	4	5	*n*
Reactive	37	158	18	4	217
Proactive	25	158	23	2	208
Interactive	50	145	9	1	205
n	112	461	50	7	*N* = 630

Qualitatively, the new descriptors for levels 1 and 2 captured the available observations as shown in Table 5.4.[18] Integrating levels 2 and 3 meant that what had previously been level 4 now became level 3. In the reactive domain, only a slight change of wording was proposed, whereby 'attends and responds to simple patterns in sound' became 'recognizes and reacts to simple patterns in sound'—since the *recognition* of patterns was felt to be a more apt description of what occurred than a child or young person giving *attention* to them. In the proactive domain, it seemed that 'produces simple patterns by repeating sounds' could constructively be expanded to embrace the production of simple patterns through *regular change* (as in examples 30, 48, and 56), and the following descriptor 'intentionally makes patterns in sound through repetition or regularity' was proposed. In the interactive domain, none of the previous examples (12, 20, and 25) nor one of the new ones (77) indicated turn-taking at this stage, so what had been described as 'takes turns, copying individual sounds that are heard and/or relishing own sounds being copied' was now proposed to

Table 5.4 Descriptors for new levels 1 and 2

Domain	New level	
	1	2 (= 'old' 2 + 3 together)
Reactive	'Encounters sounds' 1, 3, 29, 78	'Shows emerging awareness of sound' 2, 4, 7, 15, 23, 24, 35, 76
Proactive	'Makes sounds unwittingly' 2, 6, 55, 60	'Causes, creates or controls sounds intentionally' 5, 13, 23, 46, 76
Interactive	'Unwittingly relates through sound' 36, 38, 57, 73	'Interacts with another or others using sound' 9, 11, 14, 21, 32, 54

---

[18] Note that the wording for Level 1 'interactive' was modified to include a verb in line with the other descriptors.

Table 5.5 Descriptors for new level 3

Domain	New level 3
Reactive	'Recognizes and reacts to simple patterns in sound' 8, 10, 27, 41, 51, 71
Proactive	'Intentionally makes patterns in sound through repetition or regularity' 16, 30, 33, 48, 56
Interactive	'Interacts by imitating others' sounds or recognizing self being imitated 12, 20, 25, 77

read 'Interacts, by imitating others' sounds or recognizing self being imitated'. This meant that the new level 3 appeared as shown in Table 5.5.

The original level 5 had received only seven (1 per cent) of the 630 test observations across all three domains, so there was little evidence on which to base judgements as to its validity. However, there was a feeling among the research group that the reactive domain covered too broad a span of development compared with the proactive and interactive spheres of activity since, at level 5, it made reference to listeners responding to entire pieces, whereas the other domains referred only to *groups* of sounds. Extending the model to include those children and young people with SLD made it possible correct this imbalance, as we shall see.

Taking first the reactive domain, and using the same iterative process as before, a further three broad levels of attainment were hypothesized:

(d) *A developing awareness of groups of sounds and the relationships between them* (corresponding in 'typical' development to that found from the age of 7 to 11 months onwards—see M. Papoušek 1996, cited on p. 68; Moog 1968/1976, cited on p. 69; Hargreaves 1986, cited on p. 69; examples 18, 31, 39, 44, and 64).

(e) *A developing awareness of whole pieces, their structural features, the frameworks in the domains of pitch and time on which they are constructed, and of possible connotations brought about by their association with particular experiences* (corresponding in 'typical' development to that found from the age of 4 or 5 years—see Hargreaves 1986, cited on p. 69; Marshall and Hargreaves 2005; examples 22, 40, 53, 59, and 63).

(f) *A developing awareness of pieces as narratives in sound that unfold over time to create meaning, of different styles and genres, and of different performances* (corresponding in 'typical' development to that typically found from the early teenage years—see Swanwick and Tillman 1986; Swanwick 1991; examples 38, 45, 53, and 70).

Linking with this, levels 4–6 of the proactive domain were provisionally summarized as follows:

(d) *The creation or re-creation of short groups of musical sounds and coherent links between them* (corresponding in 'typical' development to that found from the age of 7 to 11 months—see the M. Papoušek, Moog, and Hargreaves citations above; examples 17, 37, 39, 47, 50, 63, and 67).

(e) *The performance of pieces of music (learnt or improvised) of growing length and complexity, increasingly 'in tune' and 'in time'* (corresponding in 'typical' development to that found from the age of 4 or 5 years—see the Marshall and Hargreaves, and Hargreaves citations above; examples 42, 62, 66, and 75).

(f) *Communication through expressive performance or through the creation of pieces that are intended to convey particular effects* (corresponding in 'typical' development to that found from the early teenage years—see the Swanwick and Tillman, and Swanwick citations above; examples 45, 49, 52, 65, and 70).

And levels 4–6 of the interactive domain were conceptualized thus:

(d) *Engagement in musical dialogues through creating and recognizing coherent connections between groups of sounds* (corresponding in 'typical' development to that found from the age of 7 to 11 months—see citations above; examples 19, 72, and 74).

(e) *The performance or improvisation of music of growing length and complexity with others, with increasingly developed ensemble skills* (corresponding in 'typical' development to that found from the age of 4 or 5 years—see citations above; examples 34, 42, 58, and 66).

(f) *Expressive performance with others, with a widening repertoire* (corresponding in 'typical' development to that found from the early teenage years—see citations above; examples 28, 43, 69, and 70).

Using the same protocol for visual representation that was used previously, this yielded the framework shown in Fig. 5.5.

The next step—to break down each of these 18 segments into manageable chunks that would assist teachers, therapists, and others to make practical use of the framework—presented the Sounds of Intent research team with a new challenge. The findings from developmental psychology, while useful up to this point, proved to be insufficiently detailed to underpin this next stage, leaving two sources of information: the observations of children and young people with PMLD and SLD engaging with music (or, in some cases, failing to) and zygonic theory. With this in mind, the researchers wondered whether, as a starting point, it would be possible to establish at each level, across the three

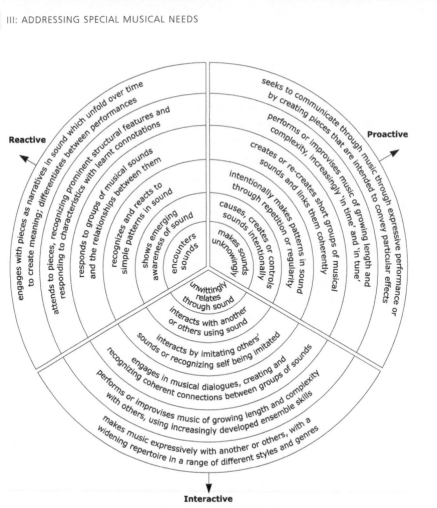

Fig. 5.5 The Sounds of Intent framework, version 2

domains of musical activity (reactive, proactive, and interactive), a common 'cognitive core' of music-processing abilities that could be used to develop the model further, enabling each segment to be subdivided into a number of discrete 'elements'. The classroom observations would be used to support their identification and verification. An immediate issue was how many elements there should be in each segment. Initial trials indicated that division into four elements offered a fair amount of detail that would nonetheless be manageable in day-to-day use.

What follows is the first attempt to produce six core level descriptors, divided into $3 \times 4 \times 6 = 72$ elements. This scheme will, no doubt, be refined through use, though even as it stands, it successfully accommodates the data gathered to date within a coherent theoretical framework.

Level 1:
'blooming, buzzing confusion'[19]

Core cognitive abilities

None; no awareness of sound as a distinct perceptual entity.

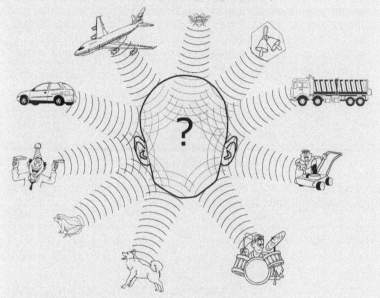

Reactive—R.1—*'encounters sounds'*

Indicated by co-workers

A   exposing children and young people to a rich variety of sounds (example 1);
B   exposing children and young people to a wide range of music (example 29);
C   exposing children and young people to music in different contexts (example 29); and
D   exposing children and young people to musical and other sounds linked with key people, places, or activities (example 78).

Proactive—P.1—*'makes sounds unknowingly'*

Indicated by co-workers

A   enhancing the sounds made by life-processes (example 6);
B   using involuntary movements to control and cause sounds (example 55); and
C   making sounds with co-active movements (example 60);
    although it may be that some children and young people are capable of
D   making sounds accidentally through voluntary movements (example 2).

---

[19] James 1890: 462.   **Continued**

Level 1: Cont.

Interactive—I.1—*'unwittingly relates through sound'*

Indicated by co-workers

A making sounds in an effort to stimulate responses (example 3);
B responding empathetically through sound to any sounds (or other gestures) that the child or young person may make (example 57);
C working with the child or young person in a variety of contexts (example 73); and
D modelling interaction through sound in the presence of the child or young person concerned (example 36).

Level 2:
'sound, silence, and variation'

Core cognitive abilities

An emerging awareness of sound as a distinct perceptual entity and of the variety that is possible within the domain of sound.

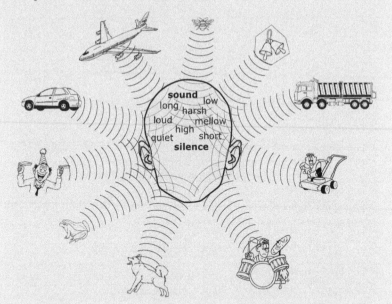

Reactive—R.2—*'shows emerging awareness of sound'*

Indicated by children and young people

A showing awareness of an increasing variety of sounds, including musical sounds (examples, 2, 4, 15, and 24); **Continued**

Level 2: Cont.

B making differentiated responses to the basic qualities of different sounds (examples 7 and 23);

C responding to musical and other sounds increasingly independently of context (example 54); and

D responding to musical and other sounds through their association with particular people, places, and/or activities (example 26).

Proactive—P.2—'causes, creates, or controls sounds intentionally'

Indicated by children and young people

A causing sound intentionally through an increasing variety of means (example 23);

B creating an increasing diversity of sounds intentionally through an increasing variety of means (example 13);

C showing increasing control over the sounds that are produced (example 46); and

D using sounds in conscious association with particular people, places, and/or activities (example 76).

Interactive—I.2—'interacts with another or others using sound'

Indicated by children and young people

A responding in sound to sounds made by another (examples 11 and 14);

B making sounds to stimulate response in sound by another (examples 9 and 21);

C interacting with increasing independence of context (examples 54); and

D interacting with an increasing number of exchanges over longer periods of time (example 32).

Level 3:
'relationships, repetition, and regularity'

Core cognitive abilities

A growing awareness of the possibility and significance of the *relationships* between the basic aspects of sounds (particularly pertaining to pitch and perceived time), of the special relationships that indicate the *repetition* of these basic aspects, and of the repetition of relationships (resulting in *regularity*)—both approximate and exact. Note that *music* cognition first seems to appear at this point.

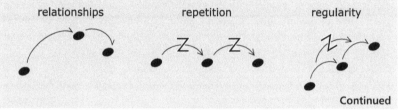

relationships   repetition   regularity

Continued

Level 3: Cont.

Reactive—R.3—*'recognizes and reacts to simple patterns in sound'*

Indicated by children and young people

A recognizing and reacting to the repetition of sounds (example 8);
B recognizing and reacting to a regular beat (example 10);
C recognizing and reacting to simple patterns formed through regular change (examples 27, 41, and 51); and
D responding to sounds used to symbolize particular people, places and/or activities (example 35).

Proactive—P.3—*'intentionally makes patterns in sound through repetition or regularity'*

Indicated by children and young people

A intentionally making simple patterns through repetition (example 16);
B intentionally making simple patterns through a regular beat (example 48);
C intentionally making simple patterns through regular change (examples 30 and 56); and
D using sounds to symbolize particular people, places, or activities (example 33).

Interactive—I.3—*'interacts by imitating others' sounds or recognizing self being imitated'*

Indicated by children and young people

A imitating the sounds made by another (example 25);
B showing awareness of their own sounds being imitated (example 20);
C imitating simple patterns in sound made by another (through repetition, regularity, and/or regular change) (example 12); and
D showing awareness of simple patterns in sound (made through repetition, regularity, and/or regular change) being imitated (example 77).

Level 4:

'groups, links, and transformations'

Core cognitive abilities

An evolving perception of *groups* through the acknowledgement of repetition or regularity of aspects of sounds (in the form of similarity, proximity and 'common fate'[20]), and the cognition of coherent relationships between them, involving (a) each group as a whole through *transformations*, or (b) aspects of each group (which effectively *link* both groups as wholes through their own inner cohesion).

---

[20] A principle of *Gestalt* perception, whereby aspects of a perceptual domain that change in a similar way are perceived as a unit. **Continued**

Level 4: Cont.

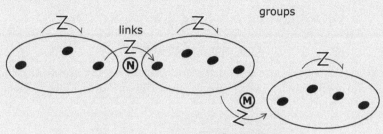

transformations

Reactive—R.4—'responds to groups of musical sounds and the relationships between them'

Indicated by children and young people

A responding to groups of musical sounds as discrete entities (example 64);

B responding to the repetition, variation, and transformation of groups of musical sounds (as in 'call and response') (examples 31 and 44)—see 'M' in Fig. 5.9;

C responding to the coherent connection of groups of musical sounds through common elements (as in 'question and answer') (example 39)—see 'N' in Fig. 5.9; and

D responding to groups of musical sounds used to symbolize particular people, places, and/or activities (example 18).

Proactive—P.4—'creates or re-creates short groups of musical sounds and links them coherently'

Indicated by children and young people

A creating or re-creating short groups of musical sounds that have distinct identities (examples 17 and 47);

B repeating, varying or transforming groups of musical sounds (as in 'call and response') (examples 17, 63 and 67)—see 'M' in Fig. 5.9;

C linking groups coherently through common elements (as in 'question and answer') (examples 37 and 39)—see 'N' in Fig. 5.9; and

D using groups of musical sounds to symbolize particular people, places, and/or activities (example 50).

Interactive—I.4—'engages in musical dialogues, creating and recognizing coherent connections between groups of sounds'

Indicated by children and young people

A imitating groups of sounds made by another ('call and response') (example 19);

B linking groups of sounds coherently to those produced by another ('question and answer') (example 72);

C producing groups of sounds in the expectation they will stimulate coherent groups of sounds in response (example 19); and

D interacting through coherent patterns of turn-taking (example 74).

Level 5:
'structures, frameworks, and probabilities'

Core cognitive abilities

A growing recognition of *structure* at the level of whole pieces, of *frameworks* in the domains of relative pitch and time (modes and tempi), and of transition *probabilities* between notes.

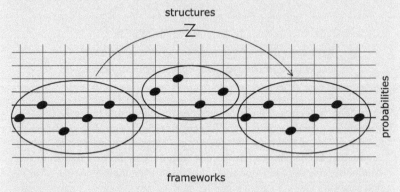

Reactive—R.5—'attends to pieces, recognizing prominent structural features and responding to characteristics with learnt connotations'

Indicated by children and young people

A   attending to pieces, recognizing prominent structural features and responding to characteristics with learnt connotations (examples 22 and 63);

B   becoming familiar with an increasing number of pieces of music, and developing preferences (example 59);

C   responding to general features whose connotations are established by convention (such as western 'major' and 'minor' modes) (example 40); and

D   responding to some pieces through connotations brought about by their association with particular experiences (example 53).

Proactive—P.5—'performs or improvises music of growing length and complexity, increasingly "in time" and "in tune"'

Indicated by children and young people

A   performing short and simple pieces of music, potentially of growing length and complexity (example 61);

B   improvising on familiar, short and simple pieces of music, potentially of growing length and complexity (example 68);

C   creating pieces of music, potentially of increasing structural coherence, complexity and length (example 75); and

D   increasingly using and maintaining conventional pitch and temporal frameworks in performance (by singing and/or playing in time and in tune) (examples 42 and 62).   **Continued**

Level 5: Cont.

Interactive—I.5—*'performs or improvises music of growing length and complexity with others, using increasingly developed ensemble skills'*

Indicated by children and young people

A performing simultaneously with others, maintaining their own parts (example 58);
B improvising with others, repeating and/or developing material and/or building on material that is presented (example 34);
C improvising with others, providing material in the expectation that it will be taken up (example 66); and
D performing increasingly in time and/or in tune with another or others (example 42).

Level 6:
'articulating the narrative metaphor'

Core cognitive abilities

A developing awareness of the 'emotional syntax' of performance (the conventions by which the matrix of pitch and perceived time may be 'warped'—for example, through 'rubato'—and the dimensions of loudness and timbre nuanced, to convey expression), and the evolving capacity to grasp the structure/content dialectic of music over time and so understand and *articulate the narrative metaphor* of pieces.[21]

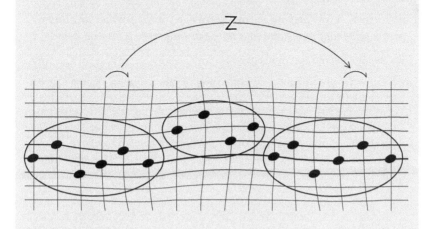

---

[21] See Ockelford 2005*d*.

Continued

Level 6: Cont.

Reactive—R.6—'engaging with pieces as narratives in sound that unfold over time to create meaning, and differentiating between performances'

Indicated by children and young people

A developing a mature musical response within a familiar style, engaging with pieces of music as narratives in sound (example 45);

B becoming familiar with an increasing number of styles and genres, and developing preferences (example 70);

C becoming familiar with different performances of pieces and developing preferences (example 45); and

D becoming familiar with different styles of performance and developing preferences (example 38).

Proactive—P.6—'seeking to communicate through music through expressive performance or by creating pieces that are intended to convey particular effects'

Indicated by children and young people

A increasingly using familiar conventions of expressive performance (examples 52 and 45);

B being able to perform with conviction in an increasing number of different styles and/or genres (example 70);

C developing the technical proficiency to meet the demands of a widening repertoire (example 65); and

D creating music (through improvisation or composition) to convey an increasing range of desired effects (example 49).

Interactive—I.6—'making music expressively with another or others, with a widening repertoire in a range of different styles and genres'

Indicated by children and young people

A being aware of and emulating expressivity of others' playing in ensemble performance (example 69);

B contributing their own expressivity in ensemble playing and in the expectation that it will inform the manner in which others perform (example 28);

C performing an increasing repertoire with others (example 43); and

D performing convincingly with others in a range of different styles and/or genres (example 70).

This information is summarized in Tables 5.6, 5.7, and 5.8. Although these tables are simple and regular in appearance, the way that level descriptors and elements relate to each other within and between the reactive, proactive, and interactive domains is complex.

Level descriptors are the most straightforward, forming a hierarchy whereby, within each domain, achievement at higher levels is dependent on the accomplishment of all those that precede. So, for example, in the interactive domain, I.4, 'Engages in musical dialogues, creating and recognizing coherent connections between groups of sounds' could only occur following I.3, 'Interacts by imitating others' sounds or recognizing self being imitated' and (therefore) after accomplishing I.2 and I.1. *Between* domains, there is a broad flow of contingency that runs from interactive to proactive and then to reactive.[22] For instance, in the proactive domain, intentionally making patterns in sound through repetition (P.3) depends on the capacity to recognize simple patterns in sound (R.3); while interacting with another or others using sound (I.2) relies on the ability to cause, create or control sounds intentionally (P.2), which in turn requires an awareness of sound (R.2).

In contrast, the pattern of contingencies that links the 72 elements lacks this simplicity. Although in some cases there is a necessary connection between elements at different levels *within* domains (for example, a pupil could not engage in intentional repetition—P.3.A—before having the wherewithal to make a variety of sounds—P.2.B) and *between* them (for instance, imitating the sounds made by another—I.3.A—similarly requires functioning at the level of P.2.B), this is not always the case. It is perfectly conceivable that a child could intentionally make simple patterns through a regular beat (P.3.B), for example, before using sounds to symbolize particular people, places, or activities (P.2.D). However, the research team felt that intricacies of this type were an inevitable consequence of the intricate nature of musical development: multi-layered and multi-stranded, with many irregularities.

Some practitioners on the Sounds of Intent team were concerned that, while levels 1–3 of the framework were well within the grasp of teachers who were not music specialists, levels 4–6 required an increasing degree of music-educational expertise. And since the PROMISE research had indicated that this was in short supply among those working with young people with complex needs, who would have the competence to use the framework? It was felt that this was an issue that those planning music provision within schools and

---

[22] Indeed, some reactive observations may best be evidenced by activity in the proactive or interactive domains. For example, the capacity to attend to complete pieces of music (R.5.A) may become apparent through a pupil's capacity to perform entire songs (P.5.A).

Table 5.6 Reactive elements in the new Sounds of Intent framework

Level	R.1	R.2	R.3	R.4	R.5	R.6
Descriptor	**Encounters sounds**	**Shows emerging awareness of sound**	**Recognizes and reacts to simple patterns in sound**	**Responds to groups of musical sounds and the relationships between them**	**Attends to pieces, recognizing prominent structural features and responding to characteristics with learnt connotations**	**Engages with pieces as narratives in sound which unfold over time to create meaning; differentiates between performances**
Element A	Is exposed to a rich variety of sounds	Shows awareness of an increasing variety of musical and other sounds	Recognizes and reacts to the repetition of sounds	Responds to groups of musical sounds	Attends to complete pieces of music, responding to prominent structural features	Within a familiar style, develops a mature response, engaging with pieces of music as narratives in sound
Element B	Is exposed to a wide range of music	Makes differentiated responses to the basic qualities of different sounds	Recognizes and reacts to a regular beat	Responds to the repetition, variation, and transformation of groups of musical sounds (for example, as in 'call and response')	Becomes familiar with an increasing number of pieces of music, and develops preferences	Becomes familiar with an increasing number of styles and genres, and develops preferences
Element C	Is exposed to music in different contexts	Responds to musical and other sounds increasingly independently of context	Recognizes and reacts to simple patterns formed through regular change	Responds to the coherent connection of different groups of musical sounds through common elements (for example, as in some 'question and answer' phrases)	Responds to general features whose connotations are established by convention (such as the western 'major' and 'minor' modes)	Becomes familiar with different performances of pieces and develops preferences
Element D	Is exposed to particular musical and other sounds being linked to key people, places, and/or activities	Responds to musical and other sounds through their association with particular people, places, and/or activities	Responds to musical sounds used to symbolize particular people, places, and/or activities	Responds to groups of musical sounds used to symbolize particular people, places, and/or activities	Responds to some pieces through connotations brought about by their association with particular experiences	Becomes familiar with different styles of performance and develops preferences

Table 5.7 Proactive elements in the new Sounds of Intent framework

Level	P.1 Makes sounds unknowingly	P.2 Causes, creates, or controls sounds intentionally	P.3 Intentionally makes patterns in sound through repetition or regularity	P.4 Creates or re-creates short groups of musical sounds and links them coherently	P.5 Performs or improvises music of growing length and complexity, increasingly 'in tune' and 'in time'	P.6 Seeks to communicate through music through expressive performance or by creating pieces that are intended to convey particular effects
Descriptor						
Element A	The sounds made by life-processes are enhanced	Causes sound intentionally through an increasing variety of means	Intentionally makes simple patterns through repetition	Creates or re-creates short groups of musical sounds that have distinct identities	Performs short and simple pieces of music, potentially of growing length and complexity	Increasingly uses familiar conventions of expressive performance
Element B	Involuntary movements are used to control or cause sounds	Creates an increasing diversity of sounds intentionally through an increasing variety of means	Intentionally makes simple patterns through a regular beat	Links short groups of musical sounds through repetition, variation, and/or transformation	Improvises on familiar, short, and simple pieces of music, potentially of growing length and complexity	Is able to perform with conviction in an increasing number of different styles and/or genres
Element C	Sounds are made through co-active movements	Shows increasing control over sounds that are produced	Intentionally makes simple patterns through regular change	Links groups coherently through common elements (for example, as in 'question and answer' phrases)	Creates pieces of music, potentially of increasing structural coherence, complexity, and length	Technical proficiency develops to meet the demands of a widening repertoire
Element D	Sounds are made accidentally through voluntary movements	Uses sounds in conscious association with particular people, places, and/or activities	Uses sounds to symbolize particular people, places, and/or activities	Uses groups of musical sounds to symbolize particular people, places, and/or activities	Increasingly uses and maintains conventional pitch and temporal frameworks in performance (by singing and/or playing 'in time' and 'in tune')	Creates music, through improvisation or composition, to convey an increasing range of desired effects

Table 5.8 Interactive elements in the new Sounds of Intent framework

Level	I.1	I.2	I.3	I.4	I.5	I.6
Descriptor	**Unwittingly relates through sound**	**Interacts with another or others using sound**	**Interacts by imitating others' sounds or recognizing self being imitated**	**Engages in musical dialogues, creating and recognizing coherent connections between groups of sounds**	**Performs or improvises music of growing length and complexity with others, using increasingly developed ensemble skills**	**Makes music expressively with another or others, with a widening repertoire in a range of different styles and genres**
Element A	Co-workers make sounds in an effort to stimulate responses	Sounds made by another stimulate a response in sound	Imitates the sounds made by another	Imitates groups of sounds made by another (as in 'call and response')	Performs simultaneously and coherently with others, maintaining own part	Is aware of and emulates expressivity of others' playing in ensemble performance
Element B	Co-workers respond empathetically through sound to any sounds (or other gestures) that are made	Sounds are made to stimulate response in sound by another	Shows awareness of own sounds being imitated	Links groups of sounds coherently to those produced by another (as in 'question and answer')	Improvises with others, repeating and/or developing and/or building on material that is presented	Contributes own expressivity in ensemble playing in the expectation that it will inform the manner in which others perform
Element C	Work is undertaken in a variety of contexts	Interactions occur with increasing independence of context	Imitates simple patterns in sound made by another (through repetition, regularity, and/or regular change)	Produces groups of sounds in the expectation they will stimulate groups of sounds in response	Improvises with others, providing material in the expectation that it will be taken up	Performs an increasing repertoire with others
Element D	Co-workers model interaction through sound	Interaction occurs with an increasing number of exchanges over longer periods of time	Shows awareness of simple patterns in sound (made through repetition, regularity, and/or regular change) being imitated	Interactions form coherent patterns of turn-taking	Performs increasingly 'in time' and/or 'in tune' with another or others	Performs convincingly with others in a range of different styles and/or genres

providing music services for them on a peripatetic basis would have to tackle, and that using the model could provide powerful evidence as to pedagogical need that may before have gone unrecognized.

With regard to the day-to-day utilization of the framework, practitioners indicated their wish for a simple quantitative system of measuring attainment to sit alongside and inform the qualitative judgements that they would be making. It was clear that any 'scoring system' that was devised would need to be sensitive enough to capture even the tiniest changes in musical engagement (or, at level 1, provision). To achieve this, it was proposed that each element be broken down into three main 'factors', defined (though not constrained) by up to five examples of activities or behaviours. For example, it was suggested that the three principal factors in R.1.A—'is exposed to a rich variety of sounds'— should be '*sources of sound*' (for instance, 'vocal', 'other "body sounds"', 'everyday objects that make sounds', 'musical instruments', and 'electronically generated sounds'); '*basic qualities of sound*' (for example, 'high . . . low', 'short . . . long', 'quiet . . . loud', 'strident . . . mellow', and 'quickly moving . . . slowly moving'); and '*nature of combination of sounds*' (for example, 'isolated', 'smoothly flowing streams', 'sequences of detached sounds', 'contrasting clusters', and 'homogeneous blends').

To assess these quantitatively, it was proposed that a scoring system of 1–5 be adopted as follows.[23] Systematic exposure to at least one source of sound, with variation in respect of at least one basic quality and one form of combination would score 1; exposure to at least two sources of sound, with variation in respect of at least two basic qualities and combined in at least two ways would score 2; exposure to three sources, basic qualities and combinations of sound would score 3; four of each, 4; and at least five of each, 5.

These scores do not paint a complete picture, however, since the frequency of the activities to which they pertain, and the degree to which these are integrated into day-to-day programmes of education and care, also need to be taken into account. Similarly, at higher levels in the framework, the consistency with which a given behaviour occurs is a crucial component of attainment. Hence it was proposed that a 'multiplier' should be introduced that would capture this aspect of music provision or pupils' engagement with it. At level 1, it was suggested that the multiplier should operate as follows. Where music and other auditory stimulation is *rarely* integrated into day-to-day programmes of living and learning, and/or there are sessions devoted to sound and music around once a fortnight or less, the factor score should be multiplied by 1. Where music and other auditory stimulation is *occasionally* integrated into

---

[23] Note that at this level, it is *co-worker* input that is being assessed.

day-to-day programmes, and/or there are sessions devoted to sound and music around once a week, it should be multiplied by 2. Similarly, where stimulation is *regularly* integrated and/or sessions occur around twice a week, the factor score should be multiplied 3. Where stimulation is *frequently* integrated and/or sessions occur three to four times a week, it should be multiplied by 4; and where stimulation is *consistently* integrated and/or sessions occur every day, it should be multiplied by 5.

At levels 2–6 (which are concerned with a young person's engagement with music), it was proposed that the multipliers should work as follows. Where behaviours were *rarely* observed (on around 1 in 8 occasions or fewer), the factor score should be multiplied by 1. Where behaviours were *occasionally* observed (on around 1 in 4 occasions), it should be multiplied by 2. Where they were *regularly* observed (around 1 in 2), the multiplier would be 3; *frequently* observed (around 3 in 4), the multiplier would be 4; and *consistently* observed (around 7 in 8 or more), the multiplier would be 5.

Given that there are four elements at every level in each of the three domains (reactive, proactive, and interactive), the maximum score that could be achieved at each level per domain would be 100. The minimum would normally be 4, falling to 0 where there was no evidence. Because the proposed scoring system would be sensitive to the frequency of occurrence of events, and since new behaviours often emerge gradually, it is quite conceivable that a child would obtain a range of scores across a number of levels, whose profile may vary with time. Such changes could be tracked with precision, and programmes of learning and leisure adjusted accordingly.

While this multi-faceted approach was felt to be both rigorous and methodical, practitioners expressed concerns as to how workable it would be in the classroom and other everyday settings, where the time available was limited, and ease of recording was essential. Technology seemed to hold the key, whereby, as before, access to the framework should be via a touch screen on a tablet PC. Each pupil would have an individual profile stored digitally on the machine (or downloaded to a central resource), including, as appropriate, dated audio and video files, and qualitative comments and quantitative measures of their attainment, based on observation. In addition, the system would offer practitioners teaching and learning materials, organized in relation to the framework—offering suggestions to specialists and non-specialists alike of how to deal with the perennial problem of working with pupils whose progress is in very small steps of *what to do next*.

In due course, it was suggested that schools should be able to access the Sounds of Intent framework, with its updatable resources, via the internet. This would also make it possible to gather certain data (that did not compromise confidentiality) at a research hub—enabling the research team to collate the attainment and progress of large numbers of pupils automatically, and build up and track a music-developmental profile of the population (and subsets of it). In the course of time, it may permit normative comparisons to be drawn, and make it possible for teachers to establish evidence-based future expectations for individual pupils. Above all, linking practitioners and researchers over the internet would enable the framework to evolve interactively through substantial user involvement.

An extended example of the kind of information and assessment protocols that would be available to co-workers[24] on the tablet PC at level 1 across the reactive, proactive, and interactive domains appears in the Appendix on p. 265.

Conclusion

A key aim of the 'Sounds of Intent' project has been to establish a model of musical development in children and young people with PMLD or SLD, and the latest iteration lies at the heart of the thinking set out in this book. The model is based on empirical evidence from two sources: 'typical' musical development in very young children, and observations of the ways in which pupils with learning difficulties engage with music; qualitative data that are framed by a new theory of how music 'makes sense'. The initial assumption that informed this work—that the musical development of children and young people with complex needs follows broadly the same course as that taken by most other people—is supported by the 'Sounds of Intent' developmental framework, which is both internally coherent and fits the data gathered to date.

The model is unlike others that have been formulated up to this point in that it focuses *only* on the development of musical interests, abilities, and preferences (while acknowledging that all auditory processing has common roots). The intention has been to avoid some of the pitfalls to which other current models have been susceptible (including the QCA's 'P-levels' for music), in which musical and non-musical elements are conflated. It appears that this conceptual blending has arisen from an ignorance of what *musical* development actually comprises, and, paradoxically, has tended to limit an appreciation of music's true capacity to inform wider learning and development. This is the subject of the next chapter.

---

[24] Teachers, teaching assistants, therapists, carers, etc.

Chapter 6

Music moves

Introduction

There is typically much more to children's engagement with music than the specialized mental processing of abstract patterns of sound: music-making requires a wide range of other skills and abilities, and provides a context that is conducive to exercising them. Because of this, as practice in schools shows (Chapter 1), music is of potential value to teachers and therapists beyond its intrinsic artistic merit: it can be used as a tool to promote learning and development in a variety of other areas (Ockelford 2000).

For example, performance, at any level, may well enhance fine motor control and coordination, while listening relies on cognitive skills such as concentration and memory. Singing can offer unique support in the early stages of language acquisition, and making music in a group provides a context and structure for socializing: participation may heighten a child's awareness of self and other, foster tolerance, and enable individuals to contribute to a larger whole. Hence just as literacy and numeracy permeate mainstream curricula, underpinning many areas of study, so music can inform the wider curriculum of children who have complex needs. A number of possibilities are worked through in detail in the four sections of this chapter that follow.

Using music in a cross-curricular role will inevitably involve a number of staff, the majority of whom, as we saw in Chapter 1, are not likely to have a background in music. However, just as the musical development of young people with complex needs can be promoted through more or less consciously adopting and (if necessary) adapting intuitive parenting skills, so participating in musical activities of the type described below is well within most people's everyday capabilities. The main issue is likely to be effective coordination in the planning, delivery, and evaluation of programmes that seek to educate *through* music, both within the formal school day and—ideally—beyond. So it is particularly important that such programmes should have clear aims, agreed in consultation with the wider team, including, as far as possible, the young people themselves. A careful note should be kept of the approaches that are adopted, so that as staff inevitably come and go, and situations change, the essential learning structure remains the same, and a pupil's wider musical environment is held intact. As is the case with education *in* music, the most effective programmes will be those that are responsive to children's growth and maturation, and evolve to anticipate them. Progress will be most likely to occur when systematic assessment and record-keeping enable future steps to be mapped out with precision. Hence attempts are made to locate what follows within developmental frameworks that are cross-referenced to the Sounds of Intent model.

Music and movement

Promoting body awareness and movement through making music

Pupil's body awareness, and the control and coordination of a wide range of movements can be fostered through playing instruments and other sound-makers. Movement is frequently required, for example, in the fingers, hands, and arms, while vocalizing utilizes the mouth, throat, and chest, and wind instruments demand varying types and degrees of breath control. Other parts of the body, particularly the legs and feet, may be involved in sound-making too (Fig. 6.1).

Whatever the movement required, the principle is that the child or young person concerned will be motivated to move in order to produce a sound (implying that he or she will be functioning in musical terms at level P.2 or higher). This may work well for pupils with the necessary motor skills or potential. However, as many young people with complex needs find move-ment particularly challenging, switches of one kind or another may be required to enable the connection to be made, since (as we have seen) technological intervention means that there need be no direct link between the

Fig. 6.1 Exploring sound-makers in the Little Room (see p. 276)

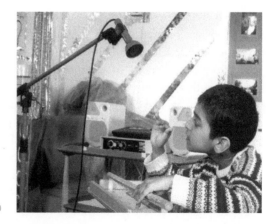

Fig. 6.2 Using the Soundbeam®

nature of the movement made and the sound that is produced. The continuing value of the device that is employed may depend on the opportunities it offers a child for progression. Systems created around ultrasonic beams linked to a MIDI system can be particularly beneficial in this respect, since by gradually altering the switching parameters that are in operation, more extensive (or more subtle) movements may be required to obtain the same sound (Ellis 1996) (see Fig. 6.2).

Pupils' motor abilities and performance skills may develop hand in hand—each potentially driving, informing, and benefiting from the other. Young people may seek (and be assisted) to copy the movements made by others to produce sounds—or relish having their own sound-making movements emulated—corresponding to interaction at level 3 of the Sounds of Intent framework. The production of groups of sounds of increasing length and complexity demands more extensive and intricate series of coordinated movements (levels 4 and 5). Finally, specialized fine motor skills may be acquired through instruction followed by conscious practice as pupils and students move along the road towards greater technical proficiency (level 6).

An auditory frame of reference

From around the age of 6 months, babies will typically move spontaneously to music (Moog 1968/1976: 56 ff.). This corresponds most closely to element I.2.A—'sounds made by another stimulate a response in sound', and, given that pupils with learning difficulties appear to tread a similar path of early musical development to that followed by most other people (albeit more slowly), it is reasonable to expect spontaneous movements to music from those with complex needs who are functioning at or beyond level 2, and who are able to move independently. This tendency can be encouraged and exploited by teachers, carers, and therapists through co-active music and movement sessions (cf. element P.1.C). Dance offers a culturally valid context—potentially appropriate to the interests and social backgrounds of the young people concerned—in which educational, recreational, and therapeutic activities of this type may be embedded.

The movements that children and young people make in response to music may be freely expressive, or characteristics of pieces they are hearing may influence, more or less specifically, the actions that accompany them. That is, music can provide an 'auditory frame of reference' for movement. This may be particularly significant for those who have no have no sight or have difficulty in processing visual information.

The strongest link between music and movement is found in rhythm, which sets the pace for action. For example, in the specially composed song (Ex. 6.1) *To and Fro*[1], the first beat of each bar alternately marks the extremes of vacillating movements such as rocking, waving, swinging, swaying, and nodding (Ockelford 1996a).

This metrical emphasis is reinforced by the structure of the melody, which is made up of short phrases that are one bar in length, assisting listeners to predict when successive downbeats will occur. Such anticipation requires the capacity to project relationships between sounds into the future, implying the integrated functioning of auditory memory and imagination. As a sense of regular pulse is formed in the mind of the listener, it is cognitively and physically synchronized with movement through the process of 'entrainment'[2] (Fig. 6.3) (see, for example, Clayton, Sager, and Will 2004).

It is of interest to note how this capacity develops in relation to the hierarchy of musical abilities set out in the Sounds of Intent framework. At level P.2 ('causing, creating, and controlling sounds'), children and young people may sometimes produce an even-sounding beat, for example by repeatedly hitting a drum. However, at this level, the regularity occurs because of evenly spaced muscular contractions, rather than arising from the conscious effort to control the sounds that are produced. Teachers can identify this higher level of functioning through previously having observed a pupil deliberately vary the speed of a pulse, in which case P.3.B ('intentionally makes simple patterns through a regular beat') would be the appropriate descriptor. Even this, though, is not the same as entrainment with an external stimulus, which demands the ability to

---

[1] From *All join in!*—a set of 24 songs to encourage wider learning and development in children with PMLD or SLD (Ockelford 1996a).

[2] The process through which pulses interact so that they occur at the same rate.

Ex. 6.1 *To and Fro*

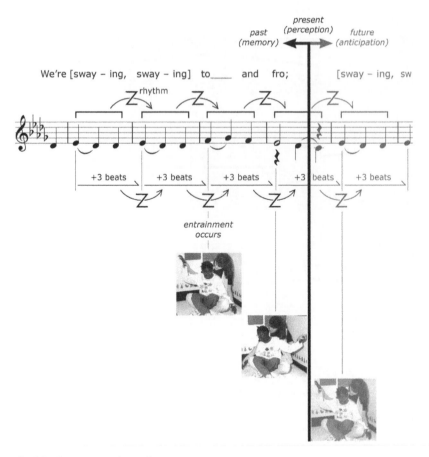

Fig. 6.3 The process of entrainment

perceive two streams of sound together and to adjust one to fit the other (I.5.D—'performs increasingly in time . . . with another or others'); in the case of *To and Fro*, something that is reinforced through R.4.B ('responds to the repetition . . . of groups of musical sounds'). This typically occurs at the age of 4 or 5 (Moog 1968/1976: 127), and so is likely to remain beyond the capacity of most young people with PMLD or SLD.

In *To and Fro*, there is a direct relationship between the tempo of the music and the rate at which actions are repeated. Other connections between music and movement are possible too. For example, loud sounds may be associated with large movements and quiet sounds with small ones. Links such as these may largely be attributed to the experience of playing instruments where there is an immediate connection between the effort that is applied and the volume of sound produced (see P.2.B and P.2.C). This principle underlies the song *Quiet and Loud*, for instance (Ockelford 1996*a*) (see Fig. 6.4).

A rise in pitch is widely considered to correspond to movement in an upward direction, and vice versa—something that is exploited in the song *Up and Down* (Fig. 6.5). While this correspondence is generally conveyed through the more or less conscious efforts of teachers and others, and appears largely to be culturally determined (Zbikowski 2002: 71 ff.), there is also some evidence that it occurs partly as a consequence of the natural way that thinking develops (Welch 1991). Either way, it implies the activation of cross-modal connections in the mind (between sound and perceptual input in another domain), which the Sounds of Intent framework suggests may occur from level 2 onwards.

Whatever their root, the power of associations between sound and movement can be considerable. Hence they offer teachers, therapists, and carers a potentially valuable tool in working with young people with complex needs. As we have seen (pp. 20 and 21), music can add an extra dimension to physiotherapy programmes, for example: motivating children to move, and enabling them to anticipate what is coming when the same short pieces are consistently used to introduce activities as well as accompany them. For example, the song *Stretch and Bend* (Ex. 6.2) has an introduction, partly to promote this special symbolic function, which music can fulfil (see pp. 101 above and 131 below).

Taking all the above into account, the connections between early musical development and movement can be summarized as shown in Table 6.1.

Music and learning
Introduction

Teachers and others can use music and other organized sound to promote their pupils' acquisition of skills, knowledge, and understanding in a number of ways. These include:

+ utilizing music and other structured auditory input to enhance sensory information obtained from the environment;
+ promoting the direct transfer of perceptual and cognitive skills from musical contexts to other spheres of activity;
+ isolating selected qualities of sound and treating them as concepts to be manipulated in pursuit of educational goals beyond music; and
+ regarding pieces of music as potential sources of information about the cultures in which they were created.

These possibilities are examined in turn.

Fig. 6.4 *Quiet and Loud*

Fig. 6.5 *Up and Down*

Sounds conveying information about the environment

Natural forces and energy in the environment effect continuous physical change, which children and young people typically perceive through sight, hearing, touch, and their other senses. For the great majority of people, vision is the channel through which most information is conveyed. Moreover, the brain often relies on visual images to inform and direct the work of the remaining senses—confirming, for example, that those strident sounds are

Ex. 6.2 *Stretch and Bend*

indeed emanating from the lead guitar, and alerting the listener to the immi-
nent entry of the solo vocalist as she takes the mike off its stand and prepares
to sing. Frequently, sight integrates the discrete, sometimes fragmented, and
potentially confusing data gathered by the other senses. For instance, seeing a
symphony orchestra enables children to know what it is like at a glance, rather
than having to rely on widely varying auditory input from the many different
instruments and, perhaps, a series of individual tactile sensations. However,
since many young people with complex needs have difficulty in processing
visual information, it may well be that, for them, sound features more prominently in the perceptual landscape than would otherwise be the case, and there
are several ways in which teachers, carers, and therapists can maximize its
impact.

One strategy is to *simplify* the auditory environment. This process can begin
by tracking pupils through a series of events in the school day, for example—
listing the sounds to which they are exposed, and assessing the effect that these

Table 6.1 Relationship between early musical development and movement

1	2	3	4	5	6
P.1.B Involuntary movements are made to control or cause sounds	*P.2.A* Causes sound intentionally through an increasing variety of means **and movements; the motivation to move may stem in whole or in part from the desire to make a sound**	*P.3.A / P.3.C* Intentionally makes simple patterns through repetition or regular change **(NB the repetition of movements, or regular change in them, are driven by auditory considerations)**	*P.4.A* Creates or re-creates groups of musical sounds that have distinct identities **through coordinated series of movements**	*I.5.D* Performs increasingly in time ... with another or others, **implying coordinating the timing of movements with another or others**	*P.6.C* Technical proficiency develops to meet the demands of a widening repertoire, **implying the development of specialized movement skills**
P.1.C Sounds are made through co-active movement	*I.2.A* Sounds made by another stimulate a response in sound **or movement**	*P.3.B / P.3.D* Intentionally makes simple patterns through a regular or regularly changing beat **(NB the even spacing of movements in time, or regular change in pace, are driven by auditory considerations)**			
P.1.D Sounds are made accidentally through voluntary movements	*P.2.B* Creates an increasing diversity of sounds through an increasing variety of **movements; hence changes in sound become associated with different types and degrees of movement**	*I.3.A* Imitates the sounds made by another, partly through imitating their **movements**			
	P.2.C Shows increasing control over sounds that are produced through increasing control over movement **(NB may include repetition or regularity that is driven by movement rather than sound)**	*I.3.B* Shows awareness of own sounds **(and movements)** being imitated.			

have. Schools are often noisy places, and it is probable that children and young people with complex needs will find some of what they hear distracting or even distressing. Moreover, they may well be unable to attend selectively to the tangle of sounds that surround them (unlike their co-workers, who, as mature listeners, will subconsciously suppress extraneous sounds). Some idea of what this is like can be gleaned by recording experiences and replaying them later. Then it may be noticeable that the noise of the tables being moved ready for lunch in the hall largely obliterated the music to which the children were intended to relax (little wonder that several of them grew more tense as the session progressed!). And it may come as little surprise, in retrospect, that the children seemed so inattentive during a session in class, since the noise of the motor-mower outside cut swathes through what the teacher was saying.

Based on findings such as these, teachers and others should consider whether it would be possible and desirable to reduce or eliminate any of the extraneous sounds that have no long-term place in pupils' learning programmes. If certain noises in the environment cannot be removed, it may be advisable to reschedule or change the venue of activities in which sound or music are particularly significant. Auditory clutter in classrooms and similar environments may be minimized by using partitions or other forms of screening to produce smaller, relatively quiet learning areas (see R.1.C—p. 114 above).

Sounds that are important may be *enhanced* or *modified* if necessary to make them more distinct (cf. P.1.A), linked to tactile and other sensory experiences, and, if appropriate, explained verbally or through other means (Ockelford 2005*b*). Extra sounds may be used to supplement other sensory input. For instance, as we have seen (R.1.D), a room may be identified through a distinctive set of windchimes suspended in the doorway, or areas used occasionally may be characterized by a particular type of music playing in the background, whose familiarity may also offer emotional security to children struggling to make sense of a confusing world (see p. 69 above). Some activities may consistently be accompanied by music in a suitable style, and, as noted above, individuals may wear carefully selected bangles or jangling bracelets, serving to augment their presence in sensory terms (cf. p. 99).

The transfer of skills

Attending purposefully to music engages a range of perceptual and cognitive processes, which usually operate subconsciously. Although some of these, such as identifying similarities, trends, and patterns among stimuli (level R.3) and assigning them to groups (level R.4) and hierarchies (level R.5), are characteristic of perception in other domains too, the development of such abilities in relation to music appears largely to be bound by that context, with no simple crossover to different spheres of mental activity. More general cognitive attributes such as concentration and memory, however, which are also fundamental to the appreciation of music (at all levels), may operate in a way which is less domain-specific, and here achievement may transfer more readily to other areas of experience, particularly those which also involve listening (Overy 1998). Bunt (1994: 111 ff.), for example, cites an extensive study that examined the effects of music therapy on children with learning difficulties, and which indicated that exposure to appropriate musical activities could indeed help children focus their attention and increase their concentration span. As he observes (p. 128), 'Over time it appears that a period of music therapy can contribute to a child's increasing ability to sustain and initiate activities'.

Sound concepts

Objects can be identified through their sound-making qualities and grouped accordingly (level R.4). For instance, pupils may be encouraged to contrast the ringing, bell-like sounds of metal with the more mellow response of wood, and to sort items on this basis. Instruments may also be grouped according to how they are played—whether sounds are made through shaking or striking them, for example.

Other concepts can be extracted from the experience of music too. For instance, the opposing notions of 'quiet' and 'loud' can be introduced or reinforced through songs such as Fig. 6.4. Similarly, the contrasting ideas of 'slowly' and 'quickly' can be conveyed musically (level R.2) (Ex. 6.3).

Number features widely in music (Ockelford 1999: 308 ff.), and it can be isolated as a concept in several ways. For example, pupils can consider the number of times a tambourine is tapped in a repeating pattern—'1, 2, 3 . . . 1, 2, 3 . . .' (possible from level R.3); the number of beats there are in a bar, the number of verses in a song, and the number of people that are playing or singing at the same time (from level I.5).

General concepts such as 'start' and 'stop' (level 2), 'the same' and 'different' (level 3), and 'together' and 'alone' (from level 4), are integral to musical structure and performance. Practical sessions provide opportunities to get to grips with ideas such as these, and offer a context for communicating with others about them (Fig. 6.6).

Music as artefact

All pieces of music and musical instruments are ultimately products of the societies in which they originated, and offer rich sources of cultural information for young people who have complex needs. Depending on their level of

Ex. 6.3 *Slowly and Quickly*

understanding, pupils' experience of pieces of music as artefacts may range from simple exposure to reasoned discussion about their construction, how they relate to other cultural products and spheres of artistic endeavour, and more broadly to the historical and geographical context in which a given composition was created.

Music and musical instruments may feature as elements in a broader multisensory cultural event (which may be appropriate for pupils functioning at all levels of the Sounds of Intent framework), including storytelling, drama, dance, and religious ritual, for example, dress and scent, drawing, painting and sculpture, and food and drink. Performers may come to the school, or pupils may experience a range of outside activities, from the exuberance of street carnivals to the relative sobriety of the gamelan. This

Fig. 6.6 *Together and Alone*

Indonesian orchestra, comprising gongs, chimes, metallophones, and other percussion instruments, produces rich textures of resonant sounds that many young people find appealing, and, with assistance, almost all are able to participate actively as performers. It is difficult to imagine a more inclusive form of music-making.

Conclusion

The opportunities for learning in the context of early musical development are summarized in Table 6.2.

Music and communication
Introduction

Many children with complex needs may well require special intervention to help them develop the communication skills that usually evolve quite naturally, with no conscious effort on the part of carers and teachers. A common approach is to *augment* receptive language through enhancing or replacing the spoken word with symbolic information in other domains that is accessible, both in sensory and cognitive terms. That is, children receive signals in a form that they can readily perceive and are capable of understanding. Two common methods are signing (Lee and MacWilliam 2002) and the use of 'objects of reference'—typically everyday items that are assigned a symbolic meaning (Ockelford 2002a). These may well be employed together: those who wish to communicate opening up on all fronts in the belief that this will increase the chances of their message getting through.

In time, following a range of appropriate experiences and exposure to communication pertaining to them, many children with complex needs may consciously try to make their own reactions, feelings, and needs known to those around. This is one of several distinct stages in the evolution of expressive communication. These are of particular significance to teachers and others working with children and young people whose development is markedly delayed.

The earliest stage is characterized by an unthinking reaction to basic needs—crying in response to physical discomfort, for example—an unwitting plea for help that may be conveyed to carers, who vest in the sounds a communicative intent, and act accordingly. This form of communication is termed 'non-intentional'. Gradually, children and young people may become aware that crying, other vocalizing, and particular expressions or gestures have an effect on others: the 'intentional' stage. Here, pupils commonly draw people's

Table 6.2 Relationship between early musical development and learning

1	2	3	4	5	6
Examples of perceptual development		**Examples of conceptual development**			
R.1.A Is exposed to a rich variety of sounds **in combination with other perceptual input**	*P.2.B* Creates an increasing diversity of sounds intentionally through an increasing variety of means **and thereby becomes aware of the physical qualities of sound-makers**	*R.3.A* Recognizes and reacts to the repetition of sounds **and is therefore potentially aware of the concepts of 'same' and 'different'**	*R.4.A* Responds to groups of musical sounds **and is therefore potentially aware of the concepts that define groups of sound-makers, such as *timbre***	*I.5.A* Performs simultaneously and coherently with others **and therefore is potentially aware of the concepts of playing 'together' and 'alone' and of the number of people performing**	*R.6.B* Becomes familiar with an increasing number of styles and genres, and develops preferences **and potentially appreciates music as an artefact within a wider socio–cultural context**
R.1.C Is exposed to music in different contexts **including uncluttered environments in which perceptual input is simplified**	*R.2.D* Responds to musical and other sounds through their association with particular people, places and/or events **implying 'sensory integration'**			*R.5.C* Responds to general features whose connotations are established by convention (such as the western 'major' and 'minor' modes) **and potentially appreciates music as an artefact within a wider socio-cultural context**	
R.1.D Is exposed to particular musical and other sounds being linked to key people, places and/or events **thereby promoting the development of sensory integration**	*R.2.A* Shows awareness of an increasing variety of musical and other sounds **and, therefore, potentially, concepts such as *slowly* and *quickly* and *quiet* and *loud***				
P.1.A The sounds made by life processes are enhanced **thereby articulating the connection between somatic and auditory sensations**	*P.2.A* Causes sound intentionally through an increasing variety of means **and is therefore potentially aware concepts such as *start* and *stop***				

Developing concentration →

Developing memory →

Table 6.3 The development of early communication

Type and phase of expressive communication	Vocal	Gestural/ visual (person-based)	Gestural/ visual (exernally based)	Tactile/haptic
Non-intentional	Cries in response to need	For example, *arches back in displeasure*	Looks at things	Touches things
Intentional	Deliberately vocalizes to show need	For example, *extends arm to attract attention*	Points to things	Consciously manipulates objects to communicate: for example, *proffers object to elicit shared attention 'hairdrier'*
Symbolic	Makes personal utterances: for example, *says 'mmm' meaning 'hairdrier'*	Makes personal signs: for example, *flaps hand for 'yes'*	Points at pictures Draws	Uses objects of reference
Formal	Speaks (using words)	Uses conventional signs	Points at symbols or words Writes (in print)	Uses Moon/Braille

attention to things by pointing, and relish the shared external interest this arouses. Next comes a growing appreciation of 'symbolic' communication, in which one thing stands for another. Flapping the hand may consistently be used to mean 'yes', for example, a humming sound may refer to the use of the hairdrier, or an object of reference such as a seat-belt buckle may indicate a desire to ride in the car. These personal gestures, sounds, and symbols may eventually become standardized in conventional signing or speech, or lead to literacy in print, Braille, or Moon (an alternative tactile reading system). At this point, communication is said to be 'formal' (see Table 6.3).

This developmental framework, which evolved from observations of the communicative (and pre-communicative) behaviours of children and young people with PMLD and SLD, quite separately from the Sounds of Intent model, corresponds to it closely in a number of respects. The 'non-intentional' phase corresponds to level 1, when pupils make sounds unknowingly, and unwittingly relate through sound.[3] The 'intentional' phase aligns with level 2, when pupils deliberately cause, create, or control sounds and use them to interact with others; and they come to appreciate that certain sounds exist as part of wider sensory experiences. The 'symbolic' phase begins at level 3 and extends to level 4. Here, some musical sounds may come to function symbolically in relation to particular places, people, or activities, acting rather like words. More typically, though, as we have seen (p. 64 ff.), rather than relating to objects or events in the external world, musical sounds are logically connected to each other through repetition, arguably through a kind of internal symbolism. The 'formal' phase of communication reads across to levels 5 and 6 of the Sounds of Intent framework. Here, features of familiar musical styles are recognized and used—in effect, a shared language.

In summary, the two frameworks are connected as demonstrated in Table 6.4. It is of interest to note that, according to this combined taxonomy, production of the simplest musical structures (stemming from the repetition of sounds) precedes the use of formal linguistic structures by some margin. As we shall see, this enables music to fulfil a unique role in promoting language development.

Sound-symbols

Music and other organized sounds (in addition to speech) typically fulfil a range of symbolic functions in everyday life. Consider, for example, the signature tunes that are used to introduce television and radio series: just a few notes are sufficient to remind regular viewers and listeners of their favourite programmes. Other familiar sound-symbols include church bells, door chimes, fire alarms, and the referee's whistle in sport. These symbols supply information about what is currently happening, what has recently taken place, or give warning of what is about to occur. They are used in preference to speech for a number of reasons: their immediate impact may be greater, for example, or they may be more aesthetically pleasing. However, it is through verbal explanation that people typically become familiar with the meaning of sound-symbols such as these.

The principle of using sound symbolically can be extended to support the receptive communication of children who have complex needs (cf. R.1.D, R.2.D, R.3.D and R.4.D), and to assist them in their efforts to communicate expressively (cf. P.2.D, P.3.D and P.4.D). As we have seen, there are various

---

[3] The exception being P.1.D: 'sounds are made accidentally through voluntary movement'—though here the developing sense of intentionality is taken to be in the movement rather than its causal effect of sound-making.

Table 6.4 The relationship between musical development and the development of communication

Phase of expressive communication	Corresponding proactive levels	Corresponding interactive levels
Non-intentional	P.1 Makes sounds unknowingly	I.1 Unwittingly relates through sound
Intentional	P.2 Causes, creates, or controls sound intentionally	I.2 Interacts with another or others using sound
Symbolic	P.3 Intentionally makes patterns in sound through repetition or regularity	I.3 Interacts by imitating others' sounds or recognizing self being imitated
	P.4 Creates or re-creates short groups of musical sounds and links them coherently	I.4 Engages in musical dialogues, creating and recognizing coherent connections between groups of sounds
Formal	P.5 Performs or improvises music of growing length and complexity, increasingly 'in time' and 'in tune'	I.5 Performs or improvises music of growing length and complexity with others, using increasingly developed ensemble skills
	P.6 Seeks to communicate through music through expressive performance or by creating pieces that are intended to convey particular effects	I.6 Makes music expressively with another or others, with a widening repertoire in a range of different styles and genres

categories of day-to-day information that can be symbolized through sound, including activities, places, and people (Ockelford 2002*a*: 15 ff.).

Sound-symbols can relate to these and other conceptual areas in two ways. There may be a direct link, where a sound is *integral* to a given activity, for instance, such as a small cluster of bells being used to represent a music session. Other sound-symbols work through being *associated* with an activity, and so operate at a more abstract level. For example, a horn may be taken to mean 'ride the bike'. This type of associative connection can also be applied to places and people. For instance, the windchimes chosen to help characterize a

Fig. 6.7 *Where are we?*

room (see p. 91 above) may also be used to represent it symbolically, while the jangling bracelets or bangles worn to enhance the individuality of key figures in a child's life (p. 143) may acquire referential status too (see Fig. 6.7).

Sound-symbols will often have tactile and visual qualities that may be exploited within multisensory communication programmes, just as some objects of reference, which are principally identified through touch and vision, have the capacity for making characteristic sounds. For example, a carved wooden rattle may be distinct and attractive visually, while a small bag of coins may make a unique jingling sound. In either case, the symbols can be used in combination with other forms of communication, including speech and signing, as part of an integrated approach.

Teachers, therapists, and carers need to give careful attention to the circumstances in which sound-symbols are used, especially in the early stages. They are not something to be learnt about in isolation, but should be introduced in everyday situations, growing naturally from pupils' first-hand experiences, *whenever the need to communicate arises*. It is particularly important, in embarking on a communication programme, to consult widely and plan thoroughly, taking account of any strong interests or preferences a child or young person may have.

Sound-symbols are likely to be used first to augment receptive communication. They may be of particular benefit to children and young people whose capacity for absorbing information in tactile or visual form is limited, and who may find objects of reference physically difficult to manage. The aim will be to move to a position where a sound that is typically associated with something or someone can be removed from this context, and, appearing as a stimulus in its own right, bring to mind the activity, place, or person with which it was originally connected. In terms of the Sounds of Intent framework, this means moving from element R.2.D ('responds to musical and other sounds through their association with particular people, places and/or activities') to R.3.D ('responds to musical sounds used to symbolize particular people, places and/or activities').

Such development may be fostered by presenting the sounding object to a child immediately before undertaking the activity of which it forms a part, or just prior to encountering the person or place with which it is associated. For example, a designated cluster of bells may be handed to a child shortly in advance of a music session, or a set of windchimes, identical to those in the doorway of the classroom, may be introduced on the way to class.

Some young people may make the link between a sound and its symbolic meaning straightaway, while the same connection may continue to elude others. For many, interactions of the type described will have to be repeated time and again, over an extended period, before their significance is grasped—highlighting the importance of a well-planned and consistent approach to communication. Gradually, it may be possible to separate the sound-symbol further and further in time from that to which it refers, and eventually, two or more symbols may be presented in succession to indicate a forthcoming sequence of events. Some pupils may progress to using 'auditory timetables', which represent a series of events (see Fig. 6.8).

Fig. 6.8 Using an auditory timetable

Once children and young people have become familiar with receiving information through sound-symbols, to indicate what is going to happen next, for example, they may be encouraged to use them in an expressive way. Pupils may be able to choose the next activity for themselves, for instance, from among a selection that is offered.

Sound-symbols may be employed retrospectively too, in reviewing events that have occurred. They can also be used, receptively and expressively, in the context of make believe—giving an added auditory dimension to stories, and enhancing the development of imaginative play. The effects chosen may be representative to a greater or lesser extent, ranging from the literal use of recorded animal sounds, for instance, to a roll on a suspended cymbal, which may be used in an entirely symbolic way to indicate the sun coming out. Deploying sound-symbols like these may be particularly appropriate for learners who are visually impaired or who have difficulty in processing visual information, for whom the colourful illustrations that feature in children's early literature may be neither informative nor aesthetically pleasing. One approach is to assemble and maintain a collection of objects, with various sensory qualities, that are relevant to each story in a class's repertoire (see Fig. 6.9).

Music and speech

As we have seen (p. 491), verbal language and music share common roots in early auditory development, and at all stages of the human experience they are combined in the form of songs and chants. This affinity can be particularly

Fig. 6.9 Storytelling with sounding objects

useful in promoting communication and fostering its development among children who have complex needs.

For example, early in childhood, as we noted above (p. 80), exposure to music may elicit vocalization (Moog 1968/1976: 59 ff.), and those working with young people with learning difficulties may exploit this tendency to promote the production and control of vocal sounds. At more advanced levels of functioning, music can play a significant role in motivating children to use language, through the many songs that have been especially written or have evolved over the years for their edification and pleasure. Whether nursery rhymes or counting songs, playground chants or action songs, game songs or songs that tell a story . . . music adds another dimension to the verbal messages presented, enlivening everyday expressions and imbuing them with extra colour and interest.

Music can also help to *structure* language. This may be particularly important for children with complex needs, who often have to contend with an unnecessarily baffling array of different words and phrases from adults who, in the face of little or no immediate reaction from those they are addressing, are culturally programmed not to repeat themselves. If at first you don't succeed in being understood, there is a strong inclination to try again, using alternative means of expression. Experience of special schools (see Chapter 1) suggests that scenarios such as the following, in which a teacher is addressing a pupil, are not untypical:

'It's time for lunch.'
Pause. No response
'Come and get something to eat.'
Longer pause. Still no response
'Aren't you hungry? I expect there'll be something nice for us today.'
Further pause, then, encouragingly
'Come on. Food! My tummy's rumbling, isn't yours?'
Final check for any response, then
'Ready, then? Off we go.'

Yet what the child seeking order and regularity may need most is simplicity and consistency. Here, music can help. By setting selected phrases to characteristic snatches of melody, reinforced where appropriate with gestures, signs, symbols, or objects of reference, the consistent delivery of key messages is assured. For example, see Ex. 6.4.

That is not to say that carefully structured fragments such as this should be *all* that is communicated, but that they should form salient features in a rich and diverse landscape of multisensory interaction.

Songs can be devised to add interest to language while structuring it tightly. The clarity of design may be enhanced through direct repetition, common in words set to music, but rare in speech alone. Consider, for example, the song *What is it?* (Ex. 6.5).

The melody of the 'goodbye' song (Ex. 6.6) relies on repetition to an even greater extent.

In song, the acceptability of *musical* repetition transfers to the lyrics, and it does not seem at all inappropriate to say the same thing over and over again. More than this, though, by allocating to important words and phrases short tunes of their own, one form of complex auditory input (speech) is supplemented with a simpler overlay (melody).[4] The message is given a stronger

Ex. 6.4 Ensuring consistency of a key verbal message by setting it to music

now it's time to   get your lunch

---

[4] Just how much simpler music is than language for the brain to process can be shown by analysing a typical nursery rhyme in terms of its 'zygonicity'—an expression of the proportion of repetition to new material that is present in a given information string (cf. Ockelford 2005*a*: 73; Cohen 1962). Take *Twinkle, twinkle, little star*, for instance: in terms of pitches, durations and timbres, the figure is 93 per cent whereas the equivalent calculation for words yields only 34 per cent. That is to say, music is far more 'redundant' than verbal language: it can tolerate far more 'noise' in the system (that may be brought about in the case of children and young people with complex needs, through fluctuating levels

Ex. 6.5 *What is it?*

identity, which is consequently more memorable, and which children and young people with complex needs may find easier to recognize. It is even possible for short snatches of melody like these to function symbolically in their own right, both receptively and expressively (see P.4.D). Hence children who find it difficult to produce speech sounds accurately may be able to make themselves understood more readily by using fragments of melody such as those shown in Ex. 5.2 (p. 90). Here, in Tabitha's short phrases, the rhythm and shape of the tunes have distinct identities, and those who are used to working with her can understand what is meant.

Finally, it is worth bearing in mind that, since there are neurological differences in the way that music and speech are processed following the early stages

---

of concentration, for example) and still be conveyed successfully. Moreover, the language found in many children's songs (including *Twinkle, twinkle*) is highly abstract and metaphorical, using concepts far beyond the comprehension of most young people with SLD or PMLD. Understanding music, on the other hand, at least at the level of pure pattern recognition, requires only the capacity to process differences and similarities in stimuli appearing within a single domain—sound. Here, the structure of the message and its content are fused into one aesthetic experience (Ockelford 2005*b*: 75 ff.).

Ex. 6.6 *Goodbye*

of development,[5] children and young people who are unable to speak, or who find verbalizing difficult, may nonetheless be able to communicate through *singing* words and phrases, or at least intoning them within a rhythmic structure. For example, Anastasi and Levee (1960: 696), in their report on a musical savant 'S', observe that 'before he could talk, S was able to hum tunes he heard on the radio or phonograph. To capitalize on this propensity, a speech therapist was engaged and S was eventually taught to talk through the medium of lyrics. To this date, a sing-song quality is discernible in his speech.'

Music and social interaction

Music has many different functions in life, nearly all of which, in the final analysis, are essentially social in nature (Hargreaves and North 1997). Although listening to music, exploring the multisensory properties of sound-makers, singing, playing instruments, and inventing new pieces potentially

---

[5] For an account of certain similarities see, for example, Maess, Koelsch, Gunter, and Friederici (2001), who report that musical grammar and the syntactic rules of speech may both be represented in the same part of the brain ('Broca's' area).

constitute satisfactory activities for pupils to do on their own, music sessions offer a unique and secure framework through which many of the skills and disciplines of social interaction can be experienced and developed. This is especially true for young people with complex needs, for whom the intricacies of verbal language and the subtle visual cueing that typically inform face-to-face communication may prove particularly challenging to discern and comprehend.

As we have seen, interaction, viewed from a musical perspective, was felt by the Sounds of Intent research team to be key to understanding and modelling musical development. In this section, musical interaction is considered in a wider context as an important strand in social growth and maturation.

Teachers, therapists, and carers may provide structured opportunities for children and young people to listen to the sounds that others are making, in a variety of contexts, and to respond appropriately to them (I.1 and I.2). For those in the very early stages of development, it may well be most appropriate for such activities to be undertaken on a one-to-one basis, with teacher and pupil, therapist and client, or parent and child working in close proximity (I.1.C), sound featuring as one element in a broader pattern of multisensory contact. Here, there is likely to be an intimate connection between the shared activity and the relationship between client and carer; the one enabling the other to occur, and permitting it to evolve (see Fig. 6.10).

In these circumstances, young people may come to initiate sound-making themselves (I.2.B), and by offering an appropriate response, co-workers can reinforce children's awareness that what they do can have an effect—contributing, perhaps, to their developing cognisance of a sentient 'other' out there. Alternating patterns of sounds and responses may be built up:

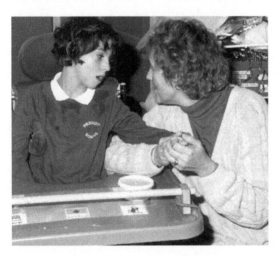

Fig. 6.10 Intense one-to-one interaction

'proto-conversations', in which the teacher, carer, or therapist reacts sensitively to the child's efforts, promoting interactive play (Rødbroe 1997: 13), as at levels I.3 and I.4.

As the Sounds of Intent framework indicates, at first, in responding to what they hear, children may produce sounds that bear no immediate resemblance to the ones with which they are presented (I.2). Teachers, therapists, and carers may nevertheless copy what the young people do, encouraging them to do the same, both vocally and using sound-makers, through providing a model of imitation (I.1.D). Initially, two adults may interact in this way themselves, with the child in attendance. Subsequently, teachers and others may act on behalf of pupils, gradually fading support as the young people themselves become active participants. Songs such as *Can you copy me?* (Ex. 6.7) can be used to set the scene for activities of this type.

Some children may be able to participate in more formal sequences of interaction, whose scripts are taken from a standard repertoire. For example, there are many nursery songs and games that set up the expectation of a particular event (such as being tickled) occurring at a given juncture, and others in which the child is required to supply particular input or undertake certain actions

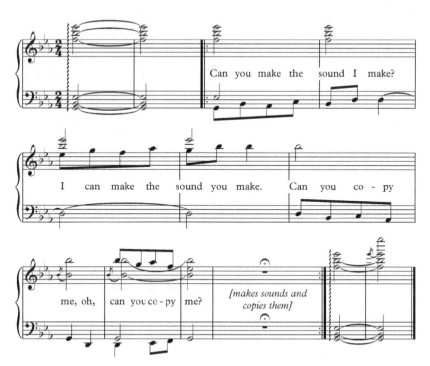

Ex. 6.7 *Can you copy me?*

from a familiar selection (for instance, 'actions' in *If you're happy and you know it*; and 'animal sounds' in *Old MacDonald had a farm*) (R.5.A). Often, the challenge for co-workers is in providing material for young people that is appropriate to their age, culture, and social background. It may be possible to make up or adapt material such as the song shown in Ex. 6.8.

Whatever its context and content, music is particularly effective in supporting the development of early social interaction. As we observed in Chapter 4, it is, in every sense, highly repetitive, with pieces generally being made up of sequences of identical or similar events, which divide time into manageable chunks, and constitute predictable patterns. Hence, it provides a secure framework for the risky business of reaching out into the far from predictable world

Ex. 6.8 *Clap your hands*

of other people, setting parameters and establishing the boundaries within which socialization can occur, and building confidence through a medium which the great majority of young children find enjoyable and motivating.

Although, as we observed above, in the early stages of development, listening to sounds can induce attendant vocalization (I.2.A), producing coherent streams of sound simultaneously is a more advanced stage (I.5), which involves listening and producing a coordinated response at the same time—or at least, switching attention rapidly between the two. However, the context of group performance can be valuable in enabling pupils whose music-making powers are limited to find a satisfactory means of musical expression. For example, producing simple, repetitive patterns on percussion may have little aesthetic appeal in the long run unless they are part of a larger experience, and their combined effect can indeed be musically pleasing and motivating (as in gamelan playing—see pp. 127 and 128).

Particular forms of social interaction can be structured through especially designed or adapted songs. These set occasions include 'good morning' routines, using material such as Fig. 6.11. On occasions such as this, it is suggested that the group sits in a circle, singing to each member in turn. Some participants may be able to choose whom they wish to sing to next. Positions in the circle may vary from one occasion to another, or a more consistent approach may be adopted if this is felt to be particularly important. If people are away, their absence may be noted. Support workers can, of course, be included in the greeting too.

In undertaking activities of this type, it is important to remember that receptive language develops before the capacity to express thoughts and feelings, and that where support workers are singing on behalf of individuals, it will make more sense of names and pronouns, and therefore assist understanding, if only one person performs, effectively functioning as the voice of the youngster concerned (cf. I.1.D). At other times, everyone can join in.

Each person can use a personal sound-maker (see p. 133), enhancing his or her presence in sensory terms, and enabling members of the group who are having difficulty processing visual information to establish the identity of participants who have no expressive language. Examples of sound-makers include: a little bell, a squeaker, a wooden rattle, a tiny tambourine, a miniature drum, a shaker, a whistle, a small net of pebbles, porcelain windchimes, and a scraper. It may be advisable not to use conventional instruments in order to avoid potential confusion in other music sessions.

Once 'set-piece' songs are familiar, it will be possible to use them in a wide range of social situations, with or without accompaniment: music can inform and enrich living and learning throughout the day.

Fig. 6.11 *Hello!*

Finally, it is worth remembering that musical activities give young people who have complex needs the opportunity for experiencing a wide range of social situations. Music-making takes place indoors and outdoors, in concert halls and sitting rooms, with small groups of friends and among thousands of strangers. Each occasion has its own atmosphere and code of conduct to which participants are expected to adhere. Hence the kinds of extrovert behaviour that are the norm at a rock concert staged in a large arena, for example, are not likely to find favour among devotees of classical chamber music, listening in the relative intimacy of a small concert hall. The extent to which pupils and students can gain awareness of these issues will vary from one individual to another: the key thing is for teachers and carers to find ways of offering them fulfilling musical experiences—experiences which typically occur in the company of other people.

Conclusion

This chapter has explored a wide range of possibilities for educating children and young people with complex needs *through* music, conceptualized in relation to four main areas of activity: movement, learning, communication, and socialization. Where possible, potential development in each of these domains has been linked to the Sounds of Intent framework, and although this work is at a preliminary stage, the early signs are that this process of cross-mapping reflects a broader conceptual coherence that augurs well for the possible future extension of the work reported in Chapter 5 into other curricular areas.

Chapter 7

About music

Introduction

Thinking *about* music and musical experiences, and discussing them, are commonplace activities in western society. Just consider, for example, in the field of popular music alone, the abundance of literature, the many hours of airtime on radio and television, and—we may surmise—the millions of conversations that each week are devoted to expressing views on the latest hits and the groups that perform them. Such communication is generally undertaken in everyday, non-technical language, that accords with our intuitive understanding and appreciation of music.

Thinking and communicating about music: pupils with PMLD and SLD

The capacity of children and young people with complex needs to reflect on music and communicate about it will depend on the extent of their listening experience, their level of perceptual and cognitive development, their capacity to respond, and, if their views are to be shared with others, their ability to make these known. For some, with PMLD, their response to music may remain at a basic level: an immediate reaction that empathetic carers may discern as a signal of pleasure or displeasure to the stimulus of the moment, for example. For others, with SLD, the expression of *preference*, with its demands on both memory and anticipation, may evolve through structured opportunities for musical reflection.

While conventional music notation is likely to have little relevance for many such pupils and students, the symbolic representation of sound does offer a wide range of potential benefits. The use of objects of reference, for example, may assist in communicating *about* music. There may be other spin-offs too, such as establishing the principle that one thing can represent another, within a context that learners find motivating.

A starting point is to identify music sessions with an appropriate object of reference, such as a cluster of bells (see p. 132). The necessary symbolic link could be made by playing the bells at the beginning of each session, and

A pupil is presented with a cluster of bells prior to a music session, which comprises a number of activities, the first involving bells

Fig. 7.1 Using a cluster of bells to signal that it is time for music

thereafter using them to anticipate sessions (p. 135) (see Fig. 7.1). Here, the principle at work is that one feature of the activity can come to represent the whole thing (cf. Ockelford 1994: 6).

Greater degrees of symbolism could be achieved in stages by reducing the cluster of bells in size, by mounting a single bell on card, by preventing this from making a sound (so only a visual and tactile representation remains), and, through further reduction or simplification, by producing increasingly abstract versions of the bell (see Fig. 7.2). Which is used will depend upon a number of factors, including a child's perceptual abilities and level of symbolic understanding, which may well be enhanced through exposure to a progressive system of augmentative communication such as that described.

Note that these symbols, which were used in a school for the visually impaired by pupils who also had severe learning difficulties, are labelled in relevant media (here, large print and Braille). Hence their meaning was clear to everyone working within a single teaching and learning environment, and the

Fig. 7.2 Symbolizing 'music' through increasingly abstract versions of a cluster of bells

system was fully inclusive (cf. Ockelford 1994: 24). Children and young people with sufficient visual abilities may use two-dimensional representations in much the same way. Again, progression may be possible, whereby pupils and students are encouraged to move from photographs to line drawings and then on to more schematic representations where appropriate.

From a single link, whether auditory, tactile, or visual in nature—or a combination of the three—the principle of representing music symbolically may be extended in a number of ways. For example, different *types* of musical activity, such as playing the drums, exploring the keyboards, listening to a CD or to music on an iPod may be symbolized in different ways. Like all objects of reference, these may function reactively as far as pupils are concerned (for instance, to let them know what is about to happen) or proactively (for example, to enable them to choose what they are going to do next).

A further refinement is for different pieces of music to be allocated symbols of their own. One approach is to use a characteristic sound—a distinct timbre—consistently when performing a piece, so that the two become associated in the child's mind. In the case of songs, such connections may be reinforced through semantic links, by choosing sound-makers that are relevant to ideas introduced in the text. Hence, *Chattanooga Choo Choo* may be represented by a train whistle, for example; *Coconut Woman* through coconut halves; and *Daisy, Daisy* by a bicycle bell.

The number of pieces that can be portrayed in this way, however, is inevitably limited by the availability of suitable timbres, and further constraints may be incurred by the need for certain characteristic sounds, which would otherwise have been appropriate, to act in a symbolic capacity in other contexts. Hence, if a significant repertoire of pieces is to be represented symbolically, a more abstract system is essential, which does not rely on auditory links. That is, pupils and students need to move from a position of representing music through objects of reference that have, or once had, an auditory association, to using symbols that are purely visual or tactile (or both), with no sounding properties.

A tactile system of this type was devised for Claire, who was blind, aphasic,[1] and dyspraxic.[2] Neither signing nor Braille were options for augmentative communication. However, Claire showed a clear understanding of what was said to her, remembering and anticipating activities, and effortlessly following

---

[1] The inability to use language; in Claire's case, she could not speak—see, for example, <http://www.aphasianow.org>.

[2] An impairment of the organization of movement—see, for instance, <http://www.dyspraxiafoundation.org.uk>.

complex series of instructions (Ockelford 1994: 28 ff.). Claire had an abiding interest in music, and she needed a way of indicating her choice of songs in lessons. So a series of tactile markers was developed, based on Claire's ability to discriminate and manipulate shapes and textures as small as one centimetre square, dimensions that were taken as a working minimum. The markers were attached to pages of her music book, enabling her to select pieces, and indicate her preferences to others. The same symbols were subsequently used to label her collection of tapes.

It soon became apparent that the symbols, which were wholly abstract, could be used in other contexts too, and so they took on the function of numbers. Eventually, they formed the basis of a tactile overlay on a talking machine that, for the first time, gave Claire a means of expressive communication that could be generally understood (see Fig. 7.3 (a) and (b)).

While Claire's combination of abilities and needs was exceptional, if not unique, the strategies adopted to enable her to communicate and control her environment in the context of music have a more general applicability. For example, it may be possible for a pupil who wishes to select a favourite CD from a collection to do so if the case is identified with a distinct colour, shape, texture, or a combination of these. Once the principle is established, two cases or more may be distinguished with contrasting labels to widen the choice available.

Colours,[3] shapes, textures, and other symbols may also be used to represent

(a)   (b)

Fig. 7.3 (a) Claire's music book and tapes with tactile markers; (b) Claire using her talking machine, with an overlay using the tactile markers

---

[3] An idea that has been used as part of mainstream approaches to music tuition—see, for example, <http://www.colourstrings.co.uk>.

different *aspects* of sound. One approach is to label the controls on CD players, keyboards, and other equipment with characteristic materials (having bright colours, contrasting textures, or cut into distinct shapes). By using these consistently, whereby the function of volume controls, for example (and therefore the notion of 'quiet' and 'loud') can be reinforced symbolically, pupils' independence in using music equipment may be facilitated. Key-guards, which leave only relevant controls exposed, may facilitate this process further.

The next logical step is to *notate* music, a concept that can be introduced in a number of ways. For example, as part of percussion activities involving counting, cards can be produced (by staff and pupils) that indicate the number of beats to be played on a drum by cutting out circles from an old drum head and fixing them onto card. Where materials such as these are used through touch, it is important to bear in mind the special challenges that are posed. For example, it may not be possible to read and play at the same time, in which case the directions for performance will have to be committed to memory before trying them out. In perceptual terms too, tactile exploration is more challenging than scanning items visually: through touch, information has to be gathered piecemeal and then reconstructed in the child's mind. It may be difficult to distinguish which features are significant and which are incidental, and to know when all relevant information has been obtained. In any case, it is good practice to keep all learning materials as simple as possible, with only salient information recorded on them. It should be stressed that the aim of introducing children and young people to representations such as these may well have less to do with their immediate worth in musical terms than with their value as an introduction to symbolic representation in visual or tactile form, or both.

Having started with a single timbre, this may be extended to two or more— by using distinctive colours or textures on the bongos; see, for example, Fig. 7.4.

It is possible to extend this idea to create multisensory 'scores'. Examples were made during a three-day multimedia project undertaken at Dorton House School, Kent by RNIB in collaboration with the London Sinfonietta, Nigel Osborne, and students of Edinburgh University, in the autumn of 1993. During the project, a number of possibilities were tried, including 'seashore' pieces, which were inspired by, and incorporated, the sounds that could be made from sand, pebbles, shells, seaweed, driftwood, and other items. The same materials were subsequently used in a representative way, by being pressed onto a series of clay tiles, which served both as score and sculpture. In a more abstract vein, pieces were contrived using 'technojunk' (small discarded items of technology), whose sound-making qualities were enhanced

Fig. 7.4 A simple musical score for the bongos using two different textures

electronically and combined with instrumental sounds to create a composition concerned with space travel and the planets, which were represented by three-dimensional 'technojunk' scores (see Ockelford 1996*b*).

Some pupils and students may find it beneficial to use overlays on 'concept keyboards'[4] linked to suitably configured software. Here it is possible to gain an immediate response from visual or tactile symbols (or both). Hence they potentially represent an intermediate stage between score and sound-maker.

In some cases, it may be possible to extend the principle of visual and tactile representation to the domain of pitch by using colours and textures. For example, by attaching small squares of coloured paper or material to the notes on a keyboard—perhaps two or three to start with—scores of simple tunes and ostinati can be constructed using further examples of the same colours or textures attached to card (see Fig. 7.5).

For some pupils who are able to distinguish a few letters (or who are close to being able to do so), 'letter' notation may be a possibility (see Ockelford 1996*b*: 46). Again, relevant notes on the keyboard may be labelled to make them easier to identify. In the system illustrated in Fig. 7.6, durations beyond a single beat are indicated by horizontal lines of appropriate length.

Comparable scores in tactile form can be made using Moon, a method of reading based on the raised shapes of letters in print, or Braille, which uses different combinations of up to six dots, through an alphabetic system termed 'Points of Contact' (see Ockelford 1996*c*) (Fig. 7.7).

Theoretically, Moon has the potential for accommodating more advanced music-notational needs too (see Jackson 1987; Aldridge 1989). However, only

---

4 A keyboard with a continuous surface that can be set up to function as differing numbers of touch sensitive cells. Overlays can be placed on the surface to facilitate access to computers for people with disabilities.

Fig. 7.5 A tactile score for the keyboard

Braille offers a fully comprehensive means of representing music in tactile form, using the method developed by Louis Braille himself (see Ockelford 1996*b*: 8ff).[5] Despite the intellectual complexities of this code, it is of value to some musical 'savants' (see Chapter 10, p. 215).

For those who can understand some elements of music theory, but are unable to read through sight or by touch, audio recording offers an alternative to visual and tactile methods of notation. For example, pieces may be recorded with accompanying explanation or instructions, including suggested fingering, breathing, or bowing, and giving an account of note-names, durations, and dynamics. Simplication and modification of the music may well be required to avoid overloading pupils with too much data at once. Even so, two or more versions of a piece may have to be recorded, each presenting different categories of information. Alternatively, the music need not be performed at all, being replaced entirely with a verbal account—a so-called 'talking score' (see Ockelford 1996*b*: 37). For example, the opening of *Au clair de la lune* (pictured above) may be presented in spoken form thus:

C C C D E hold D hold C E D D C hold hold hold

This is music notation at its simplest. More precise descriptions are possible too, using whatever terminology and music-theoretical concepts are

C C C D   E – D –
C E D D   C – – –

Fig. 7.6 'Letter' notation

---

[5] The Braille music system aims to capture whatever is written in print and encodes this using series of cells, each potentially bearing six dots.

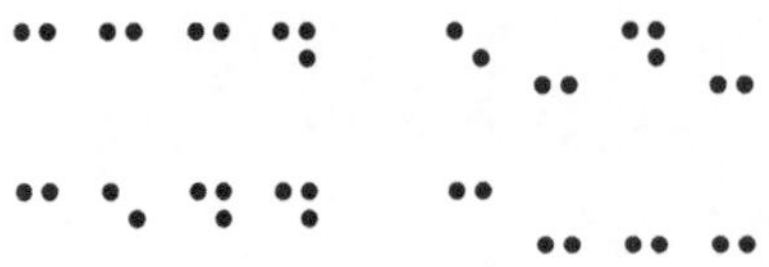

Fig. 7.7 Letter notation in Braille

appropriate. Hence a series of chord-names may be sufficient for a jazz pianist to work on, whereas a classical violinist may need to know details of nuances, phrase-marks, and indications of bowing, as well as the pitches and durations to which they refer. For some, talking scores offer a transition to notation in print, Braille or Moon; for others, they may remain the most effective way of representing music in symbolic form.

Relating 'thinking and communicating about music' to the Sounds of Intent framework

The Sounds of Intent framework is solely concerned with pupils' direct engagement with music—reactively, proactively, and interactively—and, as we shall see in Chapter 10, even the highest levels of attainment are perfectly conceivable in each of these domains in the absence of the ability to *conceptualize* what is going on, to *represent* it, and to *communicate about* it. For those steeped in traditional approaches to music education, in which concepts often take the lead over percepts (consider, for example, that in instrumental lessons the capacity to read music—at least in a mechanical sense—typically takes precedence over the ability to play by ear), this may seem counter-intuitive. Yet one only has to return to the example of Harry, the retired account, able to appreciate the first movement of Mozart's Piano Sonata, K333 (p. 66), to realize that an informal, instinctive approach to musical engagement may be more the norm in the population as a whole.

As far as those with SLD or PMLD are concerned, the principle is simple: musical concepts, symbols, and the capacity to communicate about them are likely to lag behind the immediate, perceptual, and cognitive experiences set out in the Sounds of Intent framework. It is conceivable that, in some cases, they may be at the same level, but it is highly unlikely that they will ever be more advanced. Teachers, in particular, need to bear this in mind. As I discovered (p. 257), by far the most powerful way to teach music to those with learning difficulties is through using music, rather than talking about it! Using language just erects an unnecessary barrier: for many pupils music offers a far more immediate form of communication in sound.

Nonetheless, it is possible, and potentially valuable (in analysing pupils' wider profiles) to consider how the stages in the conceptual understanding

Table 7.1 Relating the developing capacity to represent music symbolically to levels in the Sounds of Intent framework

Level	Symbolic representation of music
1	None
2	None—there may be intentional communication about sound (including musical sounds)
3	Symbolic representation of 'music'
4	Symbolic representation of different pieces of music
5	Symbolic representation of different aspects of music; simple notation (involving 'decoding' to reproduce the sounds that are notated)
6	Complex notation (involving interpretation to produce expressive performance)

and representation of music identified in this chapter potentially work alongside purely *musical* development, as set out in the Sounds of Intent framework (see Table 7.1).

Conclusion

This concludes our consideration of how the special musical *needs* of children and young people with complex needs may be met through specialist interventions. We now move on to the related topic of how to address special musical *abilities* that can occur in the context of learning difficulties. As we shall see, there is a good deal of overlap between the two, since needs and abilities are ultimately different sides of the same coin.

PART IV

IDENTIFYING AND FOSTERING SPECIAL MUSICAL ABILITIES

Chapter 8

Focus on Music

Introduction

The PROMISE research reported in Chapter 1 found that, in the view of their teachers, 10 per cent of pupils with severe, or profound and multiple learning difficulties had a particular interest in music or a noticeable flair for performing, and it is to this group of children and young people that the last three chapters of this book are devoted. The examples of performance that were given in PROMISE ranged from 'whistling' and 'vocalizing' to 'sings songs after one hearing', and from 'can tap out the rhythm of a song' to 'quick to pick out tunes' and 'loves to compose at the keyboard'. These tantalizing glimpses into what appeared to be a rich vein of musicality in some young people with significant cognitive and other impairments called for further research, and an opportunity presented itself in 2003 following a conference organized by 'FOCUS Families'[1]—a support network of parents whose children have septo-optic dysplasia/optic nerve hypoplasia.

Septo-optic dysplasia ('SOD') is a rare condition that occurs in approximately one in 16,000 children. It is defined as a combination of optic nerve hypoplasia (absent or small optic nerves), pituitary abnormalities, and the absence or malformation of the septum pellucidum[2] or corpus callosum or both, without which communication between areas of the mid-brain, such as the transfer of sensory information, is hampered. Among the likely effects of SOD are visual impairment, learning difficulties, hormonal problems, challenging behaviour, and obesity—'complex needs'. The type and range of symptoms can vary from mild to very severe (Mehta and Dattani 2004).

At the 2003 FOCUS Families conference, a number of parents reported that their children had what seemed to them to be unusually high levels of musical interest or ability. This raised a number of questions. First, were the parents' anecdotal accounts a consequence of expectations arising from a reaction to

---

[1] FOCUS ('For Our Children's Unique Sight') Families provides information, education, and support and can be contacted at <http://www.focusfamilies.org>.

[2] The 'septum pellucidum' is the membrane that normally lies between the two halves of the brain; the 'corpus callosum' is the large bundle of nerve fibres that usually connects them.

their children's visual impairment, which would not stand up to more formal scrutiny—or was there evidence that the children did indeed have a tendency to tread a music-developmental path that was markedly different from that taken by most of their non-disabled peers? Second, if exceptional musical interests or abilities *were* found among the population of those with SOD, were these characteristics related to particular physiological or neurological aspects of their medical condition, or as a consequence of the functional differences that learning difficulties and visual impairment may have induced irrespective of their aetiologies, or both? (That is, was *the SOD syndrome itself* a significant factor, or certain of its effects that were not syndrome-specific, or both these things working together?) And third, if unusual musicality were to be found among those with SOD, what were the implications for parents, teachers, therapists, and others? With little information to go on, none of these issues could be addressed satisfactorily at the time, and it was agreed that an exploratory study—'Focus on Music'—should be undertaken in order to obtain an initial understanding upon which further work could, if necessary, be built.

A research team was set up, comprising Linda Pring,[3] Graham Welch, Darold Treffert[4] and me. It was agreed that the best way of proceeding would be through informal visits to meet some of the children and their families[5] and a questionnaire. This would be distributed to parents in the UK and the US, largely through the FOCUS Families network. Through a mixed series of closed and open questions, the questionnaire would ask parents what they observed in their children in day-to-day situations as well as relaying the findings and accounts of other relevant parties, including doctors, psychologists, music teachers, and therapists. It was hoped that this approach would enable the research team to gather data on a number of children from a range of backgrounds in a relatively short timescale.[6]

Of course, gathering information in this way also had potential disadvantages. For example, the respondents were self-selecting and, despite clear

---

[3] Professor of Psychology at Goldsmith's College, University of London.

[4] Clinical Professor in the Department of Psychiatry, University of Wisconsin Medical School.

[5] Seven children were visited at home or school by Adam Ockelford or Sally Zimmermann, the RNIB Music Advisor, or both.

[6] The parents of a comparison group, volunteers whose children lived in south London and Wales and who were matched as far as possible for age and gender, but with no known disabilities or serious health issues, also completed the questionnaire for the purposes of comparison.

requests to the contrary, it was possible that an undue proportion of parents whose children were particularly musical or interested in music would participate in the study. Moreover, questions would not necessarily be tackled consistently. However, while it would clearly be important to acknowledge these factors in reporting the results of the survey, it was felt that the findings would still be relevant to those responsible for the upbringing and music education of children with SOD—and others working with children with complex needs.

The questionnaire, comprising over 100 items, was designed to elicit a mixture of quantitative and qualitative information, concerned with biographical details, special interests and talents (musical and otherwise), communication, behaviours, sociability, personality, memory, intelligence, and any other issues that parents wished to raise. It was evident from the returned questionnaires that these had typically been completed as comprehensively as was practicable—in the great majority of cases (81 per cent) by the mothers of the children concerned—and the often detailed observations that were presented evinced a significant degree of reflection and care. The publication of results to date (Ockelford, Welch, and Pring 2005; Pring and Ockelford 2005; Ockelford, Pring, Welch, and Treffert 2006) has focused only on musical interests and abilities, since no significant correlations have been found between these and the other areas of development and personality that were interrogated. This is a topic that future research could profitably explore.

In the meantime, the initial 'Focus on Music' study has been extended to embrace a new cohort of children and young people—those with 'retinopathy of prematurity' ('ROP')[7]—many of whom have coexisting developmental disabilities including cerebral palsy,[8] learning difficulties, deafness, and epilepsy[9] (Mervis, Yeargin-Allsopp, Winter, and Boyle 2000; Rahi and Cable 2003). Preliminary findings will be reported here to supplement, complement, and, occasionally, to challenge those from the SOD research.[10]

---

[7] An eye disease that can affect premature babies—see, for example, Kumar and Singha (1997).

[8] Cerebral palsy ('CP') is a broad term encompassing many different disorders of movement and posture, which result from damage to an area or areas of the brain that control the amount of tension or resistance to movement in a muscle or muscles. See, for example, <http://about-cerebral-palsy.org>.

[9] Epilepsy is a neurological condition that causes 'seizures'—sudden surges of electrical activity in the brain that usually affect how a person feels or acts for a short time—see, for example, <http://www.epilepsy.com>.

[10] By kind permission of the lead researcher, Christina Matawa, then Head of Music at Dorton House School—see <http://www.rlsb.org.uk/school>.

The research participants

In the SOD study, 32 responses were received concerning children and young people who had the syndrome,[11] of whom 16 (50 per cent) could be categorized as 'educationally blind' (that is, who learnt primarily through non-visual means) and 16 (50 per cent) partially sighted. The 32 children in the comparison group were, of course, all fully sighted. Within the preliminary ROP cohort ($N = 35$), 29 subjects (83 per cent) were reported as being educationally blind and six (17 per cent) partially sighted.

Of the research participants with SOD, 18 (56 per cent) were female and 14 (44 per cent) were male—a reasonable reflection of the equal prevalence of the syndrome in boys and girls. In terms of age, there were two children or more from every year between 0 and 8, as well as individuals who were 12, 17, 22, 23, and 27 at the time of completion of the questionnaire, giving a mean age of 6.88 years and a standard deviation of 6.73. The comparison group was matched as closely as was practicable in terms of gender and age, having 17 girls and 15 boys in the range 1.4 years to 12.4, with a mean of 7.76 years and a standard deviation of 2.96. The preliminary ROP sample ranged from 3.0 to 22.0 years with a mean of 12.8 and a standard deviation of 5.82, within which there were 20 males (57 per cent) and 15 females (43 per cent).[12]

Hence the age ranges of the SOD and ROP cohorts, extending into early adulthood, were considerably greater than those of the comparison group, and the subjects with ROP were, on average, five to six years older. Despite these differences, it is reasonable to draw certain straightforward comparisons between the samples: where parents were asked to reflect on what their children did at a particular age, for example, or where they were asked to make judgements that took into account how old their child was. In relation to other issues, however, where age *is* thought to be significant, it is considered as a distinct element in the analyses that follow.

With regard to other disabilities, 11 (34 per cent) of the SOD subjects were reported to have either 'developmental delay' (in six cases or 19 per cent), 'autism' (three cases or 9 per cent) or 'learning difficulties' (two cases or 6 per cent). Further research would be required to clarify the extent to which

---

[11] An additional four responses were received concerning children with optic nerve hypoplasia ('ONH') alone, one pertaining to a child with ONH as part of a different syndrome, and three others relating to young people with other eye conditions or syndromes.

[12] The incidence of ROP is reported to be slightly greater in males than females (Bashour and Menassa 2006).

these labels represent discrete categories. For example, it may be that 'developmental delay' and 'learning difficulties' were used to describe the same type of disability, while the relationship and interaction between autism and blindness can be highly complex (Pring 2005). In 19 cases (59 per cent), no additional disabilities were mentioned or could be inferred from other responses, and in two cases (6 per cent), where children were at or below the age of one year, the researchers judged that it was too early to say whether the infant would be developmentally delayed (for example) or not. Within the group, neither level of vision nor gender were significant factors in the existence of additional disabilities.

As far as the ROP group was concerned, a wide range of additional needs was reported in the preliminary cohort, including three young people with hydrocephalus,[13] two with hemiplegia,[14] one with cerebral palsy, one with mobility problems, one with epilepsy, two with hearing loss, two with Autistic Spectrum Disorder ('ASD')[15] and one with specific learning difficulties.[16] Surprisingly, given the proportion of children with ROP who have cognitive impairment (see above), only one research participant was said to have a disability of this nature ('developmental delay'), although from the responses to questions concerning communication, one can surmise that at least three others had learning difficulties too. This skewed profile in the preliminary sample of children with ROP may be attributed to the manner in which information about the study was disseminated—largely through professionals who on the whole were supporting pupils in the mainstream—whereas the majority of those with SLD or PMLD are known to be educated in special schools (see p. 3 above).

---

[13] The abnormal build-up of cerebrospinal fluid in the ventricles of the brain—see, for example, <http://www.hydrocephalus.org>.

[14] Weakness and lack of control down one side of the body due to brain damage (usually on the opposite side to the motor impairment)—see, for instance, <http://www.hemihelp.org.uk>.

[15] Autism is a lifelong developmental disability that affects social interaction, communication, and imagination, which makes it difficult for someone to make sense of the world—see, for example, <http://www.nas.org.uk>.

[16] 'Specific learning difficulties' involve problems with one or more of the basic processes used in understanding or expressing oneself through spoken or written language, including dyslexia, dysgraphia, and dyspraxia—see, for example, <http://www.open.ac.uk/inclusiveteaching/pages/understanding-and-awareness/what-are-specific-learning-difficulties.php>.

However, evidence from an earlier study of mine (Ockelford 1988), which evaluated the musical interests and abilities of 50 children and young people[17] who were congenitally blind, indicated that even severe learning difficulties need be no barrier to musical development. Twenty-one children (42 per cent) in the 1988 sample had ROP. Twelve were male and nine female, with ages ranging from 7 to 21, mean 14.5 years, standard deviation 4.29. Ten (48 per cent) had 'absolute pitch' ('AP'), the ability to recognize or reproduce pitches in isolation from others, which, within western populations as a whole is extremely rare—estimated at only 1 in 10,000 (Takeuchi and Hulse 1993). Yet three of these ten had severe learning difficulties and one had moderate learning difficulties ('MLD') and autism. One of the children with SLD was a prodigiously talented pianist of jazz, popular and light music (and is the subject of Chapter 10); and the young person with MLD and ASD was a competent vocalist, as well as playing the keyboard, guitar, and harmonica. Among the seven pupils with AP who did not have learning difficulties, one was a highly competent pianist (who had performed Bach's *Italian Concerto* in public at the age of 10, for example) and one, as a teenager, played keyboards and drums semi-professionally in the family's reggae band. That is to say, in terms of developing musicality and levels of achievement, learning difficulties did not appear to be a constraint. Hence it seems reasonable to hypothesize that a number of findings from the preliminary ROP study are relevant to the wider population of children with that condition—at least to those with MLD or SLD. Where it appears that learning difficulties may be pertinent to a particular finding, this is addressed in the discussion that follows.

Parents' perceptions of their children's interest in everyday sounds

Parents were asked 'Is your child particularly interested in everyday sounds (for example, vacuum cleaners, car engines)?' and were asked to select one of three responses: 'not at all', 'a little', or 'a lot'. With respect to the SOD sample, replies of 'a lot' were given on behalf of 12 of the 16 blind research participants (75 per cent), and 5 of the 16 who were partially sighted (31 per cent). In the comparison sample, the figure was 4 of the 32 (13 per cent).

There were significant differences in the number and proportion of children showing a particular interest in everyday sounds, between the blind cohort in

---

[17] The 50 pupils were those who had attended Linden Lodge School in Wandsworth—see <http://www.lindenlodge.wandsworth.sch.uk>—most recently, who had been blind at birth or shortly afterwards, as at October 1988. Hence, in many respects this represented a random selection from the south-east of England, since virtually all blind children at that time attended special schools for the visually impaired.

the SOD sample and the partially sighted sub-group,[18] and between the blind subjects with SOD and the (fully sighted) comparison group.[19]

In the preliminary ROP sample, the number of partially sighted children (six) is too small to be used for statistical analysis. However, the characteristics of the 29 blind subjects can profitably be compared with those of the blind SOD cohort and the comparison group. Thirteen responses (45 per cent) indicated that, in the view of their parents, the blind research participants with ROP were interested in everyday sounds 'a lot'. This indicates a significantly higher distribution of interest than that found among the group of fully sighted children,[20] though markedly lower than in the blind SOD cohort (although the difference between them is not statistically significant).

One explanation for the difference between the blind populations may be the greater average age of the research participants with ROP since, as we shall see, their interest in *musical* (as opposed to *everyday* sounds) is distributed at a comparably high level, and certain elements of their auditory skills tend to be advanced even more frequently. So it could be that as young children, many of those with ROP were similarly attracted to environmental sounds, but that this interest diminished with increasing maturity—perhaps becoming focused more on those sounds that had particular functional, social, or emotional significance (including language and music). Hence this could be one area where widening the ROP sample to include more children with learning difficulties, who remain developmentally younger than their chronological age would otherwise indicate, would yield results that were more in line with those of the SOD cohort.

In any case, it seems clear that for young children with little or no sight, including those with complex needs, sound offers an important source of stimulation. As one mother commented, her blind 3-year-old daughter with SOD was interested in sounds of 'anything and everything since this is a huge part of her learning experience'. Sound-making may also have an exploratory element. For instance, one 18-month-old boy with SOD constantly 'takes everyday objects and toys and attempts to make sounds out of them by banging them together, shaking, throwing'. Some infants appear to be attracted to sounds for the sheer pleasure that they can bring. For example, the mother of a 5-year-old boy with SOD noted that he 'loves repetitive sounds—[he] will press toys which make noises over and over to hear the sounds'. Sometimes, such pleasure may develop atypically and become a fixation. For instance, one

---

[18] χ^2 (1, N = 32) = 6.15, p < 0.025.

[19] χ^2 (1, N = 48) = 18.75, p < 0.001.

[20] χ^2 (1, N = 58) = 7.91, p < 0.01.

mother told of her 6½-year-old son with ROP being 'obsessed with the noise of the microwave, so much so that he becomes upset if he can't make it into the kitchen before it is finished. More recently he has become interested in the tumble drier. He lies on the floor and listens to it and gets upset when it stops. He also loves the noises of the vacuum cleaner, washing machine and dish washer.' For some young people with complex needs, such behaviours may persist well into adolescence and beyond.[21]

Parents' perceptions of their children's interest in music

Parents were next asked whether their sons and daughters showed a particular interest in *music*. With regard to the SOD cohort, the response 'a lot' (as opposed to 'a little' or 'not at all') was given in relation to all blind subjects (16 out of 16, or 100 per cent) and 13 of the 16 who were partially sighted (81 per cent). In the comparison group, the figure was 12 out of 32 (38 per cent). Analysis shows that there are significant differences between the distribution of responses in the blind SOD cohort and the comparison group,[22] and between those of the partially sighted SOD subjects and the comparison group.[23] However, there was no significant difference between the distribution of reported levels of musical interest among the blind and partially sighted research participants with SOD, and within these groups, neither additional disabilities nor gender nor age was found to have a significant effect.

So, according to parents' observations, children and young people with SOD, including those with complex needs, are much more likely to have a particular interest in music than those who are not visually impaired. As one parent, speaking about her 7½-year-old daughter, put it: 'Her music is always with her. If there is not music playing, she is singing. She listens to music while in the car, while falling to sleep, and loves to play the piano and any other instrument. It is definitely her strength in life.' Another simply said that her daughter was 'obsessed with music'.

With regard to the blind ROP group, 26 of the 29 (88 per cent) were reported to be interested in music 'a lot'. This distribution is similar to that found among blind children with SOD, and significantly different from that of the comparison group.[24] Again, parents' comments were telling. One noted

---

[21] It is of interest to note, given the findings in relation to music reported below, that all these sounds are inherently 'musical': that is, with a distinct pitch that is constant or regularly changing, and tone colours that are rich in harmonics.

[22] $\chi^2 (1, N = 48) = 17.14, p < 0.001$.

[23] $\chi^2 (1, N = 48) = 8.18, p < 0.01$.

[24] $\chi^2 (1, N = 61) = 17.62, p < 0.001$.

that her son, aged 6½, could become 'mildly obsessed with sounds/music—manipulating the sounds or listening intently for minute auditory details. This is recreation for him.' The mother of a 10½-year-old girl wrote: 'I have often wondered about the link between [her] "savant" characteristics and her blindness. . . . The music she composes flows effortlessly from idea to expression at the piano. It's an absolute joy and is as natural for her as breathing.'

The *type* of music that children and young people with SOD and ROP prefer appears to vary just as much as with any other group with similar socio-cultural backgrounds, resulting, we may surmise, from a complex cocktail of exposure, predisposition, and an evolving sense of identity (Tarrant, Hargreaves, and North 2002). The parents of 17 of the children with SOD (53 per cent) and 22 with ROP (63 per cent) noted particular musical preferences.[25] Stylistically, these varied from 'classical' to pop, from nursery rhymes to 'pub songs', and from Bhangra to traditional Highland backpipe music. On a number of occasions, specific works were mentioned, ranging from *Yankee Doodle* to the *Blue Danube* waltz, and from *Goodbye Yellow Brick Road* (Elton John) to Brahms's Waltz, op. 39 no. 15. At other times, particular artists or groups were listed, including Paul Weller, Simon and Garfunkel, The Who, Queen, Bruce Springsteen, Savage Garden, Darren Hayes, Robbie Williams, Dido, Green Day, James Blunt, and Andrea Bocelli. One 7-year-old boy with SOD was reported to be wholly obsessed with the music of Rod Stewart. Children, particularly those in the early years or with learning difficulties, sometimes appeared to be attracted by a particular sound, such as the panpipes, women's voices, or the drums, or by a certain dynamic ('loud music') or tempo (pieces with a 'fast beat'). A few dislikes were noted too: classical music ('too slow'), modern music ('too loud and raucous'), and, in the case of one 3-year-old, 'songs where a particular note is held for a long time'.

Parents' perceptions of the importance of music to their children in different contexts

Parents were asked whether they thought that music was or had been important to their son or daughter in a range of suggested contexts in which music served as a source of stimulation or comfort, to promote communication, socialization, or understanding (for example, through 'counting' songs), or to mark out events in the daily routine (cf. Chapter 6). Respondents were offered three options: 'not at all', 'a little', or 'a lot'. The numbers of those with SOD

---

[25] Thirteen (41 per cent) in the case of the comparison group.

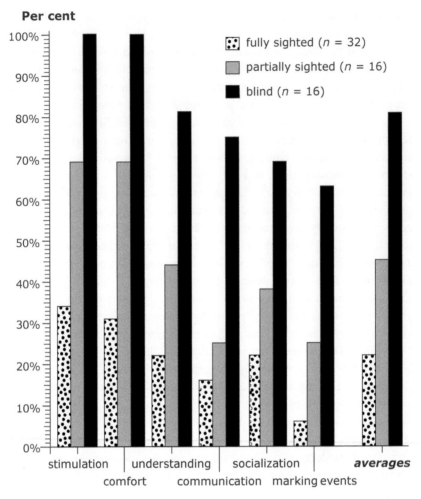

Per cent

Contexts in which music is thought to be important

Fig. 8.1 Parents' impressions of the importance of music in different contexts to children and young people who are blind, partially sighted, and fully sighted

(with the blind and partially sighted sub-groups considered separately) and in the comparison group who replied 'a lot' in each of the contexts are shown in Fig. 8.1.

Although the proportion of blind research participants with SOD whose parents provided responses of 'a lot' was consistently higher than the comparable proportion who were partially sighted, which was in turn higher than the comparable proportion of fully sighted children, the only differences in distribution that are statistically significant are those between the blind SOD cohort and the comparison group.[26] There is no consistent effect for gender or general level of development.

The frequencies with which the 29 parents of blind children[27] with ROP returned responses of 'a lot' were consistently lower than those whose children were blind with SOD, but invariably higher than those of the comparison group, yielding percentages as follows: stimulation, 90 per cent; comfort, 83 per cent; understanding, 45 per cent; communication, 59 per cent; socialization, 38 per cent; to mark out events, 17 per cent. As was the case with parents' perceptions of their children's interest in everyday sounds, it could be that this difference is attributable to the fact that none of the blind ROP subjects was in the early years, whereas around half the blind SOD subjects were.[28]

To summarize: the findings of the 'Focus on Music' surveys suggest that, in the opinion of parents, blind children and young people with SOD or ROP, including those with complex needs, are much more likely to find music important for stimulation, comfort, communication, socialization, under-standing, and to mark out daily events than their fully sighted peers. In sup-port of this view, parents made a number of vivid observations concerning the importance of music to their son or daughter. Two mothers reported having listened to particular pieces while they were pregnant which subsequently had a powerful effect on their children with SOD. A 3-month-old girl still 'reacts to her mother when she sings "Tiny Dancer" by Elton John which was played all the time she was in the womb. Her eyes get really big and she starts to try to look around.' A 1½-year-old boy cannot or will not go to sleep without the sound of the music box that was played to him *in utero*. The potentially relax-ing or comforting effect of music, particularly for younger children, was noted by other parents too. For example: 'She calms to soft gentle music' (a 1-year-old girl with SOD); 'Singing calms him down if he is upset' (a 2-year-old boy

---

[26] The levels of significance are as follows: stimulation, χ^2 $(1, N = 48) = 18.67$, $p < 0.001$; comfort, χ^2 $(1, N = 48) = 20.31$, $p < 0.001$; understanding, χ^2 $(1, N = 48) = 15.47$, $p < 0.001$; communication, χ^2 $(1, N = 48) = 16.44$, $p < 0.001$; socialization, χ^2 $(1, N = 48) = 10.00$, $p < 0.01$; to mark events, χ^2 $(1, N = 48) = 18.00$, $p < 0.001$. On average this equates to χ^2 $(1, N = 48) = 15.47$, $p < 0.001$.

[27] Again, there were too few in the sample who were partially sighted to be valid for statistical analysis.

[28] On three occasions, the differences in distribution between the blind ROP cohort and the comparison group reach statistical significance: stimulation, χ^2 $(1, N = 61) = 19.48$, $p < 0.001$; comfort, χ^2 $(1, N = 61) = 16.36$, $p < 0.001$; and communication, χ^2 $(1, N = 61) = 12.20$, $p < 0.001$. On average, across all six categories, the level of significance is χ^2 $(1, N = 61) = 7.18$, $p < 0.01$.

with SOD); 'At nursery he is calm in the music lessons' (a 3-year-old boy with ROP). As well as using familiar nursery rhymes to develop an understanding of body parts (such as 'Heads, Shoulders, Knees, and Toes', for example), some parents reported devising ingenious other ways of using music to promote wider learning and development. For instance, in the case of one 6-year-old boy with SOD who is apparently 'more fluent with repeating songs word for word than he is for carrying on a conversation . . . Songs have been made up to teach him his phone number and also how to spell his name'. It is worth noting that the connection between memory and music was mentioned by the parents of children with SOD and ROP on a number of occasions.

Parents' perceptions of the importance of music to their children at different times

Parents were also asked whether music was important for their son or daughter at particular times, or with particular activities, in particular places, or with particular people. Again, the comments made in relation to children and young people with SOD or ROP were of interest. The importance of music on journeys—especially car journeys—was noted several times. For a number of children, music was important at bedtime, and, for two, during mealtimes. Transitions (such as changing activity, moving from one place to another, or having to relate to a different person) appeared to be potentially difficult for some of the children, whose parents and teachers reported using music to help. For example, one mother described playing certain music to her son with SOD (who is rising 2) 'depending on where we are or where we're going', while the mother of a 3-year-old infant with SOD commented that 'For transitions, music helps her go from one activity to another'. The parent of a 3-year-old with SOD, who found the end of sessions at his nursery upsetting, relayed how 'his specialist teacher will sing their goodbye song. He now associates this song with home time and is then happy to leave nursery.' Similarly, consider this telling account of a girl with SOD, rising 8: 'She could sing songs before she could expressively communicate. Singing was used to motivate her or transition her from one activity to the next when she was younger or she would throw a tantrum. She would sing those songs aloud.' The importance of music appears to persist, at least into early adulthood. For example, the mother of one 17-year-old young man with ROP reported that, 'To him, music is part of his life and important all the time', while the mother of a 26-year-old woman with ROP said: 'I think [she] uses music for company. She prefers to listen to it on her own.'

The time devoted to musical activity

As well as asking parents directly about their children's interest in music and its perceived importance in their lives, the researchers enquired how much time the children and young people spent singing and playing on average each day. There were four possible categories of response: 0–1 hour, >1–2 hours, >2–3 hours and >3 hours. The results are shown in Fig. 8.2.

Although the differences between these distributions do not reach statistical significance, the data do suggest that the children and young people with SOD and ROP, including those with complex needs, spend more time actively engaged in music-making than those who are fully sighted—in the survey samples, around 80 per cent and 20 per cent more respectively.[29] Once more, one can hypothesize that the difference between these percentages is due to the average difference in age between the SOD and ROP cohorts—since children in the early years would be likely to have more time available for musical activity.

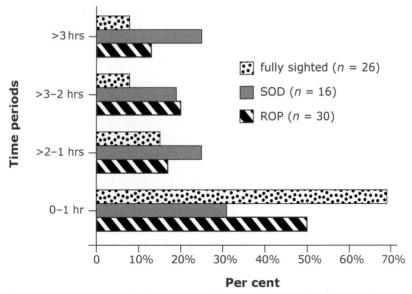

Fig. 8.2 Parents' reports of the amounts of time children and young people spend singing and playing

---

[29] Assuming mid-points in each of the time-range categories—that is, 0.5 hour, 1.5 hours, 2.5 hours, and, for the sake of argument, 3.5 hours.

Parents' perceptions of their children's musical abilities

Parents were asked whether, in their opinion, their child's musical ability was 'not as developed as you would expect for her/his age', 'about what you would expect for her/his age', 'more developed than you would expect for her/his age', or 'exceptionally highly developed'. The results are shown in Table 8.1.

In general terms, these data indicate that the subjects with SOD or ROP, including those with learning difficulties, were reckoned to have a wider spread of abilities than their non-disabled peers, whose musical development was in four out of five cases thought to be 'typical'. Among the children and young people with no sight, though, two thirds were believed to have a higher level of musical development than usual for his or her age—including around a third who were thought to be 'exceptional', around one in three was regarded as having 'typical' musical ability, and less than one in twenty was judged to be musically less advanced than one would expect (see Fig. 8.3).

Collapsing these four categories to two in relation to perceived musical ability ('typical or less developed than one would expect' and 'more developed than one would expect or exceptional') shows that these distributions are statistically distinct.[30] Using the two composite categories, the SOD and the ROP distributions are not significantly different, although both differ significantly

Table 8.1 Parents' perceptions of their child's level of musical development

Category		Less developed		Typical		More developed		Exceptional	
		No	%	No	%	No	%	No	%
SOD	Blind (n=14)	2	14	2	14	7	50	3	22
	Partially sighted (n=14)	3	21.5	6	43	5	35.5	0	0
	Total (n=28)	5	18	8	28.5	12	43	3	10.5
ROP	Blind (n=29)	0	0	10	34.5	8	27.5	11	38
	Partially sighted (n=6)	2	33	3	50	1	17	0	0
	Total (n=35)	2	5.5	13	37	9	26	11	31.5
Total	Blind (n=43)	2	4.5	12	28	15	35	14	32.5
	Partially sighted (n=20)	5	25	9	45	6	30	0	0
	SOD and ROP (n=63)	7	11	21	33.5	21	33.5	14	22
	Fully sighted (n=27)	0	0	22	81.5	4	15	1	3.5

---

[30] $\chi^2 (1, N = 90) = 10.50, p < 0.01$.

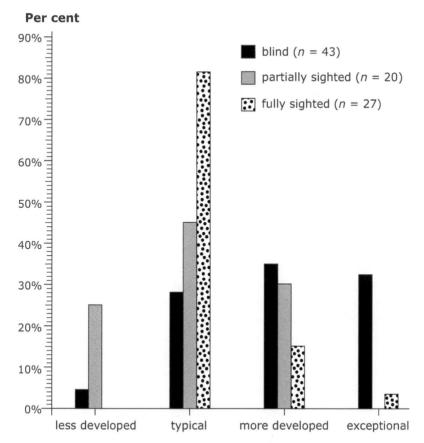

Per cent

blind (*n* = 43)

partially sighted (*n* = 20)

fully sighted (*n* = 27)

**Parents' perceptions of their children's
levels of musical development**

Fig. 8.3 Parents' perceptions of their child's level of musical development in relation to level of vision

from the comparison group.[31] It is of interest to note, too, that, as a single group, the distribution of responses pertaining to blind research participants (with either SOD or ROP) differs significantly from those relating to the partially sighted,[32] and the fully sighted.[33] The distribution of responses relating to the cohort of partially sighted subjects does not differ significantly from those relating to the fully sighted, however.

---

[31] In the case of the SOD cohort, χ^2 (1, $N = 55$) = 7.30, $p < 0.01$, and the ROP, χ^2 (1, $N = 62$) = 9.45, $p < 0.01$.

[32] χ^2 (1, $N = 63$) = 7.75, $p < 0.01$.

[33] χ^2 (1, $N = 70$) = 15.89, $p < 0.001$.

To what extent are these data, based on parental observation and opinion, likely to offer reliable indications of the children's differing levels of musical ability?[34] There are a number of issues here. First, because it would have been impracticable for most parents to use a refined set of criteria in the assessment of their child's 'musical ability', that would have required specialist knowledge, they were requested only to make a subjective 'snapshot' judgement of their child's level of musical development based on their awareness of children and young people in general. Second, it may be that some parents gave unduly favourable accounts of their child's musical abilities without realizing it. This is particularly the case with those whose children had SOD or ROP, since these parents chose to undertake a task which they knew concerned their child and music, and they may have been particularly keen to make the most of what they perceived to be a positive element in their children's lives.[35] Third, therefore, irrespective of potential bias *within* parents' accounts, the samples of children with SOD and ROP may in any case have been skewed in favour of those with particularly high levels of musical interest or ability.

A number of points are worth bearing in mind in relation to these potential difficulties, however. First, it was made clear in the literature requesting participation in the surveys that as many parents as possible should respond—whether or not they considered their child to have noteworthy musical abilities—in the interests of obtaining a representative sample. And, as the responses show, almost one in five of parents whose sons or daughters had SOD and one in ten of those who had ROP declared that they considered their children's musical abilities to be less developed for their age than they would typically have expected. (Interestingly, there were no such responses among the comparison group.) Second, a number of parents were evidently influenced by the views of the professionals working with their child. For example, one comment reads 'S's teachers have said that he has perfect pitch.[36] This was . . . a surprise [to us]', and another (which again relates to possessing AP), 'R [his teacher/therapist] says that he does. His mother and I would not know.' Third, it is worth noting that the responses given by the parents of those with SOD and ROP accord with the limited evidence that is already available.

---

[34] The parents' views and expectations of their children are, of course, important in their own right, and merit further study.

[35] Conversely, it may be that some of the parents with a disabled child gauged his or her level of musical development to be at a lower level than they would have expected, because they were being unduly cautious on account of the higher-than-usual expectations that knowledge of acclaimed 'musical savants' had induced (see Chapter 10).

[36] The term often used by musicians for 'absolute pitch'.

For example, my account (Ockelford 1988) of the musical abilities and interests of children and young people, blind since birth or shortly thereafter, with whom I worked as a specialist teacher, included two subjects with SOD and 21 with ROP (see p. 164 above). Additional (unpublished) contemporaneous notes on the musical development of partially sighted pupils of the same educational generation include four with SOD. Although relatively small in number, the SOD cohort of the 1980s displays a wide range of musicality that accords with the accounts of parents two decades later. Of the six pupils, the musical abilities of two, both of whom were partially sighted and with complex needs, were less developed than those of most children of their age, with difficulties, for instance, in pitching notes and copying simple rhythms. The musical development of a further two, of whom one was blind and one partially sighted, neither having additional special educational needs, were broadly typical. Finally, two who were blind (one of whom had learning difficulties) were judged to have exceptional musical abilities, including, in both cases, AP. One could play the keyboard fluently by ear, and the other could improvise songs vocally from an early age (one such performance appears as a case study in Ockelford, Pring, Welch, and Treffert 2006, and Ockelford 2006*b*, and is the subject of Chapter 9).

In relation to the blind pupils with ROP, their musical ability could reasonably be described as 'exceptionally highly developed' in six cases (four of which are outlined on p. 164 above); seven evinced a greater level of musical development than would typically have been expected for their age; four were 'about what you would expect'; and the musical achievements of two appeared to be lower than one would normally have anticipated[37]—a distribution that is very much in line with that produced from the 2006 parents' accounts (see Tables 8.4 and 8.5).

Absolute pitch

Nineteen of the 50 children and young people (38 per cent) in my 1988 cohort of blind pupils had AP, a figure that broadly ties in with Welch's (1988) finding, that 22 out of 34 blind attendees at special schools (65 per cent) had AP. While absolute pitch is not a prerequisite of musicianship of the highest order (less than 20 per cent of professional musicians possess it),[38] and while it is far from being the case that people with AP become musicians (at any level), it is nonetheless regarded as a necessary element in the development of exceptional

---

[37] In two cases, there is insufficient information to make a judgement.

[38] See, for example, Hamilton, Pascual-Leone, and Schlaug (2004).

musicality among people with learning difficulties (Miller 1989). Hence it appeared to be a particularly important issue to probe in the 'Focus on Music' surveys. However, this was one area where the researchers anticipated that it would be difficult to obtain reliable data from parents, even when they had access to comments from music teachers, since testing a child for AP—particularly if he or she has severe learning difficulties, and who therefore may be unable to give appropriate verbal responses—is a specialized task. In the version of the questionnaire that was sent to the parents of children with SOD and the comparison group, the relevant query was phrased as follows: 'Does your child have perfect (i.e. 'absolute') pitch?', to which the possible replies were 'yes', 'no', or 'don't know'. Parents were then asked 'If yes, please tell us what she/he can do (e.g., name notes, play notes back on a keyboard)', and they were given space to describe their child's achievements.

Unfortunately, these brief indications of what absolute pitch may enable a child to accomplish proved to give insufficient guidance for many parents, since five of the responses made on behalf of the fully sighted subjects suggested that they had AP on the basis of a single observation such as '[can] sing in tune'.[39] Five positive responses were also made on behalf of the research participants with SOD, of which only one was unambiguously appropriate. This pertained to a $6\frac{1}{2}$-year-old blind girl, who, it was reported, could name chords and their constituent notes, recognize 'any key music is being played in' and sing in any key when asked. Other answers may have been 'false positives' (particularly in the case of child who was not yet 2), and there were some responses that, judging by the associated comments, could represent 'false negatives'. For example, in relation to a girl rising 8, diagnosed with autism, who was deemed not to have AP, it was stated: 'She sings on key. Her music therapist thinks she may have perfect pitch but she is just learning what letters to associate with the keys on the piano'. Yet it is quite conceivable that a young child, or a person with severe learning difficulties, may have AP without knowing the letter-names of notes (see Ockelford, 2006b: 69).[40] Hence we cannot be sure just how many of the SOD cohort did actually have absolute pitch, though it would be noteworthy for even one subject to have AP within a group of 32 people, other things being equal.[41]

---

[39] The chances of five children in a random group of 32 from the UK having AP are, of course, vanishingly small, given the probability of any one having AP is 0.0001 (see p. 164 above).

[40] Contrast, for example, with Levitin and Zatorre (2003), who believe that AP acquisition derives from 'exposure to and reinforcement of the mapping between the sound of specific musical tones and their category labels'—yet clearly, this need not be the case.

[41] The probability among the general population is slightly less than 0.0032.

In the later, ROP, survey, a greater degree of explanation was given in relation to AP, in the hope of obtaining more reliable responses. Parents were told that 'children with perfect [absolute] pitch have an excellent memory for musical notes. This may show itself through the ability to sing a given note on request (e.g. A, G sharp, E flat, etc.) without reference to any other. It may also show itself through the ability to tell the name of a note just by listening to it.' Again, there were three possible replies to the query as to whether or not their child had absolute pitch: 'yes', 'no', or 'don't know'. The text then read: 'If "yes" or "don't know", please tell us what she/he can do (e.g., name notes, recognize the keys of pieces, play notes back on a keyboard, sing or play known songs starting on the same note without accompaniment, always sing in tune).'

As a consequence, most of the responses to the AP question in the ROP survey were less ambiguous. Examples of parents' comments include: 'Yes to all the examples above'; 'He can do all the above plus correct people who are singing in the wrong key and telling if a particular instrument is out of tune in full or in part'; 'All of the above. Also can sing notes separately from chords when asked and name the notes. Can improvise in the right key when accompanying.'

The complete quantitative results are set out in Table 8.2.

Clearly, the analysis of these data would benefit from a reduction in the number of 'don't know' responses by assigning them to a 'yes' or 'no' category. On the grounds that parents would be more likely to notice if their child *did* display abilities indicative of AP rather than fail to observe signs that they did *not*, the default assumption is that 'don't know' responses should be treated as negatives in the absence of other evidence. This leaves three cases where it seems reasonable to assume that the child *does* have AP although the parent was unsure: 'I know from the past K can tell what a note is if played as she recognized them [on] the keyboard or piano'; 'Plays notes back on a keyboard . . .'; and 'Z will copy single notes on the keyboard'. Taking these assumptions on board yields the data set shown in Table 8.3, in which 62 per

Table 8.2 Parents' perceptions of the possession of AP among children and young people who are partially sighted or blind

Status	AP?		
	Yes	No	Don't know
Partially sighted (n=6)	0	4	2
Blind (n=29)	15	2	12
Total (n=35)	15	6	14

Table 8.3 Presumed AP possession among those who are partially sighted or blind

Status	AP?	
	Yes	No
Partially sighted (n=6)	0	6
Blind (n=29)	18	11
Total (n=35)	18	17

cent of the blind subjects have AP: a rather higher proportion than I found in 1988, and one that is more in line with Welch (1988)—although the population in his study did not comprise children with ROP alone.

Combining my earlier data with these later figures gives a cohort of 50 blind children with ROP (28 male and 22 female), of whom 28 (56 per cent) had AP (17 male and 11 female).[42] Twelve of the 50 were known to have cognitive impairments, six of whom did not possess AP and six of whom did, including three with severe learning difficulties. In contrast, consolidating the SOD data for blind children from the Focus on Music study and Ockelford (1988) yields a total of 19 subjects, of whom four (21 per cent) can be said with some assurance to have had AP. One of these had learning difficulties (out of a total of seven). The ROP and SOD distributions differ significantly.[43]

This variation is relatively small, however, compared with the marked difference in the likelihood of possessing of AP as a blind person with SOD or the ROP and as a fully sighted member of the general population. There is currently no definitive answer as to why this should be so, and a detailed investigation is needed alongside the wider search that is currently going on for genetic and non-genetic components of AP. For example, in a study of over 600 musicians, Baharloo, Johnston, Service, Gitschier, and Freimer (1998) concluded that early musical tuition is an important component in the development of AP, since 40 per cent of musicians with AP had commenced music education by the age of 4. However, it was also the case that self-reported AP-possessors were four times more likely to report another AP-possessor in their

---

[42] Given the preponderance of males in the sample, these data imply a ratio of males to females with AP among those with ROP of 1.2 : 1. More research would be required to ascertain whether this gender asymmetry is characteristic of the ROP AP population as a whole—in part a corollary of the fact that there appear to be more male savants than female (see, for example, Judd 1988: 138). If so, this would represent a divergence from the equal male/female balance found among AP possessors in general (Petran 1932; Sergeant 1969; Baharloo, Johnston, Service, Gitschier, and Fremier 1998; Vraka 2008).

[43] χ^2 (1, $N = 69$) = 6.76, $p < 0.01$.

families than were non-AP-possessors, suggesting that a genetic predisposition may also be needed for the development of AP.

Given the high level of musical interest reported here among children with ROP and SOD (largely, in the latter case, as we shall see, in the absence of formal music education) it could be that a particular *focus* on music (and sound) in the early years, brought about through a lack of vision, is the crucial environmental factor in the development of AP. Early music education may, though need not, play a part: typically, children who are going to develop AP do so without the active intervention of parents, carers, therapists, or teachers. With regard to the potential genetic component, the reported incidence of AP among blind children would suggest that this must be very widespread in the population as a whole (even as high as 50 per cent, if we take an approximate average of the Welch and Ockelford figures cited above), since there are no other known genetic factors that would link this otherwise diverse group of people. Indeed, the data cited here offer support to the theory that AP begins as a universal ability, whose continuance is negated for the majority through interaction with an environment in which relative, rather than absolute, judgements are more important (Welch 2001: 10) and in which an interest in sound for sound's sake usually diminishes through the early years as, for most people, visual input quickly comes to dominate more and more.

Implications for our understanding of musical development in children with disabilities

What are the implications of the Focus on Music research evidence for our understanding of musical development in children with SOD or ROP, including those with complex needs? Are the findings of potential relevance to other disability groups?

It is possible to draw a number of inferences from the data available thus far. Of course, these can at best offer only an indication of *trends* among what we are regarding, on the basis of medical evidence, as discrete populations: further research would be required to determine with greater assurance just how similarities and differences that are identified here at a probabilistic level are likely to manifest themselves in individual cases. In the meantime, the following general observations can be made.

First, the fact that parents usually judged the levels of musical interest and ability of congenitally blind children to be higher than of those who were partially sighted—even though they all had one of two syndromes whose aetiologies are entirely different (SOD and ROP)—suggests that *level of vision* is an important factor in influencing musical development. Hence one could reasonably expect that any children born without sight, irrespective of the cause of their visual impairment, will be more likely to have higher levels of musical interest and ability than their partially or fully sighted peers. This is supported by Ockelford's (1988) study of 50 blind children cited above, in which the next largest cohort after those with ROP was a group ($n = 9$) with a condition known as 'Leber Congenital Amaurosis' ('LCA').[44] Three of the young people with LCA displayed exceptional musical ability, including two 'prodigious savants'—people with learning difficulties whose talents are outstanding by any standards (Treffert 1989/2000; see Chapter 10). These three, together with a further two individuals, had AP: a proportion of 56 per cent—the same as that found among the 50 subjects with ROP. So the LCA group provides a further example of *blindness from an early age* being a common factor in the pattern of exceptional musical development that has been observed.

Second, the fact that a number of subjects in the Focus on Music surveys who, in addition to being blind or partially sighted had learning difficulties, were reported to have a wide range of musical interests and abilities, suggests that elements, at least, of musical processing may be spared—or even supported—by certain forms of cognitive impairment. And again, if one supplements the recent survey data with information from my 1988 cohort of 50 congenitally blind children, which included accounts of pupils with ROP and LCA having musical abilities that were exceptional by any standards, despite their having severe learning difficulties, there is strong evidence that the uneven profiles of development characteristic of so-called musical 'savants' are common to a number of syndromes which have certain *functional* attributes in common. Darold Treffert, in his recent thinking on the subject,[45] puts it like this. In prodigiously talented people with learning difficulties, predisposing factors are a combination of idiosyncratic brain circuitry (incurred through damage to the left hemisphere with right brain recruitment and compensation) and some inherited or genetic elements. These form, in effect, a neurological base, upon and because of which savant talents may be built in some individuals through obsessive preoccupation, practice, and repetition that are often (though by no means always) encouraged by family, teachers, and others. In the case of blind infants, the preoccupation—noted by a number of parents in the Focus on Music surveys—is typically with sound. Given the prevalence of music in everyday environments (p. 57; Sloboda, O'Neill, Ivaldi 2001) and the potential opacity of language in the absence of visual cues and limited conceptual understanding, it is hardly surprising that *musical* sounds,

---

[44] For further information, see <http://genetests.org/profiles/lca/index.html>.

[45] Treffert (1989/2000: 390–1).

with their proclivity for internal regularity and self-sufficient structures (which, as we saw in Chapter 4, unlike words, need not refer to anything beyond themselves) become, as parents repeatedly observed, an important focus of attention for many blind children with learning difficulties (cf. Ockelford 2005*b*). Indeed, for some young people (as will become evident in Chapter 10), music can become in effect a proxy language.

Third, the fact that the prevalence of AP appears to vary significantly between the ROP and SOD populations (and, conceivably, between the SOD and LCA populations, although here the figures available are too small to draw any statistical inferences) suggests that there are important differences in the likelihood with which the syndromes may affect aspects of developing musicality.[46] That the development of AP is by no means guaranteed in any of these conditions (as well as it being linked to subjects' level of vision) suggests that the syndromes do not bear directly on areas of the brain that pertain to music processing, but operate *indirectly*, by affecting neurological function in relation to personal qualities such as motivation, perseverance, and tendency to obsession. Clearly, further neuropsychological research is needed to test this assumption.[47]

Fourth, there is evidence to support the contention (for example, Treffert 1989/2000; Heaton 2003) that AP is a necessary factor in the development of musical savants, since none of the children and young people in the Focus on Music survey or the Ockelford (1988) study with learning difficulties who did *not* have AP became exceptionally musically accomplished. However, the three subjects with prodigious talents who were learning disabled were (as Treffert would have predicted) AP-possessors. Why should this be so when, as we have seen, AP is relatively infrequently found among professional musicians (around one in five cases)? Even among blind musicians, it is by no means universal: Hamilton, Pascual-Leone, and Schlaug (2004), for example, reported finding 12 possessors from a sample of 21 (57 per cent). It seems likely, given the immense obstacle that blindness and severe cognitive impairment present to learning, that musical performance skills would quite simply never get off the ground were it not for the huge advantage that AP confers on those

---

[46] For studies pertaining to other syndromes see, for example, Lenhoff, Perales, Hickok (2001), who found 'near ceiling' levels of AP in five individuals with Williams syndrome (a neurobehavioural congenital condition caused by the microdeletion of about 20 genes in the q11.23 region of one of their two chromosomes number seven)—see <http://www.williams-syndrome.org/forteachers/musicandws.html>. See also Levitin, Cole, Chiles, Lai, Lincoln, and Bellugi (2004); Lenhoff (2006).

[47] It is of interest to note that Gaab, Schulze, Ozdemir, and Schlaug (2006) found that the neural correlates of absolute pitch differ between blind and sighted musicians.

playing, or striving to play, by ear. For those with AP, learning to play an instrument is initially a matter of discovering and practising the movements necessary to reproduce notes (usually on the keyboard) that they can already hear in their inner aural consciousness. In contrast, children without AP, striving to play even a simple melody, face the far more difficult task of attempting to match *distances between notes* (the first chosen more or less arbitrarily) with memorized *intervals*. For AP-possessors, though, once the pattern of notes is learnt, the matter of interval discovery becomes relatively easy, and (as we shall see in Chapter 10), prodigious musical savants can typically transpose music fluently to different keys.

Fifth, there is evidence from the SOD survey, where many research participants were in the early years, that a high level of *interest* in music when children are young is a necessary factor in exceptional musical development. However, it is worth nothing that, according to parents, a strong interest in music was no guarantee of outstanding musicality. On a related point, the responses to the survey suggest that the time infants spend engaged in musical activity (including listening) is an important factor in the development of musical ability, as one would expect. Specifically, the data show that no child who spent *less* than two hours a day engaged with music went on to make exceptional musical progress, while no child who spent two hours a day or *more* undertaking musical activity was described as having a low level of musical achievement.[48]

Therapy, education, and learning

Parents were asked whether their children were in receipt of any specialist musical input in the form of therapy or teaching.

Only 10 of the 65 research participants (15 per cent) with SOD or ROP were said to have music therapy sessions, and the nature of the therapeutic activity evidently varied considerably from one young person to another. Some of the sessions were on a one-to-one basis, while others involved a group. For instance, a 3-year-old girl with SOD who did not have learning difficulties 'attended a music group with singing and instruments once a week for three

---

[48] Hence these preliminary findings in a specific domain accord with and appear to extend John Sloboda's much more comprehensive research that indicates that the level of performance expertise acquired is directly related to the amount of formal practice of the relevant skill undertaken by the individual concerned (see Sloboda 1996/2005). The data here suggest that the *informal* practice of a skill (where the child is not consciously seeking self-improvement through what are typically externally determined or agreed goals) can be effective in skill acquisition too.

eight-week sessions. This really helped her rhythm and her speech blossomed through singing.' Some descriptions of the therapy seem to indicate that in reality what was being offered was music education—hardly surprising given the lack of conceptual clarity that is characteristic of the field (see Chapter 2). For instance, one young person with ROP was said to have music therapy at her sixth-form college, and the researchers were informed that 'a report can be obtained from her teacher'. The Focus on Music surveys suggest that this issue may obtain in the US too. For example, it was reported that one $7\frac{1}{2}$-year-old autistic girl with SOD 'works with her music therapist on learning the piano and also a variety of instruments'. On other occasions the nature of the activity was not clear. For instance, an 8-year-old girl who is developmentally delayed 'has music therapy at school once a week: keyboarding, piano, drumming'. At least one account suggests that communication between the therapist and parents could be improved. For example, a 17-year-old girl with severe learning difficulties 'has had music therapy at school for many years. Little known about the current therapist'.

It is of interest to compare these findings with those of the PROMISE research reported in Chapter 1, which indicated that, among children with severe or profound and multiple learning difficulties in the UK, the level of music therapy provision is very low (around 2 per cent). In comparison, the proportion reported here—almost one in seven children with SOD or ROP (irrespective of whether they are British or American)—is encouraging. This difference is attributable to a number of factors, including the fact that music therapy may be less prevalent among those with profound needs (a level of disability which the Focus on Music studies did not touch). In any case, the data presented here reinforce the view that there is still some way to go before the level of provision meets need.

None of the children with SOD was reported to have instrumental lessons, with the exception of the $7\frac{1}{2}$-year-old autistic girl mentioned above whose music therapist taught her the piano. Nonetheless, seven of the research participants with SOD were said to play an instrument (22 per cent),[49] with two being described as able to play two instruments, giving a total of nine separate instances distributed as follows (see Table 8.4). In contrast, among the 35 subjects in the ROP cohort, 24 young people played instruments, with 11 playing one, 6 playing two, 4 playing three, 2 playing four, and 1 playing five—a total of 48. Eleven (46 per cent) had specialist tuition at the time of the survey, implying that over half the group learnt and played instruments on a

---

[49] A further two in the early years were said to play *with* instruments (the keyboard and the drums).

self-directed basis. In the comparison group, 13 children (41 per cent) were said by their parents to play an instrument, with five of them playing two, making 18 instruments learnt in total. Nine of the children (69 per cent) were reported to have instrumental tuition, leaving four who were apparently managing without specialist input.

Statistically, there is no significant difference between the SOD and comparison cohorts in relation to the numbers who play and those who do not. Between the ROP and comparison groups the difference is significant, however,[50] and between the ROP and SOD cohorts.[51] The average number of instruments learnt by those in the ROP group was markedly higher too—with a third of subjects who played taking up three instruments or more.

How can we account for these differences? It could be that the advantages conferred by the possession of absolute pitch were a key factor here, since 15 of the 24 instrumentalists (63 per cent) were said to have AP—accounting for 37 of the 48 instruments learnt (77 per cent). In contrast, only three of those with AP we reported not to have taken up an instrument.

The fact that none of the research participants with SOD had lessons[52] may in part be due to the fact many of them were in the early years—before it is

Table 8.4 Number of instruments played among those with SOD and ROP, and among a comparison group

Number of instruments played	Cohort		
	SOD	ROP	Comparison
No instrument played	25	11	21
One instrument played	5	11	8
Two instruments played	2	6	5
Three instruments played	0	4	0
Four instruments played	0	2	0
Five instruments played	0	1	0
Number who play	7	24	13
Number in cohort	32	35	32
Percentage who play	22%	69%	41%
Total number of instruments played	9	48	18
Have lessons?	0	11	9

---

[50] $\chi^2 (1, N = 67) = 5.28, p < 0.025.$

[51] $\chi^2 (1, N = 67) = 14.66, p < 0.001.$

[52] Discounting the music therapy sessions in which teaching apparently occurred.

generally deemed appropriate for children formally to learn to play instruments.[53] A further (and more serious) concern, however, is the possibility that instrumental tuition may not have been considered an option on account of some of the children's learning disabilities or challenging behaviour or both—particularly in combination with a severe visual impairment. Judging from the data provided on behalf of the ROP group, which had fewer research participants with additional disabilities, sight loss alone appeared to be less of a barrier as far as accessing specialist music tuition was concerned, although the proportion having lessons was still low at 46 per cent—particularly in view of the advanced auditory development of many of these young people. The Focus on Music research team was strongly of the view that neither age nor disability should deter parents from seeking instrumental lessons for their children, nor teachers from offering them tuition, particularly as so many of the milestones of exceptional musical development for disabled and non-disabled children alike occur in the early years, when expert guidance is, therefore, particularly important.

These issues aside, it is possible to build up a picture of what may currently be happening in the cases of those young people with SOD or ROP who were reported to have acquired some skills in playing instruments, evidently with little or no formal support. We have already noted (p. 164 ff.) that, as part of their reportedly high levels of interest in everyday sounds and music, some children with little or no sight appear to be especially attracted to sound-making objects including musical toys and 'everyday' instruments with which they are likely to come into frequent contact: hand-held percussion, electronic keyboards, whistles, recorders, and the like. We may suppose that, at first, just like any other plaything, the children manipulate these, exploring in particular their sound-making qualities—intended and unintended (as at level 2 of the Sounds of Intent framework). As one mother wrote of her 5-year-old daughter with SOD, who apparently adores music of all types: 'She will ask to get instruments out and play with them', though apparently without producing anything of particular musical interest.

The researchers' observations in the field suggest that a further stage is 'playing at making music', where children are aware that the instrument they are exploring is for music-making, but, as yet lacking the ability to reproduce

---

[53] A notable exception being the 'Suzuki' approach, which advocates starting formal engagement with music early, and which has proved successful with blind and partially sighted children, including those with additional disabilities—see, for example, <http://www.suzukiassociation.org/suzukiforum/viewtopic.php?p=8813andsid=5918ed2b6ee762bedfd1dbdc068bae45>.

tunes that they know, they play imaginatively, making up snatches of music. At first (certainly for those without AP), these appear to be determined predominantly by physical patterns of movement rather than being sound-led. For example, a 3-year-old girl with ROP who lives in Venezuela, 'likes to . . . strum on guitar, play various percussion instruments we have at home (mostly Andean instruments) and [is] fascinated with a piano whenever she gets a chance to sit at one'.

The patterns of movement that infants make may but need not be remembered and repeated, though since, on the keyboard, for example, similar actions can produce different sequences of sounds according to the notes that are struck, the child's efforts judged in purely musical terms may in any case vary from one occasion to another. For example, as one mother wrote of her $7\frac{1}{2}$-year-old daughter with SOD, 'She will play a little melody on the piano and make up her own words to go along with it. She will ask [us] to come and listen but she has never been heard to repeat the same song twice.' Similarly, another parent observes that her 6-year-old daughter with SOD 'taps out her own tunes on anything that will make a noise and make up songs to accompany it'.

Some children take a further step: with persistence (we may surmise), they come to connect particular patterns of movement with the sounds that they generate. This enables them both to reproduce their own material consistently on an instrument and to recreate melodies and other musical fragments with which they have become familiar from frequent exposure (such as nursery rhymes, television theme tunes, mobile phone ring tones, and the like)—as at levels 4 and 5 of the Sounds of Intent framework. That is, they develop the capacity to 'play by ear'. For example, one parent notes that her 3-year-old daughter with SOD 'has always enjoyed playing our keyboard and is able to copy rhythms and repeat her own tunes consistently'. The mother of a 7-year-old with ROP reports that he 'can play any song that he hears on the piano. He only has to listen to the song a few times and he has it almost perfect on his own. He is now starting to make his own songs.' Another parent remarks that her 7-year-old daughter with SOD 'seems to be able to hear a melody and to emulate in a very short time . . . She has just started with formal instruction on the piano with the Primer series but would rather skip the books and just play it the way she hears it.'

The girl's music therapist wonders whether she has AP, and there is little doubt that, as we have seen (p. 176), for those learning to play by ear, this ability, which may evolve alongside the development of instrumental skills, confers enormous advantages. For example, one $6\frac{1}{2}$-year-old girl with SOD who, her mother reports, after only a few months of playing, 'is already naming chords, all keys, [and] can name any key music is being played in', also 'Learns songs quickly'. The mother of a 7-year-old boy with ROP with AP quotes from an assessment undertaken by Sally Zimmermann, the RNIB Music Advisor: '[He] can play tunes by ear and transpose these. Can harmonize with ease. Can pick up detail from someone else's playing and incorporate this into his own playing instantly. He is gifted and talented in music.' These comments suggest he may be functioning at level 5 or 6 of the Sounds of Intent framework.

There are no reports of learning to play by ear among the comparison group, who (it appears) tended to start learning an instrument at a later stage than those with SOD and ROP and, unlike their blind and partially sighted counterparts, typically through formal tuition.[54] Hence the route to starting to learn an instrument, according to the survey data, is quite distinct for the disabled and able-bodied groups. A key factor may be the degree to which self-motivation is present: in answer to the question 'Is [your child] self-motivated to play or only when it is suggested?', both cohorts of research participants with disabilities had high proportions of positive responses: 80 per cent of those with SOD ($n = 15$) and 85 per cent of those with ROP ($n = 33$). In contrast, only 48 per cent of the comparison group ($n = 23$) replied in the affirmative, yielding a statistically significant difference in population profile between this and the SOD cohort,[55] and the ROP sample.[56]

The range of instruments that had been taken up differed considerably between groups, varying in proportion to the number of subjects who played (Table 8.5). Research participants with SOD were relatively constrained in their choice, with only four categories mentioned, as opposed to seven among the fully sighted subjects and 12 in the case of those with ROP. This group was unique in reflecting a certain cultural diversity, though the keyboard (or piano) dominated in all three cohorts—perhaps on account of the its immediacy and ubiquity.

Although the numbers are small, issues of gender in relation to instrument selection are worth mentioning. The comparison group data are very much in line with those of O'Neill and Boulton (1996),[57] who found preferences among

---

[54] From the data available, it is not clear how the decision to start lessons was made.

[55] χ^2 (1, $N = 38$) = 3.93, $p < 0.05$.

[56] χ^2 (1, $N = 56$) = 8.79, $p < 0.001$.

[57] The 'Young People and Music Participation Project' undertaken by Keele University in 2001, and also led by Susan O'Neill, provides further evidence of the gender imbalance, and of the dichotomy between children's instrumental aspirations and reality in schools: see <http://www.keele.ac.uk/depts/ps/ESRC/Preportall.pdf>.

Table 8.5 Range of instruments played among those with SOD and ROP, and among a comparison group.

Instrument	Cohort								
	SOD			ROP			Comparison		
	♂	♀	total	♂	♀	total	♂	♀	total
Keyboard/piano	2	4	6	10	7	17	2	6	8
Drums/percussion	1	0	1	4	4	8	1	0	1
(Bass) guitar	0	1	1	2	4	6	2	0	2
Recorder	0	1	1	2	2	4	0	2	2
Violin	0	0	0	2	1	3	1	2	3
Bagpipes/backpipes	0	0	0	3	0	3	0	0	0
Cello	0	0	0	0	2	2	0	0	0
Clarinet	0	0	0	0	1	1	1	0	1
Tabla	0	0	0	1	0	1	0	0	0
Tin whistle	0	0	0	1	0	1	0	0	0
Flute	0	0	0	0	1	1	0	0	0
Trumpet	0	0	0	0	0	0	1	0	1
Euphonium	0	0	0	1	0	1	0	0	0
Total	3	6	9	26	22	48	8	10	18
Percentage	33%	67%	100%	54%	46%	100%	44%	56%	100%
Number of instruments	2	3	4	9	8	12	6	3	7

9- and 11-year-old girls for piano, flute, and violin, and among boys of the same ages for guitar, drum, and trumpet, and with Ofsted (2004), who found the same, marked biases in a study of music services in 15 Local Education Authorities, which between them covered some 54,000 pupils. The general imbalance that Ofsted found in relation to the proportion of girls (60 per cent) and boys (40 per cent) learning instruments is also reflected in the comparison group totals—56 per cent and 44 per cent respectively. The data relating to children with SOD who play instruments—meagre as the numbers are—are also consistent with the wider trends. Many of the ROP data, however, seem to point in a different direction. For example, there were more reports of males than females learning the piano/keyboard and the violin, and a preponderance of females tackling the guitar, while equal numbers were said to have taken up the drums/percussion. Overall, there were more males (54 per cent) than females (46 per cent) learning instruments, and the level of difference with the mainstream Ofsted sample was statistically significant.[58] Clearly, further research would be needed to bottom out the matter of how disability and gender interact in this context (cf. Ockelford 2006*b*). For example, is it the case that attitudes to disability, or expectations concerning exceptional musical ability, or perhaps a combination of both, have overridden preconceptions in relation to gender? And if this effect does exist, is it disability-specific?

With regard to the standards of performance achieved by subjects, those with SOD were, with one exception,[59] judged to be at the level of beginners. Children in the comparison group were, on the whole, also described as beginners, although one girl of 11, who had just taken Grade 3 examinations on the piano and violin, was said to be at an 'intermediate' level on both instruments, as was another girl who played the piano and clarinet. Another girl, almost 9 years old, was described as being at an 'intermediate' level too—on the violin. She had recently received a distinction in her Grade 1 examination and had been chosen to take part in a week's tuition at a Suzuki school of music in the US in 2005.

Clearly, the labels 'beginner' and 'intermediate' were subject to different interpretations, since another child who had achieved Grade 1 on the piano and was at the level of Grade 1 or 2 on the violin, was described as a 'beginner' on both instruments. With the ROP group, things were very different. Twelve instances of 'advanced' instrumental skills were reported (11 male and 1 female), 19 'intermediate' (9 male and 10 female) and 22 (7 male and 15 female) at the level of 'beginners'. Examples of 'advanced' performance included a 7-year-old boy, who was said to be able to 'play any song that he hears on the piano. He only has to listen to the song a few times and he has it almost perfect on his own.' A 12-year-old boy was reported to play the piano (at Grade 4 level), drums (in a group), the bagpipes, and guitar. Another young man (aged 17) 'has taken part in several solo piping competitions, a very serious hobby, properly regulated from Scotland, coming 2nd, 3rd and 4th in different competitions. He plays all his instruments very well with feeling and confidence; he tours the karaoke circuit often and he has performed on keyboard and vocals in public and for our local town mayor.' Another 17-year-old had been 'identified as gifted on piano and violin at the age of 10'.

How does one account for the differences in relation to the level of achievement between groups? Clearly, further research is required, though possible factors would seem to be the possession (or non-possession) of AP, the degree

---

[58] χ^2 (1, $N = 54{,}048$) $= 4.01$, $p < 0.05$.

[59] A 22-year-old man whose mother reported that he had been able to play the piano and organ 'well at four years old but never followed up, so lost a lot of his skills'.

of self-motivation, the potentially limited choice in undertaking other artistic ventures for those with sight loss and (for some) complex needs, and social expectations in relation to blind children and music becoming a self-fulfilling prophecy (Merton 1968).

Conclusion

This chapter put the spotlight on special musical *abilities*, and, through the use of parental surveys and observations by researchers, found a range of factors that appear to play an important role in the exceptional musical development of young people with learning difficulties. A crucial element appears to be the *level of vision* of the child concerned. For example, among those born blind (or who lose their sight shortly after birth), the incidence of AP is markedly higher than in those who are partially or fully sighted. The situation is far from straightforward, however, since not all blind children with learning difficulties develop AP. Furthermore, the incidence varies from one syndrome to another. Hence a number of interrelated factors may well be in play in the development of early musicality, and parents, teachers, and therapists need to be alert to the possibilities, to ensure that musical potential is not overlooked. The danger is that unthinking prejudices will become barriers to pupils' attainment. Clearly, the message is to approach all learners with an open mind, and to foster engagement with music as soon as possible.

Chapter 9

Influential measures

Introduction

Kyroulla Markou's research, reported in Chapter 2, indicated that all music therapists and most teachers working with children and young people with complex needs use improvisation in their sessions and lessons (see Fig. 2.3). At the same time, a key issue was raised with regard to improvised interactions between teachers and pupils, and therapists and clients: how do such relationships actually *work* in musical terms? Who influences whom, and how? According to Markou, teachers and, more particularly, therapists consider that they adopt a child-centred approach (Fig. 2.2)—but what direct evidence is there to show that they succeed? Which party does, in fact, exert the greater influence? Who, ultimately, is in control?

Until recently, it has only been possible to approach questions such as these *indirectly*, through eliciting teachers' and therapists' views (after the event) as to the nature of the musical engagement that has taken place, and subjectively attempting to gauge its impact. While these approaches have a certain intrinsic validity, it is important to acknowledge their limitations. It is easy to imagine, for example, that a therapist may have felt that she was wholly focused on the needs of a particular pupil or client, responding empathetically to his musical input, when, in fact, it was *she* who was determining the greater part of the content and the broad direction of their improvised dialogue in sound.

Zygonic theory, which sets out to explain how music 'makes sense' through its self-deriving structure (see Chapter 4) offers a new way forward, enabling a moment-by-moment analysis to be undertaken of the ebb and flow of musical influence in improvised events that involve two participants or more. It does this by tracking the derivation of musical elements presented by the contributors from the material that each provides and (potentially) from external sources.

In the context of a single case study, this chapter explores one such interaction, between a pupil with special needs ('K'—a $4\frac{1}{2}$-year-old girl with SOD who formed part of the research reported in Chapter 8) and her teacher (the author—'AO'), which was previously videoed and transcribed (see Ockelford, Pring, Welch, and Treffert 2006; Ockelford 2006b; 2007b). The analysis that is undertaken also enables certain aspects of K's evolving musicality to be assessed. As we shall see, she is highly precocious in musical terms—functioning at level 5 and in some respects at level 6 in the Sounds of Intent framework—and, therefore, musically unlike most children and young people with PMLD or SLD, though by no means all. However, the advanced nature of the musical interaction that occurs has the advantage of testing the new analytical technique to the full, and it will become evident that the approach could easily be adapted to the less intricate interactions that occur at lower levels.

The session

The session with K was originally intended to enable AO to assess her musical abilities and potential.[1] The assessment had been requested by K's class teacher, who had observed that her new pupil particularly enjoyed singing and that (as far as she was able to judge) K's efforts appeared to be unusually advanced for a child of her age. All that was known of K's musical background was that she had a small keyboard at home, which apparently kept her occupied for significant periods of time, although she had never received any formal music tuition.

AO began the session by suggesting to K that she might like to sing something, whereupon she immediately set off unaccompanied with *Supercalifragilisticexpialidocious* from *Mary Poppins*. K's singing was enthusiastic though somewhat raucous. Despite the fact that her vocal technique was limited, which meant that her intonation was not always perfect, K's rendition had a secure tonal centre (the key of D), which was established without reference to a fixed pitch. K evidently relished the novel experience of making music with someone listening, and she was pleased to repeat the song with great gusto at an even faster tempo, this time with a piano accompaniment.

It was immediately evident that K was a natural and uninhibited young performer, who thoroughly enjoyed making music and was capable of communicating forcefully through sound. The fact that her rendition began recognizably in the key of D major (although K was unaware of this or any other formal musical concepts or specialized terminology) and remained in that key (notwithstanding the immaturity of her vocal production) indicated that K was likely to have absolute pitch. In addition, she exhibited a reliable sense of rhythm that was nonetheless flexible enough to accommodate different tempi.

---

[1] At the time, AO was working as a specialist music teacher at Linden Lodge School in Wandsworth, which catered for visually impaired children, including those with additional disabilities.

A number of issues remained to be resolved, however. How effectively was she able to process harmony, for example? Could she create her own music? And if so, at what level was K capable of assimilating and developing material that was provided and fashion this into a coherent structure within a recognizable stylistic framework? Answers to these questions were sought by suggesting that K should make up a new song about her pet dogs (Jack and Elisha), of which she was known to be particularly fond. AO played four chords—F major, D minor, G minor[9], and C major—on the piano with a gentle swing rhythm, and added a simple vocal melody to set the scene. After two iterations of the sequence, K intuitively took the lead and, against the continuing four-chord ostinato, improvised a song that lasted for around 90 seconds (see Ex. 9.1).

AO's initial impression, as the teacher-accompanist, was of an unfolding extemporization of genuine musical expressivity within a continuously evolving but coherent musical structure. It was clear that K had an active musical mind that was able to create new material intuitively, quickly, and confidently within a broadly familiar style. Beyond these immediate reactions, however, the taped record of the session meant that it has been possible to transcribe K's efforts, enabling her improvisation to be analysed systematically in relation to a number of musical criteria, and the teacher–pupil musical interaction quantified on a moment-to-moment basis. In particular, K's improvisation will be assessed here in relation to the three potential sources of material from which she could draw: (*a*) the unfolding melody, as initiated by AO and subsequently taken up by K; (*b*) the piano accompaniment provided by AO; and (*c*) other pieces in similar style.

K's song

Does K's song 'make sense' as a piece of music—and, if so, through what structural means? According to zygonic theory (introduced in Chapter 4), musical coherence requires at least one salient feature from each event to be felt to *derive* from another or others.[2] Features include pitch, harmony, tonality,

---

[2] That is not to say that, in order to be coherent, K's improvisation should have consisted only of repetition. Through 'perceptual binding' (the cognitive glue through which the different properties of an object cohere in the mind to form the notion of a single thing—see, for example, Snyder (2000: 7)) and *Gestalt* perception (through which discrete events are reckoned to form larger wholes—see, for instance, Deutsch (1999)) sounds, or groups of sounds, may differ from each other in some respects while being the same in others. Hence (as we shall see), similarity and diversity work in parallel in the creation of musical material that is at once original though coherent.

I Have a Dog

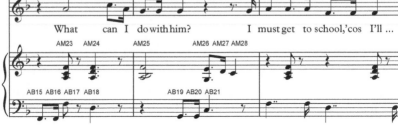

Note: 'AV = 'AO voice'; 'KV' = 'K voice'; 'AM' = 'AO melody'; and 'AB' = 'AO bass-line'.

Ex. 9.1 K's song

Ex. 9.1 Cont.   **Continued**

Ex. 9.1 Cont.

inter-onset interval, duration, metre, timbre, and loudness. The cognition of derivation between musical elements such as these is predicated on the presence of 'interperspective relationships'[3]—cognitive constructs through which, it is hypothesized, percepts may be compared (cf. Krumhansl 1990: 3). In most circumstances, interperspective relationships are formulated unthinkingly, passing listeners by as a series of qualitative experiences. However, through introspection, they may be captured conceptually and assigned values, commonly expressible as a difference or ratio.

Fig. 9.1 shows how interperspective relationships may be symbolized using an arrow with the letter 'I' superimposed. Superscripts indicate the features concerned, each represented by its initial letter—here 'P' for 'pitch' and 'O' for 'onset'. Relationships can exist at different *levels*, with 'primary' relationships potentially linking percepts directly, 'secondary' relationships connecting primaries, and 'tertiary' relationships comparing secondaries (Ockelford 2002*b*).

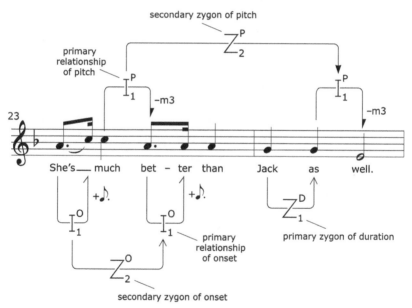

Fig. 9.1 Zygonic relationships presumed to be at work in the creation and cognition of K's song

---

[3] 'Interperspective': a term coined by Ockelford (1991) to mean 'between *perspects*' (that is, '*per*ceived a*spects*') of music; used in contradistinction to the term 'parameter', which is reserved solely to refer to the physical attributes of sound. Hence the perspect 'pitch', for example, most closely corresponds to the parameter 'frequency', though the connection between the two is far from straightforward (cf. Meyer 1967: 246).

The level of a relationship is indicated by the appropriate subscript (here, '1' in each case). The values of the pitch relationships (shown near the arrowheads as '–m3') have two components, 'polarity' (which here is negative, showing that the intervals are descending) and 'magnitude' (a minor third). Similarly, the values of the relationships of onset indicate both temporal polarity and magnitude (a dotted quaver).[4]

Interperspective relationships through which imitation is cognized are deemed to be 'zygonic' (Ockelford 1991: 140 ff.) and, as we observed in Chapter 4, may be depicted using the letter 'Z' (see p. 65). Here, refinements will be made to this form of representation, to enable more detailed musical analysis to be undertaken. In Fig. 9.2, the *primary zygonic relationship of duration* ('D') reflects the apparent derivation of the note-length used for the word 'as' from that pertaining to the preceding 'Jack'. The *secondary zygons of pitch and onset* (indicated through the subscripts '2') show imitation at a more abstract (intervallic) level. Note the use of *full* arrowheads, which signify relationships between values that are identical. *Half* arrowheads are indicative of difference, and are used in a zygonic context to show approximate imitation.

A full zygonic analysis of K's song (which is too extensive to be reproduced here) confirms the informal observation that successive notes do not pass by as isolated entities, but sound logically connected to each other through similarities in pitch or rhythm which bind them together in the mind to form short melodic 'chunks' (as in level 4 of the Sounds of Intent framework). As we shall see, these chunks are themselves linked through various forms of sameness and similarity. Here, an analysis of K's first phrase will suffice to illustrate the principles involved.

K's song begins as she picks up on the fourth octave E that AO's vocal line leaves in the air, and which is reinforced in his accompaniment. From here, K moves back to the adjacent F, following the change from tonic to dominant harmony, which she would have been able to anticipate from the same harmonic transition between bars 2 and 3. This opening melodic interval is a retrograde[5] version of the ending of AO's last vocal phrase—illustrating how, from the outset, K takes the material that is offered and stamps her authority on it. K's initial F is followed by 11 others, together constituting a pitch structure of the simplest kind (potentially derived through a network of identical

---

[4] Observe that arrowheads may be open or filled—the former showing a link between *single* values, and the latter indicating a *compound* connection within or between 'constants' (typically, values extended in time)—implying a network of relationships the same. For a fuller explanation, see Ockelford (1999).

[5] That is, backwards.

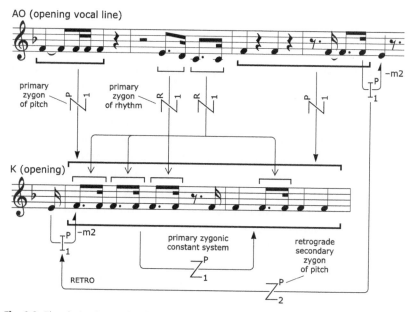

Fig. 9.2 The derivation and coherence of K's opening phrase

primary zygonic relationships that are known as a 'constant system'; Ockelford 1993: 180 ff.). This repeated series of notes, which at first appears to over-extend itself against the accompanying harmonies (conflicting with the concluding dominant chord in the second half of bar 6), could be heard as a device for K to buy time while deciding what to do next. However, analysis shows that the series of Fs actually grows organically from the preceding material, deriving from two sources: the pitches echo the initial repetitions of the melody, and the rhythm adopts the dotted-quaver/semiquaver pattern first heard in the second half of bar 2. This means that K took two distinct elements from the opening phrases of the melody (supplied by AO) and fused them in her continuation, a form of musical development typical of many styles that simultaneously offers coherence and variety (Fig. 9.2).

K's forceful delivery of the repeated pitches adds to the sense that she is asserting her place in the partnership that is about to unfold: both musically and socially, building a foundation for the action to come. This starts immediately: in the very next phrase (bar 7), there is a sense of release as K's melody springs up from the constraints of the opening repetitions using a new, syncopated rhythm. Despite the sense that things are moving off in a new direction, though, both pitch and rhythm again derive logically from what has gone before: the 'dotted' motif again pressed into service and two similar ascending melodic intervals (from F to A, and A to C) deployed to straddle the phrases.

This method of connecting chunks, through secondary zygonic relationships—rather like using a musical 'ladder' to link different ideas—is one that K adopts a number of times (for example, between bars 16/17 and 22/3). Her other favoured approach is to use a primary zygonic relationship—taking a pitch at or near the end of a phrase and using it to start the next (see, for example, the connections between phrases in bar 8, 18/19, and 20) (Fig. 9.3).

These two approaches to connecting chunks of musical material are typical of many styles (Ockelford 2004) and are identified in the Sounds of Intent framework (P.4.C—'links groups coherently through common elements'). However, there is another way of linking segments, which involves the repetition (or variation) of chunks *as a whole* (acknowledged in P.4.B). Although, arguably, this is the most widespread of all music-structural techniques, it is not one that K adopts. The nearest she comes to it is in bars 17–24, when a pattern of three descending pitches is successively transposed and varied, mirroring and reinforcing the rhetorical form of the verbal narrative at this point: ('*one* for her biscuits, *one* for her water, and *one* for her meat'). Exact transposition of the intervallic descent, which would have required a B flat at the beginning of bar 19, appears to have been overwhelmed by K's desire for a convincing concord at this juncture (with the emphasis on the repeated word 'one'). So it is that K demonstrates the intuitive ability to weigh up and manage conflicting musical (and extra-musical) demands, and—in the midst of her improvisation—the capacity to select the option best able to meet her expressive intentions (see Fig. 9.4).

Why does K not make greater use of the commonplace method of repeating or varying chunks as a whole? It may be on account of the improvised nature of the exercise that K was undertaking, in which building a coherent structure depended on remembering material that had just been made up at the same time as continuing with the creative process (which may well have interfered with the memories that had recently been formed). By intuitively adopting the approach of having each successive chunk pick up where the previous one left off, K made fewer demands on her memory and gave herself greater freedom to follow her musical or verbal whim of the moment. A corollary of this free-flowing approach is that there is no particular pattern to the links between chunks in K's song: while the moment-to-moment connections on the musical surface are convincing enough, there is no hierarchical arrangement of the segments—no deeper structural repetition or development. The climax, which occurs at the end of the improvisation, is signalled by a change of register and effected through a high, sustained tonic F (sung 'fortissimo'), rather than occurring through a feeling of structural inevitability.

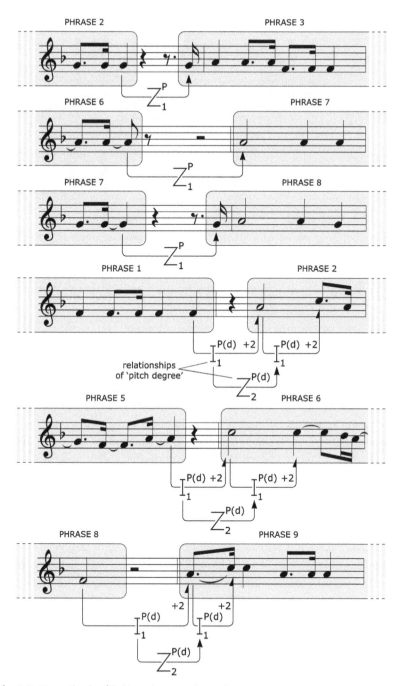

Fig. 9.3 K's methods of linking phrases coherently

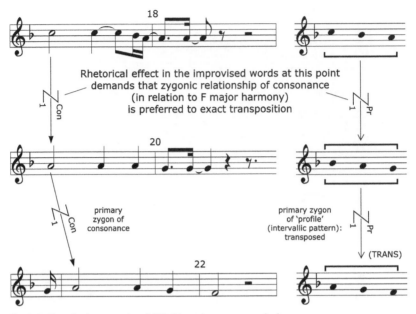

Fig. 9.4 The single example of K linking phrases as a whole

Hence, taking all this evidence into account, it is reasonable to assert that K had grasped a number of the key principles of how western music (within the tonal vernacular of the early twenty-first century) is structured (indicating functioning at levels R.5/R.6 of the Sounds of Intent framework), and that she was able to use these to create new tunes that would make sense to listeners (suggesting attainment at levels P.5/P.6). We know that K developed this capacity with no formal intervention on the part of others—purely through being exposed to a range of music and through expressing herself by singing. Just as the great majority of people absorb the syntactical rules of their native language without conscious effort (simply by listening and trying things out for themselves), thereby acquiring the ability to create original but coherent and comprehensible linguistic utterances, so K evidently had done the same in the domain of music. Her intuitive awareness of certain elements of *musical* syntax within familiar styles enabled her to formulate new, stylistically authentic *musical* statements. Of course, this is not in itself exceptional; almost all young children make up songs that are coherent by absorbing, copying, and extending what they hear—infant 'meme engineers' (Barrett 2003).[6] It is through

---

[6] See also, for example, Moog (1968/1976: 128–33); Hargreaves (1986: 60 ff.); Barrett (2006).

considering the way in which the structural techniques that K employed interacted with the accompaniment that was provided that we can glean more about the unusual nature of her developing musicality.

The influence of the accompaniment

Zygonic theory was used to gauge the impact of the accompaniment on K's creative efforts by assessing each note[7] in relation to its probable musical sources, which could be found either in AO's melodic opening (bars 1–4), the extemporized piano melody (equivalent to the uppermost RH notes), the bass ostinato or K's vocal line.[8] For every note, up to ten zygonic relationships[9] were considered in relation to pitch, melodic interval, harmonic context, and rhythm. These were weighted as follows: pitch scored 2 for exact repetition, and 1 for the transfer of pitch-class to a different octave; melodic interval scored 2 for identity, 1.5 for approximate imitation, and 1 for inversion or retrogression; harmonic context scored 2 for exact repetition, 1.5 for variation, 1 for transposition and 0.5 for transposed variation; and rhythm scored 4 for identity, 3 for approximate derivation (including a change of relative location within the relevant metrical level), 2 for repetition of duration or inter-onset interval only, and 1 where the sole connection was the variation of duration or inter-onset interval. Since each aspect of every note could be considered to be derived from up to ten others, further weighting was necessary, whereby each raw score of derivation strength was multiplied by a factor based on the theorized salience of the zygonic relationship concerned, such that the sum of the factors pertaining to the given feature of a particular note was invariably 1.

For example, K's seventh pitch (labelled K7 in Fig. 9.1) could be considered to derive from K6, K5, K4, AM13, K3, K2, AV12, AM11, AV11, and AM10—the

---

[7] Hence the analysis was as fine-grained as it was practicable to make it. Longer pieces could be investigated using more substantial musical gestures as the primary unit of analysis.

[8] This work was undertaken by AO, utilizing his intuitions as an experienced music analyst, performer, and educator. The principal disadvantage of this approach was the possibility of bias through idiosyncratic interpretation of the underlying structural relationships. The advantage was his intimate knowledge of the situation in question—in particular what was going through his mind as the accompanist. Future analyses along these lines could (though need not) be based more on the consensus of a number of people's views. Indeed, it is anticipated that a significant proportion of the analytical activity could be undertaken by computer (searching for combinations of similarity and salience through appropriate algorithms).

[9] Chosen for pragmatic reasons—other analyses could involve more or fewer relationships per feature than this.

order determined by their temporal adjacency to K7.[10] The pragmatic decision was made to separate each of the factors used to moderate the raw scores pertaining to a series such as this by a common difference (implying a linear decrease in the strength of their zygonic influence). In this case, with ten factors required, the values used to modify the raw derivation scores were 0.182, 0.164, 0.145, 0.127, 0.109, 0.091, 0.073, 0.055, 0.036, and 0.018 respectively. The result of applying these proportions to the raw scores was a series of 'derivation indices'.

The indices for each feature were summed separately in relation to the material improvised by AO and K. The total potential derivation index for each note ranged between 0 and 10 from either of the two sources (AO or K). With regard to K7, the subtotals pertaining to AO- and K-derived material are shown in Fig. 9.4: pitch has a derivation index of 0.618 from AO and 1.382 from K; melodic interval, 0.334 from AO and 1.666 from K; harmonic context, 1.335 from AO and 0.666 from K; and rhythm, 1.620 from AO and 2.136 from K. This yields a total derivation index of 3.907 from AO's material and 5.850 from K's. Given the maximum total derivation index of 10, the sum of these two figures (9.757) leaves a residue of 0.243, reflecting aspects of K7 that cannot be accounted for through derivation from other material in the song. This, then, is a measure of the 'originality' of the event in question (K7) in relation to the improvisation up to that point (see Table 9.1).[11]

The usefulness of these figures in interpreting the relationship between AO's and K's contributions lies principally in the ratios between them—taken either as averages over a given period or in terms of event-by-event patterns of variation. For example, the derivation indices for the piece as a whole are shown in Table 9.2. That is to say, 70 per cent of AO's production was generated from other of his material, with a little under 13 per cent deriving from K's input. In contrast, only 50 per cent or so of K's melody is attributable to the emulation of her own efforts, with approximately 36 per cent based on AO's introductory vocal melody and piano accompaniment. This is powerful evidence that, while improvising her own structurally and expressively coherent

---

[10] On the grounds that, other things being equal, their temporal adjacency corresponds to their relative salience and therefore implicative strength. Factors that could impact on this assumption include the possibility of an event pertaining to a larger perceptual unit. Hence it is thought that the bass note at the beginning of bar 5 (third octave F), for example, more strongly derives from the bass notes at the beginning of bars 3 and 1 respectively than the temporally more adjacent Fs in the vocal and piano melody lines (something that is reinforced through common and differing octaves respectively).

[11] The issue of material derived from other pieces is considered briefly in the third section of the analysis.

Table 9.1 Measures of derivation and originality in K's material

Pitch—derived from AO					Pitch—derived from K				
Event number	Relative position	Raw score	Weight factor	Derivation index	Event number	Relative position	Raw score	Weight factor	Derivation index
AM13	4	2	0.127	0.254	K6	1	2	0.182	0.364
AV12	7	2	0.073	0.146	K5	2	2	0.164	0.328
AM11	8	2	0.055	0.110	K4	3	2	0.145	0.290
AV11	9	2	0.036	0.072	K3	5	2	0.109	0.218
AM10	10	2	0.018	0.036	K2	6	2	0.091	0.182
Totals	**5**	**10**	**0.309**	**0.618**	**Totals**	**5**	**10**	**0.691**	**1.382**

Interval—derived from AO					Interval—derived from K				
Event number	Relative position	Raw score	Weight factor	Derivation index	Event number	Relative position	Raw score	Weight factor	Derivation index
AM12	6	2	0.083	0.166	K6	1	2	0.222	0.444
AV12	7	2	0.056	0.112	K5	2	2	0.194	0.388
AM11	8	2	0.028	0.056	K4	3	2	0.167	0.334
Totals	**3**	**6**	**0.167**	**0.334**	K3	4	2	0.139	0.278
					K1	5	2	0.111	0.222
					Totals	**5**	**10**	**0.833**	**1.666**

Harmonic context—derived from AO					Harmonic context—derived from K				
Event number	Relative position	Raw score	Weight factor	Derivation index	Event number	Relative position	Raw score	Weight factor	Derivation index
AM9	2	2	0.267	0.534	K6	1	2	0.333	0.666
AV10	3	2	0.200	0.400	**Totals**	**1**	**2**	**0.333**	**0.666**
AM2	4	2	0.133	0.267					
AV4	5	2	0.067	0.134					
Totals	**4**	**8**	**0.667**	**1.335**					

Rhythm—derived from AO					Rhythm—derived from K				
Event number	Relative position	Raw score	Weight factor	Derivation index	Event number	Relative position	Raw score	Weight factor	Derivation index
AV12	4	3	0.133	0.399	K5	1	4	0.200	0.800
AM11	5	3	0.111	0.333	K3	2	4	0.178	0.712
AV8	6	4	0.089	0.356	K1	3	4	0.156	0.624
AM7	7	4	0.067	0.268	**Totals**	**3**	**12**	**0.534**	**2.136**
AV6	8	4	0.044	0.176					
AM5	9	4	0.022	0.088					
Totals	**6**	**22**	**0.466**	**1.620**					

Grand totals		
From AO	'Original' material	From K
3.907	**0.243**	**5.850**

Table 9.2 Comparison of the influence of AO on K, and K on AO

	AO's material generated from			K's material generated from		
	AO	K	Original	AO	K	Original
Sum: derivation indices	1827.04	329.60	453.36	369.59	522.77	147.63
Average derivation index	7.00	1.26	1.74	3.55	5.03	1.42
Number of events	261			104		

melody, K was able to attend to the piano accompaniment and (apparently without conscious effort) take on board a range of musical ideas that were presented. Moreover, within the musical interaction that occurred, AO's influence on K was almost three times greater than K's impact on AO—a somewhat sobering statistic for a music educator who at the time felt that he was providing a responsive foil for K's efforts! In fact, zygonic analysis indicates that the flow of musical ideas was largely from teacher to pupil. One wonders how asymmetrical the patterns of influence are in other more 'typical' music-educational and therapeutic contexts, notwithstanding teachers' and therapists' beliefs concerning the child-centredness of their approaches.

The derivation indices also enable us to track how the influence of one performer on another varied over time. For example, during K's first phrase (notes K1–K13), the derivation index from AO's material falls from 9.476 to 0.927, whose trend closely matches a linear descent ($R^2 = 0.817$)—the principal exceptions being K9 and K10, where K introduces a rhythmic pattern similar to one used in AO's introduction (Fig. 9.5).

This decline in K's use of AO's material through the phrase reflects K's increasing self-assertion (noted above) and, as one would expect, is matched inversely by an increasing use of her own improvisation to generate further ideas. At the same time, K's use of original material fluctuates at a low level (Fig. 9.6).

Subsequent phrases show different derivational patterns that cannot be reported in detail here. However, the mean derivation indices pertaining to phrases will be used to give an overview of trends at a deeper structural level. These show K drawing significantly on AO's material in her first phrase, less so in the second, and more again in the third and the fourth. Subsequently, there is a gradual decrease in AO's impact over phrases five to nine—the central part of K's improvisation with the descending sequence at its heart—during which K's efforts become ever more self-sufficient. In contrast, AO's influence is felt more strongly in K's tenth phrase, whose lack of verbal coherence suggests that K may be running out of steam. Indeed, after rallying briefly in the eleventh phrase, K's creative flow almost completely dries up at the beginning of the

Derivation index

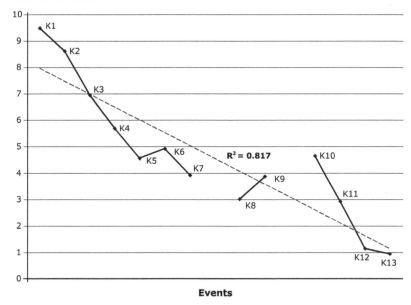

Events

Fig. 9.5 The decreasing derivation of K's material from AO during her first phrase

Derivation index

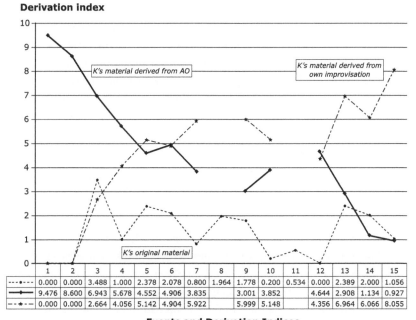

Events and Derivation Indices

Fig. 9.6 The increasing use by K of her own material during her first phrase

Mean derivation index

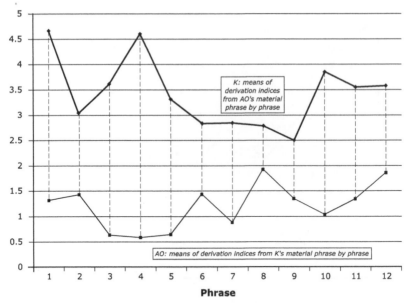

K: means of derivation indices from AO's material phrase by phrase

AO: means of derivation indices from K's material phrase by phrase

Phrase

Fig. 9.7 The inverse relationship between K's and AO's derivation of material from each other during the song

twelfth, and she draws heavily on material in the accompaniment to sustain her vocal line (although in the concluding notes she finally wrests back the initiative). K's global pattern of derivation from AO, invariably lower than AO's derivation from K, is inversely related to it with a striking consistency (82 per cent). That is to say, during the improvisation, as K chose to rely less on AO for material, AO tended to rely more on K, and vice versa—perhaps through an intuitive desire on the part of one performer or both to ensure coherence in the improvised texture as a whole (Fig. 9.7).

Analysing indices of 'originality' reveals further issues of structural significance. For example, itemizing all K's events that had an originality index ≥ 0.25 (that is, when a quarter or more of material was derived other than from the improvisation) yields 13 entries as shown in Table 9.3.

Although different features are implicated (including melodic interval, duration and inter-onset interval) K's originality is most frequently expressed in the domain of harmonic context (in 62 per cent of cases). On some occasions, this appears to be a consequence of K's melodic intent overriding the harmony provided (for example, in the second half of bar 6 and at the end of bar 10), although her continuations make sense of these things in retrospect: as we have already observed, the repeated Fs in bar 6 serve as a springboard for

Table 9.3 K's originality manifests itself largely through harmonic context

Event	Originality	Pitch	Proportion	Interval	Proportion	Harm. context	Proportion	Duration	Proportion	Inter-onset int.	Proportion	Highest
K12	2.800	0.000	0.000	0.000	0.000	2.000	0.714	0.800	0.286	0.000	0.000	H
K14	6.000	0.000	0.000	2.000	0.333	1.000	0.167	2.000	0.333	1.000	0.167	H/IOI
K15	5.182	1.000	0.193	0.500	0.096	1.500	0.289	1.126	0.217	1.056	0.204	H
K17	3.666	0.666	0.182	1.500	0.409	1.500	0.409	0.000	0.000	0.000	0.000	H/Int
K27	5.400	1.000	0.185	1.500	0.278	1.500	0.278	1.100	0.204	0.300	0.056	H/Int
K28	2.767	0.382	0.138	0.611	0.221	0.466	0.168	0.654	0.236	0.654	0.236	D/IOI
K35	2.691	0.000	0.000	0.400	0.149	1.000	0.372	0.601	0.223	0.690	0.256	H
K49	5.636	2.000	0.355	0.000	0.000	2.000	0.355	0.000	0.000	1.636	0.290	H
K91	2.657	0.490	0.184	0.000	0.000	0.167	0.063	0.400	0.151	1.600	0.602	IOI
K92	3.109	0.399	0.128	0.000	0.000	2.000	0.643	0.710	0.228	0.000	0.000	H
K94	2.953	0.327	0.111	0.472	0.160	0.500	0.169	0.544	0.184	1.110	0.376	D
K103	3.346	0.818	0.244	0.892	0.267	0.000	0.000	0.762	0.228	0.874	0.261	IOI
K104	4.255	0.946	0.222	0.309	0.073	1.000	0.235	2.000	0.470	0.000	0.000	D
n=13 sum		8.028	1.943	8.184	1.985	14.633	3.863	10.697	2.761	8.920	2.448	
Average		0.618	0.149	0.630	0.153	1.126	0.297	0.823	0.212	0.686	0.188	

the next phrase, while the F at the end of bar 10 is sustained to reach over into the F major harmony that starts the next sequence. However, there are other times when, rather than having arisen as a by-product of melodic goals, K's harmonic originality seems to have been intrinsically motivated; see, for example, K27, where K's A flat produces an astringent minor ninth chord on the supertonic[12] bass provided. A further measure of K's harmonic creativity can be gleaned from the number of ways in which she melodizes a given harmony within the ostinato pattern. For example, K overlays the second chord in the sequence (which in AO's original version comprises a simple D minor harmony—D, F, A) at different times in the course of her improvisation with D, F, G, A, B flat, and C, using a range of melodic devices (described below).[13]

Despite the substantial impact of AO's improvisation on K's melody, the derivation is largely at a 'general' level, whereby each feature almost invariably stems from a number of sources, and the relationships concerned rarely have the salience to stand out from their coherence-creating neighbours and acquire specific structural significance. There are exceptions, however, which function either through a series of relationships working in parallel or by prominent percepts being repeated in temporal apposition. For example, the syncopated rhythm first heard in the piano in bar 12 reappears in the vocal melody in bar 15 (and then again in the piano in bar 24), while from bar 30, K repeatedly derives A flats and Fs from the accompaniment.

The derivation of material from other sources

The third and final issue to be addressed is the extent to which K uses material from other pieces in her improvisation. For this to occur implies that the music improvised by AO (and by K herself) triggered features common to many other pieces—stylistic influences—that were subsequently pressed into service in the new work, or specific memories of other compositions, or both. Direct borrowing is not a requirement for musical coherence (although it is encountered widely in traditional jazz—see Berliner (1994: 103 ff.)), and it is not an approach that K adopts.[14] The utilization of more general features is far

---

[12] That is, the note above the tonic, in this case G.

[13] Similarly, while K's phrase-lengths indicate her evident cognizance of the underlying harmonic structure, they are not bound by it, ranging in duration from two beats to nine. Here, the influence of the improvised words appears to have been particularly important. Moreover, in the manner of a mature musical dialogue, K sometimes left the piano to play on its own (notably in bars 11 and 12), partly to regroup her own thinking, no doubt, though nonetheless affording a convincing feeling of 'give and take'.

[14] AO does, however, quoting 'Dream, Dream, Dream' by the Everly Brothers in bars 20–3.

more important in the construction of musically meaningful pieces, however, and K's improvisation does indeed fit comfortably within the stylistic envelope of the western musical vernacular of the late twentieth/early twenty-first centuries, in terms of the tonal and rhythmic frameworks that are used (level P.5.D). More than this, though, K utilizes a range of melodic devices that indicate a certain musical sophistication, including passing notes (in bars 15 and 16) and appoggiaturas (see bar 25), as well as elements redolent of the Blues style, in particular the flattened third, first introduced in bar 10.[15]

Conclusion

There are three main findings that can be drawn from the analysis of K's musical interaction with AO.

First, it appears that the zygonic approach may indeed be of value in interrogating certain aspects of the ebb and flow of musical interaction involving two participants or more in the context of music education or therapy sessions involving improvisation. Although labour-intensive at this stage, key elements in this type of analysis could be automated, leaving the practitioner/researcher to check and refine the data gathered using an appropriate computer programme. The techniques set out here could be used more widely to support the assessment of certain aspects of children's music-making in relation to the Sounds of Intent framework—informing the aggregation of a bank of comparative data that would enable individual efforts to be contextualized. Clearly, this may be of benefit to music therapists and educationists seeking to evaluate the effect and effectiveness of their interactions with children with disabilities and other special needs. Moreover, as music-analytical techniques such as those used here are further developed, it is interesting to postulate the extent to which the scrutiny of the purely musical elements of an improvisation with two people or more may shed light on aspects of broader personality and human relationships—including the capacity and willingness for imitation, resistance to change, resilience, and so on.

Second, there are findings of significance in relation to K's evolving musicality. For example, it is evident that, within a familiar style, she can grasp a repeating pattern of harmonies and create material that not only conforms to what is provided but develops and extends it, structurally and expressively. However, there is a lack of thematic correspondence between voice and accompaniment that may have arisen as a consequence of the considerable musical skill and experience that are needed to attend to someone else's contribution

---

[15] Although this is hinted at by AO in bars 5 and 6.

and remember it at the same time as creating material oneself. More broadly, the fact that certain common approaches to the logical connection of material are not used and the concomitant absence of a deeper structure may be specific to this improvisation or could indicate where future avenues of K's learning may lie. Although K has evidently achieved a great deal by dint of her own efforts, it is also clear that there is much more that remains to be done, and she would undoubtedly benefit from working with a teacher willing to engage with her musical interests, able to guide her development, and with the capacity to work flexibly with her in extending her musical horizons.

Third, K's ability to construct a mature musical narrative that is at once both expressive and coherent, drawing upon a range of stylistically appropriate music-syntactical techniques, appears to show an exceptional level of musical ability.[16] However, her efforts should be contextualized in the knowledge that, as we saw in Chapter 8, precocious musical talent may well be unusually prevalent in young children with SOD who are blind (Ockelford 2003; Pring and Ockelford 2005) and more widely among the severely visually impaired population (Miller and Ockelford 2005; Ockelford, Pring, Welch, and Treffert 2006; Ockelford, Welch and Pring 2005)—irrespective of other disabilities they may have (Ockelford 1998b). K's improvisation supports these and other findings (for example, Ockelford and Pring 2005; Ockelford 2007b) that the essential elements of advanced musical understanding, many of which are typically conceptualized and codified in the process of music education, can develop and thrive at a purely intuitive level. The enduring message for researchers and teachers alike is the capacity of the mind to absorb and intuitively utilize sophisticated musical strategies with no formal tuition at all—an issue considered in depth in the chapter that follows.

---

[16] The extent to which her verbal improvisation is typical, both in its own right and in relation to the music, are the potential subjects of future research.

Chapter 10

Fragments of genius

Introduction: uneven profiles of musical development

Creating, controlling, and causing sounds through the exploration of sound-makers, including the voice and musical instruments, are activities of potential relevance and interest to the great majority of children and young people with complex needs, including many of those who are in the earliest stages of development (cf. Ockelford 1998*b*: 44 ff.). However, competence in areas such as musical performance, improvisation, and composition—in the sense of having the capacity to plan and reproduce series of sounds faithfully to an inner intention, in emulation of what is heard, or through instruction (implying functioning at levels 5 or 6 of the Sounds of Intent framework) is characteristic of rather fewer pupils with severe intellectual impairments. Making music in this sense requires a cluster of abilities, including a sufficient level of auditory development to process pitch, rhythm, and other qualities of sound effectively; a range of motor skills, coordinated with what is heard; concentration, memory, imagination, and motivation; and, in many cases, an awareness of the presence and needs of others.

Certain of these qualities may be found in some young people with moderate learning difficulties, whose attainment in music is commensurate with their general level of functioning. For others with disabilities, however, the situation is more complicated since the attributes that together comprise 'musicality' may, to a certain extent, develop and function independently of each other and independently of other abilities, such as the capacity for using verbal language. Hence pupils may well have *uneven profiles of development*, both within the domain of music and more broadly.

Discrepancies between different areas of attainment may arise for a number of reasons. For example, a physical impairment may constrain the potential for technical accomplishment, vocally and instrumentally, while a hearing impairment may interfere with the evolution of auditory perception. Then, as we noted in Chapter 8, children and young people may develop an exceptional skill or skills in the context of learning disabilities—so called 'savants' (see, for example, Miller 1989).[1] Treffert (1989/2000: 15) defines two levels among

---

[1] Areas of savant skill include music (the most prevalent), art, mathematics, 'hyperlexia' (a

those with what he terms 'savant syndrome': 'talented savants', whose skills are remarkable only in relation to their disability; and 'prodigious savants', whose ability is spectacular by any standards. Nettelbeck and Young (1996: 52) additionally distinguish those with 'splinter skills', which reflect levels of competence only marginally above a person's general level of functioning. However, while these discrete categories may have a certain conceptual value, experience suggests that savants' skills are better regarded as existing on a number of continua (Ockelford 2000), as the following descriptions show.

Descriptions of six savants

A (21, male—LCA—blind with moderate learning difficulties) plays a number of instruments, including the recorder, clarinet, saxophone and piano. His speciality, however, is percussion, particularly the timpani, drum kit and vibraphone, on which he performs to a high standard. He has performed widely in youth orchestras and bands, and has a wide knowledge of western classical and popular music. A has a truly remarkable ear, with a highly refined sense of AP that functions effectively whatever the source of sound, and enables him to hear how the most complex harmonies are made up. Both his short-term and long-term memory are outstanding. For example, he was able to learn a Debussy *Arabesque* on the piano by hearing the music only once (a page at a time). However, A finds it difficult to reproduce what he can hear in his head on the keyboard, where his efforts tend to be rather uncoordinated. Hence having learnt the *Arabesque* aurally in a short space of time, he then spent many weeks practising it from memory, and was never able to achieve (for him) a satisfactory standard of performance. A enjoys improvising and composing in a wide range of styles. He has a rudimentary knowledge of music theory and terminology, though he cannot read music.

B (6, male, partially sighted—unknown medical condition—with moderate learning difficulties and right hemiplegia) plays chords on the keyboard with the left hand alone, to accompany songs and other pieces performed by others. His harmonic repertoire is limited to basic diatonic combinations. His sense of AP functions in most musical contexts. His feeling for rhythm is secure within familiar idioms (largely rock 'n' roll). He usually learns pieces by listening to them several times over a period of a few days. B shows no interest in improvising or composing, and does not use conventional music terminology. He is unable to read music.

C (12, male, blind—SOD—with severe learning difficulties) can play the choruses of two pop songs on the piano that he taught himself over a long period of time—a single melody line in the right hand, and the bass in the left. He can sing along as he plays, and his performances are rhythmically secure. Both songs use diatonic notes only. C can

---

precocious ability to read words combined with a significant difficulty in understanding verbal language—for further details see, for example, <http://www.hyperlexia.org>) and 'calendrical calculation' (the ability to name the days of the week for dates in the past and future—see, for example, O'Connor, Cowan and Samella (2000); Rimland and Fein (1988: 478)).

recognize the notes of the scale of C major around the centre of the keyboard. He currently shows no ambition to extend his repertoire.

D (27, male, blind—ROP—with severe learning difficulties)[2] is a highly accomplished pianist, with a remarkable technique: despite idiosyncratic fingering, he is capable of great rapidity and freedom of movement around the keyboard. His extensive repertoire, which consists largely of light music of the twentieth century, jazz and pop, can be played with equal fluency and virtuosity in any key. D has performed extensively in public, in the UK, Europe, and the US. He has an exceptionally well-developed sense of AP, which enables him to identify pitches with a high degree of accuracy whatever their source, and reproduce large clusters of notes almost instantaneously. He can handle passages of considerable rhythmic complexity. D's approach to learning is examined in detail below, though he generally learns new material by listening to it repeatedly over a period of a week or more. During this time, renditions of pieces gradually 'come into focus'—D's version eventually becoming almost entirely faithful to the original, before serving as a framework for subsequent improvisation. Here he can display creativity and even wit, as different styles are merged. D has not composed original pieces, however. His knowledge of music theory is limited to the names of notes and those of simple chords. He is unable to read Braille music. (See Ockelford 1991; 2007a)

E (11, female, blind—SOD—with moderate learning difficulties) enjoys singing pop songs, which she learns relatively quickly, and performs by imitating the style of the original singers. She regularly appears in public. E has AP, which extends to most musical contexts. She is currently learning to accompany herself on the keyboard using basic chords, and already shows a facility for transposition. As yet, she has not improvised (vocally or instrumentally) or shown an interest in composing. She knows the names of the notes, but is unable to read music.

F (18, male, blind—ROP—with moderate learning difficulties, with a diagnosis of autism) performs simple classical pieces on the piano and improvises fluently on the blues harmonica. His sense of AP is confined to the middle range of the piano. He has a good grasp of basic musical concepts and terminology, and can read Braille music. F has an extensive knowledge of popular music of the last 40 years.

Commentary

These six people are in many ways typical of the population of musical savants as a whole—in so far as anyone within such an idiosyncratic group can be considered to be 'typical'. They are predominantly male (cf. Hill 1974, who reports a 6:1 male-to-female ratio in savants, based on accounts of 105 individuals); all are visually impaired (cf. Judd 1988: 137 ff., who in his summary of 18 cases notes that 10 are blind), with two cases of ROP (cf. Miller 1989: 33 and 34), two of SOD and one of LCA (see Chapter 8); and all have or have had

---

[2] Derek Paravicini—whose musical memory and creativity are described below.

difficulties with language, displaying echolalia,[3] verbalism,[4] overextension, and underextension,[5] or confusion with pronouns (cf. Webster and Roe 1998: 85 ff.).

Indeed, it has been suggested (for example, by Miller 1989: 193 ff.) that the failure of language to evolve adequately at a crucial stage in a child's early development may be a decisive factor in savants' acquisition of exceptional musical skills. It is supposed that music, which structurally shares some of the features of language (though not its semantic content), comes to function in some respects as a proxy for verbal communication in the auditory domain. This tendency may be exacerbated by visual loss, which, particularly in combination with learning difficulties, can hinder the development of semantic understanding, while fostering, nevertheless, an attention to sound as a potentially pleasing source of sensory stimulation (Ockelford 2005b: 64 and 65). Hence, where infants' neurological capacity for processing musical sounds is unimpaired, there is the distinct possibility of their developing a special interest in music, which, given severe sensory and intellectual constraints, can become obsessive. This theory is supported by the findings of Rimland (1978) who charts the age of onset of musical savant abilities. Most frequently, these manifest themselves at the age of 2, typically a period when expressive language begins to develop rapidly, while by the age of 4, two-thirds of those who are going to be savants are already showing exceptional abilities. However, the fact remains that the vast majority of children who have complex needs (including visual impairment) do not develop special musical skills—even when music features prominently in the environment.

It may be that the overriding issue in savant development is simply the strength of a child's determination to make music. It could be argued that savants are astonishing not so much in terms of what they can do, but on account of the fact that, in the vital early stages, they typically learn to do it entirely by dint of their own efforts. D, for example, at the age of 2, against seemingly impossible odds—with only a very limited understanding of what he was doing, and no visual model to guide him; with no external incentive, no assistance, and no purposeful language—began to teach himself to play the piano. By the time he was 4 his aural development had already out-stripped that of most adults, and he could play the piano fluently, if somewhat

---

[3] Repeating words or phrases, often with little or no regard for their meaning—see Andersen, Dunlea, and Kekelis (1984).

[4] Using words or phrases for the sake of their sounds rather than their semantic content.

[5] Respectively, imbuing words with too many meanings or too few.

chaotically, capable of playing by ear anything that was within the reach of his small hands (and, as we shall see, his elbows!).

Given key similarities in their paths of musical development, to what extent do functional commonalities exist between these highly individual people? According to Treffert (1989/2000: 16) *memory* provides a common thread that runs through all savant skills, and it is indeed an important factor in all the six cases outlined. However, there are important interpersonal differences: only *A* appears to have the auditory equivalent of 'eidetic' memory (that has been a part of savant folklore ever since Mark Twain took an interest in Blind Tom in 1869)[6]—being able to recall long and complex passages of music after just one hearing. The remaining five rely on their ability to remember pieces—often, for sure, a substantial repertoire—in the long term. Just how short-term and long-term memory function and interrelate in *D*'s case is considered later in this chapter.

Then, the six savants' motor skills vary considerably, from *D,* who has an exceptional technical facility on the keyboard, to *B* who has only limited powers in his left hand. The savants differ in their musical interests, too, in the instruments they play (although the piano or keyboard are most usual), and in the contexts in which they prefer to utilize their skills. Some enjoy public performance, and indeed show a remarkable sense of occasion, while others are content to play for themselves. The savants show a varying sensitivity to musical structure in performance—some, such as *C*, appearing to be more 'mechanical', while others, like *E*, being capable of highly expressive performances. Some can improvise or compose, while others show little or no interest in generating new material. The savants' knowledge of musical terminology and concepts, while generally limited, varies significantly. Only one (*F*) reads music, and all learn by ear more or less effectively, greatly assisted, in every case, by having AP. However, the extent of this ability varies from one savant to another in terms of range and the types of sound for which it functions.

Similarly, the effectiveness with which the individual notes that make up chords can be detected—a key skill in reproducing music aurally that has more than one part—differs from one savant to another. Although the differences between some people's chordal disaggregation abilities are immediately apparent in everyday musical situations (such as playing the piano by ear), with others, whose music-perceptual skills are exceptional by any standards (*A* and *D* in the examples given above), the precise extent of their auditory processing powers (and therefore possible differences between them) can be hard to discern. This aspect of their music-perceptual make-up could only be evaluated

---

[6] See <http://www.twainquotes.com/archangels.html>.

through systematic investigation, and it is to this area that we now turn our attention.

Researching savants' abilities 1: disaggregating chords

Since it is such an important element in a prodigious savant's battery of musical abilities, a study was recently undertaken[7] to ascertain, in the first instance, just how many simultaneous notes A and D were able to perceive as distinct entities in a variety of harmonic contexts. The experiment used a 'listen and play' protocol, whereby 20 four-, five-, six-, seven-, eight-, and nine-note chords were created for each of the savants to hear in turn and reproduce as accurately as they could. The chords ranged from simple diatonic harmonies to chords of the seventh, ninth, eleventh, and thirteenth with a range of chromatic inflexions;[8] to polytonal aggregates reminiscent, for example, of certain compounds used in Stravinksy's *Rite of Spring*, and clusters of major and minor seconds, that to most people would appear to be little more than noise (see Ex. 10.1).

The chords were recorded digitally for the experiment using a Korg SP-200 88 note touch-sensitive hammer action keyboard linked via MIDI to a laptop computer, monitored through Edirol MA-10A speakers. Each had a duration of one second, separated by nine seconds of silence from the next chord in the series.

The chords were played to A and D in separate sessions using the same equipment, in batches of 20, after which breaks were offered (though these were declined). Each savant was asked to copy what he heard as accurately he could. This approach was adopted because previous observation had indicated that D could not reliably assign pitch labels to clusters of notes, even though he could play them back with startling immediacy and, it seemed, accuracy. For the purposes of comparison, an experienced jazz pianist with AP, used to playing by ear, 'S', also undertook the test, under the same conditions.

The accuracy of the renditions was ascertained through the production of a score using *Finale* music notation software, supplemented with video and audio recordings. To date, only a preliminary analysis has been undertaken, using a simple scoring system, whereby each correct pitch receives one mark, and the number of marks per chord is treated as a proportion of the maximum possible. Additional notes have been ignored.[9] Examples of nine-note chords (produced by D) are shown in Ex. 10.2.

---

[7] By Linda Pring, Katherine Woolf, Evangelos Himonides, and me.

[8] That is, more complex, dissonant combinations.

[9] It is intended to adopt a more sophisticated approach for the more refined analyses using zygonic theory that will be published in due course. However, the method used here is adequate for the task in hand, and provides useful indicative results.

The results for *A, D,* and *S* for each chord size were as follows. As the linear trend lines indicate, the performance of all three subjects deteriorated as the number of notes per chord increased, although in *D*'s case the reduction was on average slighter (around 1.5 per cent per additional note from a starting point of no errors) and less predictable than *A*'s (whose performance declined by approximately 4 per cent for each note added from an initial score of 99 per cent). *S*'s pattern of responses differed noticeably from those of both savants: beginning with a success rate of just over 80 per cent for four-note chords, the accuracy of his efforts diminished by about 6 per cent for every increase in chord size. Hence with the nine-note chords, he was achieving little more than a 50 per cent success rate.[10] (See Fig. 10.1)

In one sense, these findings are straightforward: two prodigious savants appear to be able to disaggregate simultaneous sounds of the same timbre (that for the great majority of listeners would blend into a single, homogeneous harmonic percept) more effectively than a professional musician with AP. Moreover, the auditory capacities of the savants themselves apparently differ—particularly with chords with seven notes or more.[11] However, informal observations made during the experiments suggest that there is more to be gleaned about the strategies each subject used and their attitudes to the task.

For example, *D*'s responses were made without hesitation and, indeed, with a certain relish, it seemed to the researchers. After a few chords that were played 'straight', he started to arpeggiate the simultaneous clusters of notes that he had heard and then began noodling playfully on each harmony in the few seconds that were available before the next stimulus sounded. This led to him being asked on a few occasions to 'copy *exactly* what he heard', which had the effect of temporarily curtailing his musical peregrinations. With regard to scoring *D*'s efforts, his miniature improvisations were not taken into account.

---

[10] These data do not take into account the potentially confounding effects of chance (clearly, the greater the number of pitches per chord within a limited range, the higher the probability of striking a correct note at random) nor of the limitations of fingering (once a finger is assigned to a note on the keyboard, the range of other notes that are within reach is limited).

[11] Paired sample t-tests (between *D* and *A, D* and *S,* and *A* and *S*) indicate significant differences between each of the subjects in relation to the entire series of chords. With four-, five-, and six-note chords, there are no significant differences between the performances of *D* and *A*; with seven-, eight-, and nine-note chords, the difference in performance between *D* and *A* is significant. The performances of each of the savants and *S* differ significantly in relation to each chord size.

Ex. 10.1 The chords used in the pitch disaggregation experiment

Ex. 10.1 Cont.

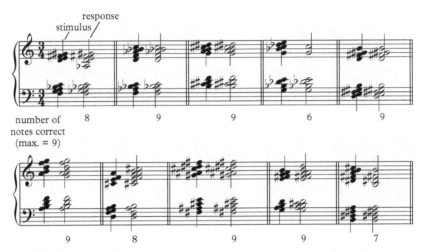

Ex. 10.2 Examples of *D*'s responses

D showed no signs of fatigue or loss of concentration over the 20 minutes or so in which the 120 chords were played, amounting to some 780 individual stimuli.

A, with a greater level of general awareness and understanding, followed the instructions he was given more faithfully, with no musical digressions.

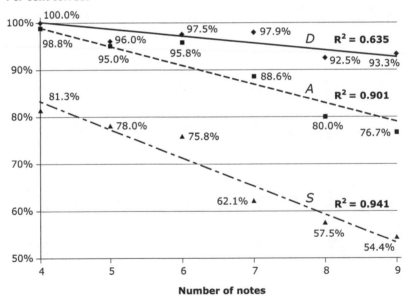

Fig. 10.1 Trends in the ability to disaggregate chords increasing in size for *D*, *A*, and *S*

However, given a keyboard technique that was less fluent than *D*'s, it was clearly an effort for him to get his fingers over the right notes in time. Observing him in action, it appeared to the researchers that *A* was physically groping to recreate the sounds that he could evidently continue to hear in his head for some seconds at least after the stimulus had ceased. In fact, on more than one occasion, he was still striving for the correct combination of notes when the next chord sounded. Hence, in scoring *A*'s responses (unlike *D*'s), it was largely the *last* thing he played each time that was taken to be his intended response. It was the researchers' belief that, with more time, *A* could have achieved better results, and that problems of coordination gave only a restricted view of his auditory processing capacity.

S was alone in being able to reflect verbally on the task and the strategies he employed as the increasing number of notes per chord evidently made things more and more difficult for him. He described how he attended primarily to the top and bottom notes and subsequently 'fitted in' the middle ones as best he could.[12] This strategy became more difficult to implement with the large clusters, however, when the top note (in particular) was difficult to disembed from those immediately adjacent to it. *S*'s account is borne out by the quantitative analysis shown in Table 10.1, which summarizes the accuracy of responses in relation to the positions of notes within chords.

The data show *S*'s reliance on the outermost pitches in all but the largest chords, when his performance diminished throughout the range. Nonetheless, across the entire series of 120 chords, he reproduced the lowest notes most consistently, followed by the highest, with the inner parts lagging some way behind. Interestingly, this pattern was only partly in evidence in the savants' intuitive efforts: they played the top notes correctly less often than those in the middle. With *D*, his habit of 'rolling' the chords up from the bass (he invariably replicated the bottom notes of the stimuli without error)[13] meant that he occasionally 'ran out of fingers' by the time he got to the top. And although *A* did not intentionally arpeggiate his responses in the same way, a comparable strategy is evident, with his faultless realization of all the bottom notes. As with *D*, he consistently reproduced the inner parts better than the notes that were topmost in the chords (where his average score was slightly lower than *S*'s).

---

[12] The same approach was described by a further control—*Y*—who subsequently tried a similar exercise (though with insufficient trials for purposeful analysis).

[13] He did, however, add notes *below* the given bass from time to time—additions that are ignored in this analysis.

Table 10.1 The differing importance of the position of pitches within chords to the three subjects (%)

Subject	Relative position	Number of notes per chord						Mean
		4	5	6	7	8	9	
D	Top notes	100.0	87.5	95.0	95.0	80.0	90.0	**91.3**
	Bottom notes	100.0	100.0	100.0	100.0	100.0	100.0	**100.0**
	Middle notes	100.0	97.5	97.5	98.1	93.3	92.8	**96.5**
	Overall	**100.0**	**96.0**	**97.5**	**97.9**	**92.5**	**93.3**	**96.2**
A	Top notes	98.0	88.0	95.0	75.0	45.0	62.5	**77.3**
	Bottom notes	100.0	100.0	100.0	100.0	100.0	100.0	**100.0**
	Middle notes	99.0	95.7	95.0	89.0	82.5	75.4	**89.4**
	Overall	**98.8**	**95.0**	**95.8**	**88.6**	**80.0**	**76.7**	**89.2**
S	Top notes	100.0	100.0	95.0	75.0	50.0	45.0	**77.5**
	Bottom notes	95.0	95.0	100.0	80.0	75.0	55.0	**83.3**
	Middle notes	99.0	65.0	65.0	55.9	55.8	55.7	**66.1**
	Overall	**81.3**	**78.0**	**75.8**	**62.1**	**57.5**	**54.4**	**68.2**

Overall, the data strongly suggest that even the nine-note chords did not define the limits of the savants' abilities—particularly *D*'s (Derek's)—and the opportunity to informally test him further came in the course of filming for CBS's *60 Minutes* television programme that was aired in the United States in 2005. As the account of the programme on the CBS website puts it:

Ockelford keeps trying to figure out how Derek's brain processes music. Most people—musicians included—can make out about two or three notes at a time. Ockelford devised a test to see how many notes Derek could hear at once, and then repeat. Stahl[14] gave the test to Derek, initially playing four notes at the same time. Derek was able to instantly play back all notes. Next, Stahl played Derek 10 notes at the same time, which sounded like noise. Derek was able to repeat that too.

'Derek's hearing a different sound world. For us, we can perhaps hear the melody and the bass and the drums. But he can actually hear 10 different instruments at once. That's incredible,' Ockelford said.

But even though he could repeat exactly what Stahl played, when asked to count the notes, Derek was lost. Stahl played a four-note chord and Derek said, 'Two, is it one, is it?'

'He could separate the notes out … and yet, he couldn't tell me how many. He couldn't even tell me there were four,' Stahl said.

'That really shows Derek's brain in action, doesn't it?' Ockelford said.[15]

---

[14] Lesley Stahl, the presenter of the segment.

[15] See 'The Mysterious Gift of Musical Savants' at <http://www.cbsnews.com/stories/2006/06/12/60minutes/main1703281_page5.shtml>.

Derek's brain was certainly in action as he reproduced the two ten-note chords that Lesley Stahl played for him—both with 90 per cent accuracy, and therefore very much in line with the trend identified in Fig. 10.1. Accordingly, it seemed very likely that his ability to disaggregate chords is greater than this, and more than his ten fingers allow him to display. Derek's habit of arpeggiating chords appeared to offer a way forward, however, since by playing notes as a series that he had heard simultaneously, his digital limitations could be circumvented. And in a television documentary that was made about him in 2006,[16] Derek reproduced chords played by a full symphony orchestra with no hesitation, by scurrying up and down the keyboard. Although these efforts await formal analysis, it was clear to the many musicians who were present that Derek's efforts accorded perfectly with what they were playing—though (as with the earlier chord experiments) he did not appear to be limited by only what he heard, gleefully embellishing on the 20 to 30 distinct parts that were sounding.

There is no doubt that the remarkable speed and ease with which Derek can process extensive aggregations of simultaneous notes is a huge benefit to him in playing by ear. This highly unusual perceptual skill is necessary though not in itself sufficient to enable him to assimilate pieces so efficiently by ear in the way that he does, however, and further experiments were undertaken—and are planned for the future—to explore other elements in his array of musical abilities. An account of one of these follows.

Researching savants' abilities 2: Derek and the 'Chromatic Blues'

The experiment described here forms part of the 'REMUS' Project—'Researching Exceptional MUsical Skill'—which is a joint initiative of the Royal National Institute of Blind People, the Psychology Department of Goldsmith's College, and the School of Arts and Humanities at the Institute of Education, University of London.[17] The study is one of a series that aims to glean new insights into the nature of savants' musical ability, in particular learning, memory, reproduction, and creativity, and to use these findings to generate models of the mental processing involved, adopting a fusion of music-psychological and music-theoretical approaches (see Chapter 4). The

---

[16] Entitled 'The Musical Genius'; see <http://www.five.tv/programmes/extraordinary people/musicalgenius>.

[17] Led by Adam Ockelford, Linda Pring, and Graham Welch.

underlying methodological assumption is that the musical pieces and fragments that savants produce following exposure to controlled musical input—
specifically the extent to which their responses can be considered to derive
from the stimuli with which they are presented—provide powerful evidence of
the underlying cognitive processes.[18] That is, the research assumes (and hopefully demonstrates) that it is reasonable to deduce the latter from the former.
It is intended that the findings will be used to underpin new didactic
approaches in working with savants (and others)—and the first steps towards
this are taken in the final section of this chapter.

Initially, four experiments were planned with Derek, based upon the ways in
which he was known to learn pieces. It is not intended that these four
approaches should give a complete account of Derek's usual means of learning: indeed, in order to facilitate comparison, they were designed not to
involve direct intervention of a didactic nature. However, the experimental
conditions were meant to be as natural as it was reasonably possible to make
them—a crucial factor in research with savants where ecological validity is
often necessary to obtain representative and meaningful results.

The four conditions are as follows:

- 'Listen and play' (described in detail here).
- 'Just listen' (in which Derek hears a piece twice in each of two sessions per
  week, but does not attempt to play it until the eighth session).
- 'Play along' (in which Derek plays at the same time as listening to a piece,
  to be played twice in each of two sessions per week, and his progress monitored).
- 'A bit at a time' (in which Derek hears and copies successive fragments of a
  piece in each of two sessions per week, his progress being monitored).

A piece was especially composed for the 'Listen and play' experiment and
given a name that Derek would find memorable: the *Chromatic Blues*. It was
important to create new material because it is difficult to find pieces that one
can safely assume that Derek has not heard before (and he is not able to say
consistently whether he knows a piece or not just by being told its title).
Moreover, it was felt that composing an original piece would make it easier to
create others of comparable style, complexity, and length for the subsequent
experimental conditions, thereby offering some equivalence between them.
The following criteria were used to inform the composition of *Chromatic Blues*

---

[18] Cf. John Sloboda (2005: pp. vi and vii), who writes of the 'core psychological tradition,
where overt human behaviour is the central form of data, and explanatory frameworks
are developed in primarily intentional and functional terms'.

(determined through the researchers' awareness of repertoires with which Derek is known to be acquainted, and informal accounts of his memory and technical ability).

- The style should be broadly familiar to Derek.
- There should, in addition, be specific features that were unusual within the style, offering higher degrees of salience.
- The piece should be of sufficient difficulty for Derek to find it challenging though possible to learn after a number of hearings, given its complexity, tempo and length.
- It should be well within his capacity to play, so that technical considerations should not interfere with issues of music-processing.

Created within all these constraints, *Chromatic Blues* took the form shown in Ex. 10.3.

The piece was recorded digitally using the same equipment and software as that employed for the chord experiment (see p. 218 above).

Statistically, it comprises 312 events that occur within 49 seconds (an average rate of 6.37 events per second). Structurally, *Chromatic Blues* may be represented as shown in Table 10.2.

The 'Listen and play' experiment with Derek was conducted over 13 sessions, spaced over two years. It is just the first session that we will be concerned with here, which was run according to the following protocol:

- Derek was asked to listen carefully to the recording of the *Chromatic Blues* being played.
- Derek was asked to play the *Chromatic Blues* as well as he could. Derek was thanked, but with no evaluative comment.
- Derek was asked to listen carefully to the recording of the *Chromatic Blues* again.

In order to bring the amount of data for subsequent analysis within readily manageable proportions, only excerpts were transcribed from most of Derek's responses: bars 0.4 to 2.3[19] ('Excerpt 1'), 4.4 to 6.4 ('Excerpt 2'), 8.4 to 10.3 ('Excerpt 3'), 12.4 to 14.4 ('Excerpt 4'), and 18.3 to 20.4 ('Excerpt 5').[20]

---

[19] That is, from the opening anacrusis to the third beat of the second bar.

[20] In later renditions, which closely resembled the original, there was no ambiguity as to which bars corresponded to which. However, Derek's earlier versions did not consistently bear such self-evident correspondence with the original, and decisions regarding which bars to transcribe (and so subsequently to compare) were made (a) on their relative position within the rendition and (b) on their strength of derivation from corresponding excerpts in the original (judged in the manner set out below).

Ex. 10.3 Piece composed especially for Derek to learn

These excerpts were chosen by the researchers since they were felt to be representative of the *Chromatic Blues* as a whole, varying in salience according to their position within the piece (which included the beginning and the end), their musical complexity and perceived stylistic conformity. Also, Excerpt 1 was identical to Excerpt 3 in the original, while Excerpt 4 was a transposed version of Excerpt 2, enabling subsequent internal comparisons to be drawn within each rendition. Transcriptions were undertaken by one of the researchers based on the automated notation available from the MIDI files which were checked aurally using the digital audio data.

Ex. 10.4 shows Derek's first rendition.

In order to use transcripts such as these to gain an understanding of Derek's musical mind in action, the crucial question is: where does he obtain his material? Hence the first stage of analysis was to evaluate the *strength of derivation*[21] of each of the five excerpts (listed above) from:

- their probable source in the original (where there was doubt, the most similar excerpt was chosen, consistent with its location relative to the other excerpts); and
- their probable source in Derek's rendition (where passages were repeated or transposed).

The perceived strength of derivation cannot be measured just by examining the physical qualities of sound since it is ultimately a subjective measure, which is determined in part by musical and in part by non-musical factors.[22] In the case of the *Chromatic Blues*, it was decided that the strength of derivation should be measured principally by considering pitch and rhythm. These variables were chosen because they were regarded as having the greatest salience in the task that Derek was asked to undertake.[23]

---

[21] The notion of 'strength of derivation'—similar to the concept of 'derivation indices' used in Chapter 9—combines the concepts of 'salience' (Ockelford 2004) and 'zygonicity', which was developed in the context of pitch-set analysis to give some measure of the perceived similarity of musical groups of events (see p. 137; Ockelford 2005a).

[22] An example in relation to *Indian Love Call* is described below (p. 239).

[23] It is planned to examine other characteristics such as loudness, tempo, and rubato in other studies.

Table 10.2 Structure of the *Chromatic Blues*

Segment	$A_{1.1}$	$B_{1.1}$	$A_{2.1}$	$B_{2.2}$	C
Function	**Theme A** exposition	**Theme B** exposition	**Theme A** reprise	**Theme B** transposed, modified	**Coda**
Tonal regions	I→(V of ii)	♭VII→V	I→(V of ii)	♭III→V	I
Range (beat.bar)	0.4–4.3	4.4–8.3	8.4–12.3	12.4–18.3	18.4–20.4
Excerpts analysed	Excerpt 1 0.4–2.3	Excerpt 2 4.4–6.4	Excerpt 3 8.4–10.3	Excerpt 4 12.4–14.3	Excerpt 5 18.4–20.4

The algorithm that was used for determining the strength of derivation of one excerpt from another is set out in the footnote below.[24] In essence, this considers each note separately in relation to pitch and rhythm and asks: 'to what extent (if at all) can this be deemed to derive from the corresponding note in the 'source' excerpt'? This analysis is undertaken in relation to three textural strands—the melody (at the top), the inner parts (considered as a single item) and the bass-line—reflecting the way that the piece was constructed (and in line with the investigation into chordal disaggregation—see p. 224

---

[24] The strength of derivation of rhythm is determined as follows. Align the two series of 'onset + duration' events to ensure maximal congruence. 'Onset + duration' events may be omitted from either series, provided that their sequence is not compromised. If an 'onset + duration' pair is omitted, the following onset can be measured from the next most recent event to have occurred, or, in the case of two onsets or more, from a new 'data zero'. For each match count 1. For an incorrect duration but correct onset, count 0.5. Total score = $\#Z(R)$ (that is, the number of zygonic relationships of rhythm). Let the total number of sequential actual and potential rhythmic relationships between excerpts = $\#Rel$. The total of score for strength of derivation of pitch is $ZYG(R)$ ('zygonicity' of rhythm), where $ZYG(R) = \#Z(R)/\#Rel$. The strength of derivation of pitch is similarly determined as follows. Align the two series of pitch events to ensure maximal congruence. Pitches may be omitted from either series, provided that their sequence is not compromised. For each match count 1. For an incorrect octave but correct pitch-class, count 0.5. Discounting exact or partial matches involving pitch-class, identify among any remaining pitch events intervallic matches. These must be between sequentially adjacent events; hence the minimum number of events involved in any intervallic match is two. For each event involved in an intervallic match, count 0.5. Total congruence score = $\#Z(P)$. Let the total number of sequential actual and potential pitch relationships between excerpts = $\#Rel$. The total of score for strength of derivation of pitch is $ZYG(P)$ ('zygonicity' of pitch), where $ZYG(P) = \#Z(P)/\#Rel$. The total of score for strength of derivation of pitch and rhythm is $ZYG(P+R)$ (zygonicity of pitch and rhythm), where $ZYG(P+R) = (\#Z(P)+\#Z(R))/(\#Rel.2)$.

Ex. 10.4 Derek's first rendition of the *Chromatic Blues*

above).[25] Inevitably, this method for calculating the 'strength of derivation' has limitations. For example, material that was originally heard in the bass may find its way into the inner parts of the reproduction, and the algorithm would only pick this up if movement *between* parts were treated as a special case. Overall, however, the results do appear to be intuitively as well as logically satisfying.

We are now in a position to build up a phenomenological account of Derek's rendition, beginning with the opening bars, using as evidence the data on derivation gleaned qualitatively or quantitatively from the transcription. This analysis will be used to construct hypotheses as to the nature of the mental processing underlying Derek's output.

In the first session, aspects of the opening of Derek's rendition can be considered to be derived in a straightforward way from the opening of *Chromatic Blues*, with events being reproduced in their original order. Rhythmically, for example, the origin of 80 per cent of Derek's material is attributable in this way, as opposed to 39 per cent in the domain of pitch: an average of 59 per cent. Hence a good deal of what Derek produces remains unaccounted for—a tendency which characterizes his rendition as a whole. Logically, the remaining material could either have been created afresh, or have stemmed from elsewhere in *Chromatic Blues* or from other pieces. Moreover, since material can be derived from a multiplicity of sources (Ockelford 2005*a*: 114), those features of his rendition that had direct sequential equivalents in *Chromatic Blues* may additionally have originated elsewhere.

These potential sources will now be considered in turn in relation to the opening bars. A music-analytical approach will be adopted, which seeks to identify relationships through which fragments of musical material can reasonably be considered to be derived from one another, according to the similarity and relative salience of the events concerned.[26]

---

[25] See also Huron and Fantini (1989); and Huron (2001), who give empirical evidence of our capacity to process a textural density of three auditory streams.

[26] An important factor in the current context is the researchers' detailed knowledge of Derek's repertoire, which informed the accounts of possible connections between pieces that follow. Clearly, this method, which relies so heavily on the intuitive judgements of people who know Derek well, has potential difficulties, in particular, a lack of objectivity. However, it is important to emphasize the status of the analyses that follow: they are only intended to be indicative of the *type* of musical connections that appear to be present (and therefore, as a further step to be taken in due course, of the *type* of cognitive processes that created them). This is as much as can be attained through current music-analytical techniques, which are, by nature, subjective. But, to reiterate, it is the *principles* they illustrate that are more important than the verifiability of any particular aspect of them. Methodologically the approach adopted here is comparable to that used, for example, by

With regard to material derived from elsewhere in *Chromatic Blues*, it appears that the first four bars were a particularly rich vein for Derek to tap. Analysis suggests that the transformational techniques he adopted included the reordering of material in the domain of pitch, whereby, for example, the contour of the *second* phrase (which begins in the same way as the first) was used at the *beginning* of his version (through relationship 'O'). This emphasizes the D major harmony that was particularly salient in the original (as it provided an unusual tonal goal for the second phrase of the melody) (see 'P'). In addition, the ascent in the bass-line from F to F sharp in bar 1 seems to echo the transition from C to D flat in the original, effectively transforming a highly unusual move this early in proceedings into one that (as we shall see) is stylistically commonplace ('Q'). Further reordering occurs as the descent to middle C that ends the first phrase is moved in Derek's rendition to the end of the second ('R'). In the domain of rhythm, the opening phrase (without the acciaccatura) is used twice, conferring a straightforward symmetry on proceedings that is not found in the original ('S'). Hence, it appears that in the process of creating his version, Derek separated elements of pitch and rhythm and resynthesized them to produce material that was closely related to the original, though distinct from it (see Fig. 10.2).

In parallel with these connections, it seems that Derek borrowed material from other pieces, both generally (through stylistic features) and specifically (from individual works; a technique that is characteristic of traditional jazz, as we noted above—see p. 210). Fig. 10.3 shows some of the potential strands of derivation that the researchers believe may have played a part in the formulation of the opening bars of Derek's first rendition of *Chromatic Blues*. For example, it is suggested that the first two bars of the bass-line in Derek's rendition derive from a standard bass riff (exemplified here in an excerpt from Count Basie's rendition of *The Dirty Dozens*, 1929) (through relationship 'T'), whose harmonic pattern also constitutes a widely used Blues 'turnaround' ('U'). Moreover, the bass-line and harmonies of the first four bars of Rendition 1 closely resemble those used in the chorus of *Paper Moon* ('V'). It is impossible to say the extent to which these pieces (with which Derek was known to be very familiar) and others that could be identified *actually* played a part in the creation of Rendition 1—though the probability of complex, integrated patterns of pitch and rhythm such as those identified resembling others by chance is statistically remote. In summary, then, Fig. 10.3 is intended to offer

---

John Livingston Lowes (1927) in his detailed investigation into the sources of Samuel Taylor Coleridge's imagery; as Margaret Boden points out (2004: 127), ' "evidence" and "probably" are the best we can expect in investigations of this kind'.

Fig. 10.2 Derivation of the opening material of Derek's first rendition from the opening bars of *Chromatic Blues*

an indicative and partial account, rather than one that is prescriptive or exhaustive.

How were these differing materials, culled from a diversity of sources, brought together within a new and coherent musical whole? In relation to the first four bars of Derek's rendition, the position may be summarized as follows (see Fig. 10.4). The pitch contour of the melody is based on the movement from middle C to the C an octave above, followed by a return to middle C

Fig. 10.3 Derivation of material from other sources

through approximate retrogression of the opening motif (through relationship 'W'). These two gestures are also connected through repetition, whereby the last two notes of the initial figure are used to kick off the second ('X'). This reiteration is mirrored in the bass-line with the movement from G to C and the harmonic shift from ii to V, together giving the effect of picking up from where the first gesture left off and then taking it in a new direction ('Y'). Rhythmically, the two halves are identical ('Z').

It is possible to synthesize musical fragments from a variety of sources in this way thanks to the 'chameleon' effect (Ockelford 2005*b*: 99 ff.), whereby

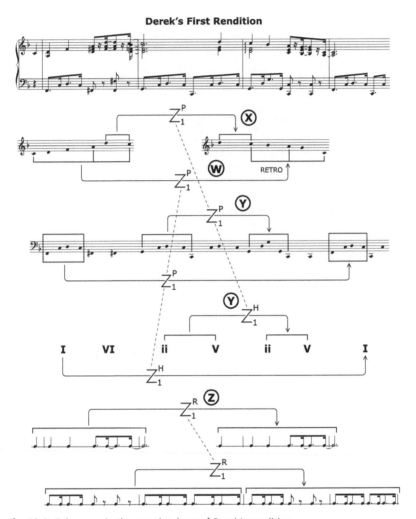

Fig. 10.4 Coherence in the opening bars of Derek's rendition

certain features of chunks of music can be modified without their identities being compromised, enabling them to coexist within a common framework of tempo, tonality, timbre, and loudness. Specifically, Derek adopts a tempo of 107 crotchet beats per minute (slightly faster than the ♩ = 100 of *Chromatic Blues*), and uses the same metrical framework (common time). Both *Chromatic Blues* and Rendition 1 utilize sets of context-specific transition probabilities in the domain of pitch that give the sense of the tonality of F major, and, broadly speaking, the feel of the 'Blues'.

The chameleon effect is one way in which the creation of the opening bars of Derek's rendition represents a balance of forces between the deployment of extant materials and the need for what is produced to make musical sense on a moment-to-moment basis. Inevitably, it is the latter that dominates, as (for example) the construction of the second melodic gesture illustrates. Having ascended an octave and arrived at the harmony G minor^{7}sus^4 (from F via D^7), the stylistically attuned ear would typically expect a melodic descent and a return to the tonic (F). To achieve this, Derek has to create a new link (the D–C taken from the end of the first phrase, setting in place a scalar motion which continues to the A) before being able to deploy a modified version of the ending of the first motif from *Chromatic Blues*.

The dominance of the internal forces of coherence becomes more and more evident as Derek's rendition progresses (see Ex. 10.4). For example, in *Chromatic Blues*, following the opening four bars, there is a highly chromatic passage (labelled 'B$_{1.1}$' in the structural analysis shown in Table 10.2). This is linked to opening ('A$_{1.1}$') via the pivot note D, which serves successively as the root of the D major harmony with which the opening section ends (in bar 4) and the third of the B flat major chord with which the chromatic sequence begins. However, in Derek's rendition, this link is not available since his first section ends on middle C. Hence, he was more or less compelled to take another tack (irrespective of whether he could remember what actually occurred at this point). What possibilities were open to him? Working within the constraint that he had to be as faithful as possible to the original, Derek did the musically obvious (perhaps the only) thing and returned to the opening for the source of his next swatch of material. However, given that he was aiming to emulate *Chromatic Blues* as far as he could, this left Derek with the structural difficulty of the need for contrast (including key change) at this juncture. His solution was to reharmonize the end of the first phrase in A minor, incorporating the stylistically unusual transition from D major (bars 5 and 6). The A minor tonality continues into the second phrase, at first through straightforward reharmonization (bars 6 and 7) but subsequently through transposition and modification of the melodic descent first heard in bar 3, yielding a more authoritative A minor cadence (bars 7 and 8).

At this point, Derek's solution to the problem of tonal contrast presented him with a further challenge. Structurally (following the *Chromatic Blues* model), a return to the opening is demanded, both tonally and thematically. Hence, within a very short space of time (beats 2 and 3 of bar 8) he needed the music to modulate from A minor to prepare for a return to F (through its dominant, C). This he achieved with a V-I sequence that continues into the reprise of the opening, logically binding the two sections together (through the series of harmonies D–G–C–F). Derek then repeated bars 1 to 4 (with only minor changes in detail), again utilizing the structure of *Chromatic Blues* divorced from its content. It is fascinating to think that Derek was presumably aware (at some level) that by repeating what he had first played in Rendition 1 he was inevitably producing something that—once more—was different from the original. But we can also assume that he intuitively knew that musically it made more sense to repeat an 'error' rather than to try for a more accurate recall of the opening theme at the second attempt.

At this juncture, then, Derek had produced a piece in the form $A_{1.1}$ $A_{1.2}$ $A_{2.1}$. In order to continue to follow the *Chromatic Blues* structural model—$A_{1.1}$ $B_{1.1}$ $A_{1.2}$ $B_{2.2}$ C—albeit approximately, a further version of A would be required, modified so as to produce an unambiguous sense of completion, with a strong perfect cadence in F major . . . and this is precisely what we get. The opening melody appears for a fourth time, but the feeling of forward motion engendered by the rocking motif in the bass is curtailed, replaced with spread chords. The impending sense of closure is reinforced by a move to the subdominant (B flat), which replaces the G minor harmony. Finally, within this four-bar section (functioning as '$A_{1.3}$' in structural terms) Derek's rendition nods in the direction of the coda of *Chromatic Blues*, through an additional perfect cadence in the final bar in which RH quaver triplets (incorporating blues notes) extend upwards to fifth octave F, while the bass reaches down two octaves. These similarities with the *Chromatic Blues* coda are sufficient to capture something of its spirit, capping the piece off through the injection of a new rhythm and texture. Once more, the legacy of the preceding phrase meant that some development of the original material was inevitable.

In summary, it is evident that the requirement for musical coherence in Derek's rendition produces a range of solutions, some of which appear to have been hastily constructed in response to moment-to-moment needs (such as the move to A minor in bar 6, and the return to F major in bars 8 and 9), while others suggest a greater degree of structural anticipation, such as the reduction in the level of activity in the final phrase initiated at its outset through the chords in bar 13. With regard to the derivation of material from *Chromatic Blues*, there is, as we have seen, significant use of both its content and structure in section $A_{1.1}$. In the following sections $A_{2.1}$ $A_{1.2}$ and $A_{1.3}$, however, only structural relationships are appropriated—although, inevitably, given the repetition in *Chromatic Blues*, this results in some of the original content being replicated too (as in section $A_{2.1}$). It is only in the final bar (the coda) that an unambiguous sense of derivation returns.

So what is the status of Derek's rendition in musicological terms? While the foregoing analyses show that its opening is made up of motivic threads and patches taken from other pieces (including the *Chromatic Blues*, with a strength of derivation based on the five excerpts set out in Table 10.2 of 31 per cent), it is evident from the first four bars alone that Derek has created an original piece. The rising pitch contour of the opening gesture, comprising intervals that increase arithmetically by semitones (a major second, minor third, major third, and perfect fourth),[27] is, as far as the REMUS researchers are aware, shared by only one other piece in the standard repertoire (*Indian Love Call* from *Rose Marie* by Friml), and here the rhythmic framework is very different.[28] That is to say, in the manner of typical of composers working in the western tradition, Derek has fashioned something new by borrowing, transforming, and recombining materials with which he is familiar. Hence it is reasonable to assert that he is genuinely 'creative' in a musical sense.[29]

What does this musicological analysis suggest to us about Derek's mental processing? What is it reasonable to infer? Clearly, it is important to acknowledge at once the methodological limitations inherent in this approach, to contextualize the validity of what follows. For example, while we can assume that the music Derek produced bore some relationship to his mental representations of *Chromatic Blues*, it would not be safe to presume that the mappings between model and product were exclusive or regular. That is, it seems highly likely—indeed, almost certain—that there were elements of the traces in Derek's memory that were never realized in sound. Partly, as we have seen, this situation will have arisen due to Derek's (unwitting) aim of producing something that was musically coherent based on imperfect recall. Beyond this, however, it will also have been the case that the motor processes required for the

---

[27] For psychomusicological considerations of this phenomenon, see Ockelford 1999: 517 and 2002*b*: 207; Narmour 2000: 364.

[28] A piece with which Derek was *not* familiar.

[29] The degree of novelty required to create an original piece of music is surprisingly small, as my analysis of Mozart's Piano Sonata K333 shows (see p. 66; Ockelford 2005*a*: 35 ff.). Here, a zygonic approach indicates that K333 shares with others of Mozart's piano sonatas, for example, an 86 per cent similarity in the distribution of relative note-lengths, a 92 per cent similarity in the distribution of inter-onset ratios, a 92 per cent similarity in the distribution of pitches, a 77 per cent similarity in the distribution of melodic intervals, and an 89 per cent similarity in the use of harmonies. Hence, in statistical terms, the sonatas are very closely related. Their originality lies in their moment-to-moment features, though even here the differences between pieces may be small, as the derivation of the opening of K333 from J. C. Bach's sonata op. 5 no. 3 testifies. In musicological terms, Mozart's *creativity* lay in his ability to craft something original within such tight stylistic constraints. Mozart's greatness as a composer—his musical genius—lay in his ability to have created something of lasting musical worth within such constraints. That is not a claim the researchers are seeking to make in relation to Derek. To assert that Derek is musically 'creative', it is sufficient to demonstrate that he is capable of producing abstract sonic artefacts that are '*new, surprising and valuable*' (Boden 2004: 1 and 256 ff.).

reproduction may have influenced what he played (through the use of purely kinaesthetic schemata that may have been triggered) and, indeed, that these same over-learnt motor patterns may have been the source of musical material that bore no direct auditory relationship to that contained in *Chromatic Blues*. Nonetheless, it can be argued that the music that Derek produced provides sufficient evidence for a number of reasonable assumptions to be made about the cognitive processing that lay behind his efforts.

We start by reaffirming the assumption, based on past experience of working with Derek, that, since he was requested to do so, he would have tried to make his version of *Chromatic Blues* as faithful as to the original as he could. It is reasonable to conclude that, because he did not reproduce the piece accurately, it lay beyond the capacity of his working memory. So what *did* he remember? And—just as importantly—what was he *not* able to recall? It is immediately apparent that what Derek did not do was to recreate *Chromatic Blues* sequentially up to a certain point and then stop (as would a computer with a buffer of limited capacity). As we observed above, in producing his rendition, at once an act of creation and reconstruction, he utilized specific items from the beginning and end of *Chromatic Blues*, higher-level structural attributes from the piece as a whole, and features (such as tempo and metre) that were present throughout. That is to say, he appears to have built up and stored a bundle of musical fragments and attributes from various locations in the original piece, of varying lengths, types and degrees of abstraction. With regard to the opening bars, for example (see Fig. 10.2), a *fragment* that was preserved in terms of both pitch and rhythm was the opening motif in the bassline. Subsequently (from the second half of the first bar) it was only the rhythm that was recalled accurately. An *attribute* that was stored was the tonality. Derek's *Chromatic Blues* memory bundle should not be conceived of as a collection of auditory traces (and their abstractions) laid down like rock strata, with no interaction, each layer consolidated at a certain point in time. Rather, it seems likely that the system dynamically evolved as *Chromatic Blues* unfolded, and continued to develop during his rendition (and in the period that followed).

These observations beg a number of questions. For example, why did certain items find their way into Derek's *Chromatic Blues* bundle and others (apparently) not? Under what conditions were the memories of items from other pieces stimulated? How did the process of 'creative reconstruction' work?

First, we consider the issue of the selection and storage of items in the bundle and their durability. The fact that *Chromatic Blues* apparently exceeded the capacity of Derek's working memory inevitably meant that there would have been competition among its elements, whereby some would be captured and retained while others would not. We may surmise that among the determining factors in this process were *salience*, including the immanent qualities of a particular item and how these related to the perceived attributes of surrounding stimuli in terms of similarities and differences (cf. Ockelford 2006a); *structure*, including the degree of internal regularity of an item which may permit its parsimonious encoding (Ockelford 1999: 115 ff.); *resilience*, the degree to which an item can retain its encoded identity among a welter of interference from rivals; and *reinforcement*, brought about through the repetition of items (see Ockelford 2004). It seems that these factors frequently took effect in combination. Consider, for example, the opening rhythmic motif in the right hand of *Chromatic Blues*, which Derek reproduced accurately (though without the grace note)—indeed, it forms the basis of much of his Rendition 1, being used eight times. We can assume this motif had particular salience, being among the first things that Derek heard, with no pre-stimulus interference; it had moderate rhythmic regularity that proved to be resilient in the face of competing post-stimulus input; and it was heard twice in the course of *Chromatic Blues*, offering reinforcement.

Second, we consider the manner in which memories of items from other pieces were stimulated. The indicative analysis in Fig. 10.3 suggests that memory traces were activated through the perception of new items with which they shared varying degrees of similarity, which were variously incomplete, which comprised perceptual features or the relationships between them (of varying degrees of abstraction—see Ockelford 2002b), which pertained to one piece or more, and which were in nature either 'veridical' (relating to particular episodes) or 'schematic' (relating to probability matrices—'style systems'— deriving from many such episodes) (Ockelford 2006a). Evidently, one memory trace was able to stimulate another (in the case of the Bass Riff and *Paper Moon*, for example), resulting in only an indirect relationship between features of *Chromatic Blues* and Derek's rendition. The process of stimulation was rapid and unthinking.

Third, how did the process of 'creative reconstruction' work? This can be understood using the analogy of a cognitive 'central processor' whose primary input was the auditory information deriving from the digital recording of *Chromatic Blues* and whose secondary input comprised Derek's memories of other pieces: fragments, attributes, and style systems. The two outputs were the imagined auditory trace of his rendition and the necessary motor instructions to realize this on the keyboard.[30] From Derek's rendition, we can surmise that

---

[30] Just how the motor output functioned, and how this and the auditory output interrelated, are major topics in themselves, and beyond the scope of this book.

the guiding principles under which the central processor operated were to produce something that made 'musical sense' that resembled, as far as possible, *Chromatic Blues*. In the case of potential conflict, the former would take precedence over the latter. From what Derek produced, it is evident that the central processor must have the capacity

- to hold fragments and attributes of varying types in readiness for use—both from immediate perceptual input and from the memory traces that this input may stimulate;
- to establish a multi-dimensional style system that is congruent with new and remembered elements;
- to select items or features from the available 'bank' that would fit with each other—albeit with modification—within the (evolving) style system;
- to transform these as necessary, through the addition, deletion, or modification of material;
- to synthesize the selected elements, integrating them 'vertically' (harmonically) and 'horizontally' (melodically) within the unfolding matrix of pitch and perceived time;
- to create new material within the style system, as required, to provide links between given material, to fill potential gaps and to ensure coherence; and
- to track and direct the musical narrative simultaneously at different levels to ensure both short- and longer-term coherence.

Remarkably, all these operations must occur in 'real time' as an improvisation proceeds, and in Derek's case appear to have taken place quite unwittingly, with no conscious thought on his part; certainly, afterwards, he was unable to reflect at all on what he had done.

What does the *Chromatic Blues* experiment tell us about Derek's abilities in relation to others'? First, it is evident the great majority of people—including most musicians—would not have the capacity to engage with the task in a meaningful way. To put this in context, consider an experiment undertaken by John Sloboda, in which eight musicians and non-musicians struggled to recall a short folk melody accurately even after six hearings (Sloboda 1985/2005) … and that was just a vocal line: remembering and reproducing *Chromatic Blues* is a far more difficult task in terms of its complexity (up to six notes at once, many of which are non-diatonic),[31] its length, and the requirement of reproducing what is heard on a keyboard.

---

[31] That is, in this case, lying outside the F major scale.

In order to obtain some sort of meaningful comparison, a jazz pianist with AP, used to learning by ear (subject '*S*' in the chord experiment) also undertook the *Chromatic Blues* experiment. Although the data have yet to be completely analysed, it is evident that Derek's performance is superior with regard to the speed and accuracy of his learning, though both pianists appear to have adopted similar creative approaches in order to 'make musical ends meet': modifying features and fragments of the *Chromatic Blues* material that *were* recalled in order ensure moment to moment coherence, as far as possible, within the overall constraint of trying to produce an accurate rendition. This suggests that both Derek and *S* used similar cognitive strategies in order to keep the music flowing.

In fact, evidence of real-time music-transformational abilities of this type occurs widely in children's vocal improvisation (see p. 95 above), suggesting that they are commonplace. For example, Ex. 10.5 shows the transcription of a spontaneous attempt to sing 'Happy Birthday' by a boy aged 3 years and 9 months ('*T*'). He misjudges the first contour—overshooting the initial leap—but then modifies the *second* phrase with the same degree of 'error' in order to maintain the rising pattern of pitch that leads the ear to the highest note of the piece, which occurs early in the third phrase. So, just as Derek's musical mind must have computed that, by starting the second phrase of his rendition with fifth octave D and C (Ex. 10.4), he was committing a surface 'error' in order to maintain the deeper level connection between the opening phrases, so *T*'s internal 'music processor' must similarly have preferred to adhere to structure rather than content in modifying phrase 2 of 'Happy Birthday' to follow logically from phrase 1—implying that he was functioning at level P.4 of the Sounds of Intent framework. That is to say, Derek's intuitive capacity for manipulating the elements of music during the act of creative reconstruction does not seem to differ qualitatively from the abilities that people typically possess. Apparently, what makes him stand out is the effectiveness with which he perceives musical stimuli, and the accuracy and rapidity with which he can realize these on the keyboard.

The important point, though, is that these skills have been *learnt* but not *taught*, tying in with a view held in the past by those struggling to come to terms with teaching those with learning difficulties that people such as Derek are 'ineducable'. However, in common with all the other six case studies cited

Ex. 10.5 Three year old's rendition of *Happy Birthday*

above, there is no doubt that Derek has benefited enormously from appropriate music-educational programmes over the years, and it is to this issue that the remainder of this chapter is devoted.[32]

Teaching pupils with special musical abilities and learning difficulties

Programmes of learning will be most successful if they take careful account of a pupil's profile of abilities and areas of need, both musically and in terms of general development. Music teachers may be able to obtain the necessary information from the accounts of others, as a result of tests, and through observation. They should bear in mind, though, that their initial interactions with a pupil—musical and otherwise—are likely to be skewed by lack of familiarity on both parts. It is important for them to appreciate too that those who first suspected a young person of having special musical abilities may well have made that judgement on the basis of limited relevant experience, and a pupil's skills and potential may have been exaggerated. Conversely, it is quite possible for exceptional talent to be underrated, or even to go unnoticed, when it springs up in the unexpected context of severe learning disabilities.

Since savants are almost invariably self-taught in the early stages, their patterns of learning often evolve distinctively and remain idiosyncratic. Some may have little or no concept of what it is to be 'taught' in the formal sense, nor understanding of the conventional roles of pupil and teacher, and their first music lessons may well comprise activities that they initiate. In these circumstances, teachers may necessarily begin simply by listening, waiting for an appropriate moment to offer comments or suggestions, or to communicate directly through music: playing or singing along discreetly, or imitating what is heard in any pauses that present themselves. Here, it can be beneficial for teacher and pupil each to have a similar instrument to play, since this assures an affinity in sound without compromising a child's personal space. Sharing an instrument may be an unfamiliar notion, as this account of my first attempt to teach Derek, having met him once before, shows (Ockelford 2007a)!

---

[32] Conversely, those with special musical abilities, whose motivation to attend to organized sound may be unusually strong, may derive particular benefit from programmes that use music to promote wider development and learning. For example, it may be especially appropriate to teach certain concepts through music (see pp. 119 ff.); sound-symbols (see Chapter 7) may be highly refined—particularly for pupils with absolute pitch; savants' memory for songs and other musical material may be valuable in a range of contexts (see, for example, pp. 113 ff.); and their capacity for performance may foster the development of social skills (pp. 139 ff.).

As I had done at Linden Lodge, I reached forward and this time as gently as I could, started to improvise a bass-line below what he was doing. The notes were barely audible to me, but Derek was on to them immediately. His left hand shot down to where my fingers had trespassed, shooed the intruders away with a flick, and instantly picked up from where I had left off.

Round 1 to Derek.

Leaving my chair, I walked round to the other side of the piano and started improvising an ornamented version of the tune high up—as far away as I could from his right hand. In a flash he was there again, pushing my hand out of the way. Then once more he began imitating what I had just played before extending it to fit in with the changes in harmony.

End of Round 2, and Derek was clearly ahead on points.

Still, by following me to the extremes of the keyboard, he had left the middle range of notes temporarily exposed and, surreptitiously leaning over Derek's shoulders, with a feeling of mischievous triumph, I started to add in some chords. My victory was short-lived, however. Without for one moment stopping what he was doing, he tried to push me away with the back of his head. This time, though, I was minded to resist.

'Do you mind if I join in, Derek?'

My words fell on deaf ears. Ignoring me, he pushed with increasing force, all the time continuing to play. His message was unequivocal, so I decided to let him have his own way. For now. As soon as the coast was clear, his hands darted back to the middle of the piano, to fill in the chords that were now missing, before scampering outwards again to catch up with the abandoned tune and bass-line.

'You need an extra hand, Derek,' I joked, as in my mind I conceded Round 3 to him. By a knockout.

As teachers respond musically to their new pupil, they need to pay scrupulous attention to how he or she in turn reacts to them. Doubling the melody as the child plays may be tolerated, for example, but not deviating substantially from it. An open-minded, flexible approach is most likely to succeed, with teachers prepared to modify their input to accommodate a pupil's potentially roving musical focus. By providing an arresting model of musical responsiveness, the aim is to encourage pupils to evolve a sensitivity to the direction that others are taking, and a willingness to follow their lead. By stimulating the aural imagination of pupils—even tantalizing them with novel harmonies and rhythms that are currently beyond their grasp—the hope is that they will be fired with enthusiasm to explore new and exciting musical territories.

Matters of technique are likely to present a particular challenge, especially for those working with savants who have previously taught themselves, for in the likely absence of vision, and with limited understanding, aspects of their playing may well be unconventional. For example, Derek, aged 4, with very small hands but a huge determination to play the complex musical textures he could resolve aurally, used his wrists and even his elbows on occasions to play notes that would otherwise have been beyond his reach.[33] The main melodic line was typically placed in the middle of the texture and picked out with the thumbs, giving it a characteristic percussive prominence.

While technical idiosyncrasies such as these are ultimately neither 'right' nor 'wrong', certain methods of playing undoubtedly enable performers to fulfil their musical aims more effectively than others—indeed, some passages may even be rendered impossible unless a particular fingering (for example) is adopted. However, the prospect of changing aspects of a savant's technique, which may have evolved wholly intuitively, can be daunting too. Children with severe learning difficulties may have little capacity to reflect consciously on what they do, and lack the receptive vocabulary to make description or analysis of their efforts meaningful. Moreover, the challenges they face may be compounded with physical disabilities. Hence teachers may opt for compromise: seeking to modify a pupil's technique only where it is judged to be essential; adopting, where appropriate, an evolutionary rather than a radical approach to change; and, in a positive way, acknowledging and accepting the effects on performance—technically, stylistically, and in terms of repertoire—that a child's disabilities may have.[34]

Because of savants' likely visual, cognitive, and language impairments, where technique is to be developed, teachers may have to rely to a great extent on demonstration (rather than explanation).[35] This may be based on the pupil seeing, feeling, or listening to what is going on, or a combination of the three. Partially sighted children and young people, for example, may be able to learn effectively from visual demonstration, provided that it is undertaken at an appropriate pace, with adequate repetition, and with the observer sufficiently near at hand. In this way, he or she will have the best chance of building up a coherent picture of what is happening from what may well be imperfect or incomplete visual information and cognitive processing. Pupils who are blind or who have very little sight may benefit from feeling what their teacher does: 'hand under hand' as he or she plays the keyboard, for instance; or, from behind, getting a sense of the position and movements of the bowing arm in

---

[33] Eddie, the young savant with whom Leon Miller worked, apparently adopted the same approach! (See Miller 1989: 30)

[34] As the six case studies set out earlier in this chapter indicate, the skills of some savants, such as A, extend naturally to two instruments or more, while the special abilities of others are more narrowly focused (typically on the piano or other keyboard). For them to learn a second instrument may be as challenging as for any other person with complex needs.

[35] However, musical activities may provide a motivating context in which verbal communication skills—expressive and receptive—can be practised (see pp. 128 ff.).

playing the violin. This is usually preferable to attempting coactive movements face to face, when sets of muscles work in opposition rather than together. Listening, and seeking to emulate the quality of sound made by the teacher or other performers, may be a crucial factor in technical development too, since the pupil's desire to reproduce what is heard may encourage the necessary motor activity without needing conscious attention.

Whatever approach is adopted, the development of technique is likely to require many hours of painstaking work on the part of pupil and teacher alike. For example, Derek (aged 5) tended to play passages of consecutive notes by jumping from one to the next using the same finger—or sometimes even a series of karate chops with the side of his hand! Despite the extraordinary dexterity this entailed, it was clear that his playing would benefit enormously from incorporating the standard finger patterns associated with scales and arpeggios.

I decided to start with some five-finger exercises, the foundation of all keyboard technique: just up and down the keys, one note for each finger and the thumb. Would Derek find that sufficiently engaging? How would he react? But these questions were supplanted in my mind by a more immediate problem: how was I going to be able to get at the piano for long enough to play the notes that he was supposed to be copying?

Sitting next to him on the piano stool, I tried holding both his wrists with my left hand to give my right free rein on the keyboard. I reckoned that I only needed about ten seconds. But that was nine too many for Derek. He wriggled out of my grip in no time and struck the C that I had managed play before being overwhelmed. I was afraid of hurting him if I held his wrists any tighter, so I had to try something else.

'Right, Derek,' I declared, 'we're going to play a game. You're going to sit over the other side of the room while I play something on the piano, then you can come over and see if you can copy it.'

I didn't really expect to him understand what I'd said, but in any case, without waiting to see his reaction, I picked him up and plopped him down on the floor at the far end of the nursery. I strode back to the piano and quickly played the five-finger exercise. I'd only just finished when Derek, who'd been amazingly quick out of the starting blocks and had fairly scuttled across the room, was pushing me out of the way. That done, he reached across the stool, and played what I had—well, a version of it. He used both hands to play a series of chords, up and down. I had to laugh at his antics.

Then he stopped, waiting. This was a game whose rules he had somehow immediately grasped.

So I picked him up again, sat him as far away as I could from the piano, raced back and played the exercise once more—this time starting on the next note up, C sharp. Again, my thumb was barely off the last key when Derek was back with his response.

And so we continued up the chromatic scale, until we'd tackled all twelve different keys. That brought us back to C, and it felt right to stop there. Derek seemed to sense that feeling of completion too, and he was content to return to his familiar routine of taking requests for pieces to play. He still wouldn't let me join in, I noticed, but I didn't mind: I was convinced that the five-finger-exercise game had provided the break-through that I had been looking for. Now I had something to build on.

It was then a short step in the lesson that followed to leave Derek where he was on the piano stool, and to engage in the 'play-copy' dialogue with no physical intervention on my part at all. In due course, I started to imitate what *he* was doing too, enabling us to have a genuine musical 'conversation'. And it wasn't just a matter of a musical ball bouncing between us like echoes in an alleyway. Whatever you lobbed at Derek would invariably come hurtling back with interest, and it was challenging to keep up with his musical repartee, which combined wit and ingenuity with an incredible speed of thought.

With no words to get in the way, a whole world of sophisticated social intercourse was now opened up to him. It was the second 'eureka' moment of his life: having first discovered that he was able to play what he could hear, now he came to realise that he could communicate *through* music. Indeed, for Derek, music came to function as a proxy-language, and it was through music that his wider development was increasingly channelled.

However, Derek's fingering remained as eccentric as ever, and as he had no conceptual understanding of his thumbs and fingers as distinct entities, and was consequently unable to manipulate them appropriately in response to ver-bal direction, the problem of how to help him develop his technique remained. Although he could copy the notes that I played just by listening, he could not, of course, see how I held my hands at the piano, which fingers I used, and the fact that my elbows didn't figure at all in what I did!

To plug this gap in his experience, I tried putting his hands over mine, one at a time, so that he could feel the shape of my hand and, to an extent, what my fingers were doing. We tried it for a few weeks, but it didn't seem to make any difference: whenever it was his turn, Derek just carried on as before.

So I tried a different approach. I held his right hand on mine.

'Look, Derek, here's my thumb,' I said, giving it a wiggle as his fingers curled around it.

'Now, where's yours?' I guided him to feel his right hand with his left.

'That's it! Now, let's put your thumb on C, middle C.' He allowed me to help him find the correct note and to push it down with his thumb.

'There you are.' And I sang, 'thumb'.

Next I uncurled his index finger and placed its tip on D. He pressed the note.

'Second finger,' I sang.

And so we continued with his third, fourth and little fingers, before coming back down to the thumb. He sang along enthusiastically, and couldn't resist adding in an accompaniment below. When we swapped over to his left hand, he treated the five-finger exercise like a bass-line, and added tunes in the right. No matter, I thought. The main thing was that, for the first time in his life, he'd manage to play using something approaching a conventional technique. On that simplest of foundations we would sub-sequently be able to build.

Little did I appreciate at the time just how long Derek's technique would take to reconstruct. For a total of eight years we worked together, weekly and then daily, spending hundreds of hours physically going over all the basic fingering patterns that make up a professional pianist's stock-in-trade. From five-finger exercises we moved on to full scales: major, minor and chromatic, as well as some of the more exotic varieties—the so-called 'modals', the whole-tones and the octatonics. Scales had the additional complexity of requiring Derek to tuck his thumb under his fingers while his hand was travelling in one direction, and to extend his fingers over his thumb while it was coming back in the other. I had to use both my hands to help him get this action right. We also tackled arpeggios: major, minor, and dominant and diminished sevenths, followed by some of the more unusual forms—French sevenths, augmented triads and chords of the added sixth. Long after my threshold of boredom was a distant memory, Derek would be keen for more. There was something about the orderliness, not only of the scales and arpeggios themselves, but also the regular way in which they related to one another, that he clearly found deeply satisfying.

However, in spite of the tens—perhaps hundreds—of thousands of willing repetitions, Derek never did learn to tell which finger was which! And even today, if you ask him to hold his thumb up (rather than his fingers), he still can't do it reliably, and the capacity to distinguish one hand from the other continues to elude him. While this seems odd—incredible, even—given his dazzling virtuosity, with hindsight I've come to realise that being able to put a name to concepts such as 'left' and 'right' wasn't the most important thing. What really mattered was achieving that very first aim I identified when I initially watched Derek play: that his technique should develop sufficiently so as not trammel his vivid aural imagination. And that, over the years, is exactly what *did* happen. During all those hundreds of hours of practice he absorbed many of the standard fingering patterns, quite without being aware of it, and these slowly became assimilated into his own playing. Today his technique, as a mature adult performer, although still far from conventional, enables him to do whatever his musical imagination demands.

As Derek's story and the other case studies show, savants generally learn pieces 'by ear'—re-creating music by hearing and remembering it, as opposed to using notation. This is a complex skill, which entails building up internal musical models—aural images of pieces that are held in the mind, that are subsequently related to the physical movements and control required to play an instrument.[36] Developing this ability is largely a process of trial, error, and determined effort and, as the case studies on pp. 214 and 215 show, the capacity of savants to play by ear varies considerably.

It is widely believed that the ability to play by ear is (like other savant skills) a 'gift'—and is not teachable. In reality, though, it is a skill that can be learnt (and taught) like any other; indeed, the motivation to practise is a highly significant factor in its development. For those for whom playing by ear does not come intuitively or who are in the early stages, teachers can assist their

---

[36] The concept tends to be used in the context of melody and harmony instruments, such as the piano, violin, and recorder, although it is more broadly applicable than this—to drums, shakers, and other untuned percussion, for example.

learning in a number of ways: through explanation (in so far as this is helpful), demonstration, and physical guidance, and by providing, among other repertoire, a series of pieces that are carefully graded according to the number and range of pitches they use. These need to be pitched in a key best suited to the instrument in question.

Take, for example, the selection of folk and popular songs shown in Table 10.3, whose range increases upwards from the tonic. The songs are shown here in E major, which beginners on the keyboard, piano, or organ may well find easiest to start with.[37]

For beginners on the violin, however, D major would be an obvious choice. The usual pattern of technical development on other instruments may suggest a different route: for example, working towards pieces whose pitches range from dominant to dominant; see Table 10.4. Here, the key is G major—suitable for the recorder, for instance. Each set of songs shown is intended only to indicate a potential framework for learning, outlined with a few examples. In

Table 10.3 Songs using an increasing range of pitches (from tonic to tonic)

Songs	Required pitches							
Au clair de la lune (opening)	E	F♯	G♯					
It's me, O Lord (chorus)	E	F♯	G♯					
Super Trouper (chorus)	E	F♯	G♯	A				
Love of the Common People (chorus)	E	F♯	G♯	A				
Jingle Bells (chorus)	E	F♯	G♯	A	B			
When the Saints Go Marching In	E	F♯	G♯	A	B			
It's a Heartache	E	F♯	G♯	A	B	C♯		
Oh, Susanna!	E	F♯	G♯	A	B	C♯		
Everyday (1st section)	E	F♯	G♯	A	B	C♯	D♯	
All My Loving (chorus)	E	F♯	G♯	A	B	C♯	D♯	E'
Kookaburra	E	F♯	G♯	A	B	C♯	D♯	E'

---

[37] The assumption that C major makes the simplest starting point is a construct driven by music theory, and may in any case be inappropriate for children and young people who are severely visually impaired or who have difficulty in processing visual information (as are most savants), since an uninterrupted sequence of white notes offers no clues at all to those using touch to locate the keys.

reality, many more pieces will be needed—ideally, culturally relevant and of genuine interest to pupils. The relative scarcity of tunes suitable for the early stages, which utilize only three or four notes, is offset by the fact that there is no need to use complete pieces, as the examples show.

The number of pitches that make up a tune is only one aspect of the challenge it presents to performers learning by ear. Teachers also need to give due regard to the intervals used in pieces: leaps are generally harder to gauge than movement by step, while repeated notes (at a moderate tempo) are particularly easy to realize instrumentally (as, for example, in *Love of the Common People* and *Karma Chameleon*). Rhythmic complexity is a crucial factor in the equation too, and the rate at which notes occur.

As their repertoires increase, the hope is that pupils and students will develop a growing feeling for the different function that each note of a scale typically performs in relation to the others—an awareness of 'tonality' (level 5 in the Sounds of Intent framework). Having established by listening which scale a tune uses (major, minor, pentatonic, and so forth), this will enable them to gauge within it the place of each of its constituent notes; to hear, for instance, that *Clementine* begins on the tonic (G in the example given) and *The Sloop John B* begins on the dominant (in this case D). Although this process is

Table 10.4 Songs requiring an increasing range of pitches (from dominant to dominant)

Songs	Required pitches							
It's me, O Lord (chorus)				G	A	B		
Au clair de la lune (opening)				G	A	B		
Karma Chameleon (chorus)			F♯	G	A	B		
Nkosi, Sikekel' i Afrika (chorus)			F♯	G	A	B	C	
Mull of Kintyre (chorus)	D	E		G	A	B		
Old MacDonald Had a Farm	D	E		G	A	B		
This Little Light of Mine	D	E	F♯	G	A	B	C	
The Sloop John B	D	E	F♯	G	A	B	C	D'

described here using the concepts and terminology of music theory, tonality may be understood purely at an intuitive level, as most savants show.

The two frameworks shown in Tables 10.3 and 10.4 are only examples of possible approaches. For instance, rhythmic expertise can be built up by exploring a series of passages that display an increasing range and diversity of inter-onset times between successive notes, and degree of syncopation. Within the realm of pitch, a more closely defined strategy than that indicated is to work exclusively through pieces that use a pentatonic scale (such as *Mull of Kintyre* and *Old MacDonald had a Farm*). Whatever the initial framework, transposition may represent an appropriate further step in some contexts and with certain instruments. For example, using the notes of the E major scale, *It's me, O Lord!* and *Au clair de la lune* can be played not only on E, F sharp, and G sharp as shown, but also on A, B, and C sharp (effectively in A major) and B, C sharp, and D sharp (functionally, B major). Similarly, *Love of the Common People* and *Super Trouper* can be played on B, C sharp, D sharp, and E, as well as E, F sharp, G sharp, and A. Beyond this, tunes can be selected in which accidentals function as chromatic inflexions, such as the B flat in *Karma Chameleon*, or as signals of modulation (a raised fourth degree showing a transition to the dominant, for instance).

One of the main challenges facing teachers is sustaining their pupils' enthusiasm for what is likely to be a modest repertoire of musical fragments when they start practising to play by ear, which are subject, furthermore, to a great deal of repetition. By making music with others, however, or through the judicious use of recorded material, even the most basic snatch of rhythm or melody can potentially form part of a satisfying, even sophisticated, musical texture. Pieces that use ostinati (short passages that are repeated a number of times) are particularly suitable. Ostinato-based structures are characteristic of many styles, and children may enjoy African drumming or playing pieces on the gamelan, as well as providing the bass-lines for songs ranging from *Summer is A-Coming in* to *Feelin' Groovy*. Melodic ostinati often have a limited pitch range and so fit comfortably into schemes such as those proposed in Tables 10.3 and 10.4.

Performing in textures comprising two parts or more can promote aural awareness, including children's sense of harmony, and their feeling for harmony and line working together. Indeed, group performance can provide a useful introduction to learning to play harmonies by ear. Here, a systematic approach can be adopted comparable to that proposed for melodies, with its incremental increase in the range of notes used. It is even possible to start with one chord (almost invariably the tonic) which can be used, for example, throughout the first section of *Au clair de la lune*. Common two-chord

Table 10.5 Songs requiring an increasing number of chords

Song	Required chords					
Au clair de la lune	I					
Kookaburra	I			IV		
Clementine	I				V	
Love of the Common People (chorus)	I			IV	V	
When the Saints Go Marching in	I			IV	V	
Jingle Bells (chorus)	I			IV	V	
This Little Light of Mine (chorus)	I			IV	V	
The Sloop John B	I			IV	V	
Oh, Susanna!	I			IV	V	
Everyday (1st section)	I			IV	V	vi
It's a Heartache	I		iii	IV	V	vi
Karma Chameleon	I	ii	iii	IV	V	vi

combinations are I and V, and I and, IV. However, it is with the three chords I, IV, and V that the most significant threshold is reached—these harmonies being sufficient to support a large number of melodies (see Table 10.5).

Hence, contrary to popular belief, playing by ear is something that can be improved with practice, and, whatever pupils' level of achievement—no matter how unusual their talent may be—teachers can assist them in further developing in this area. For example, to what extent are a pupil's skills restricted stylistically? If she or he can process simple diatonic chords in the context of rock 'n' roll, for instance, can this be extended to the chromatic combinations and higher discords characteristic of jazz? Pupils may be able to learn melodies relatively easily in the major mode, but are they equally at home with tunes that use the blues scale? Just how good is their ability to transpose—can they play completely fluently in every key? Rhythmically, are they more comfortable with pieces in 2, 3, or 4 time than those built around 5s or 7s, and have they experienced the complex rhythms of some Indian and African music, for example? How quickly is new material assimilated? How well is it retained? Like other skills, the use of memory may be improved through use.

A natural development of the ability to play pieces by ear is the capacity to improvise; in fact, the two skills may well evolve alongside each other. However, some savants find the concept difficult to grasp, and, on hearing an improvisation, assume (we may surmise) that it is just another piece to be learnt. Teachers can help them understand the process by playing a familiar tune and then embellishing it, or by improvising fragments of melody over an established pattern of harmonies—explaining what they are doing if this is appropriate. They may then encourage their pupils to do the same, by taking it in turns to play and listen, or by improvising with them as they perform. At first, rather than producing new material, some pupils will simply copy what they have just heard, and it may be many sessions before original ideas start to appear. Indeed, some savants never move beyond the stage of direct imitation. Others, having attained a certain competence in improvising, may be helped to refine their efforts through exposure to renditions of the same piece in different styles. Eventually, these versions may merge in the pupil's mind, and, exceptionally, re-emerge within a new idiomatic framework—a characteristic of musical maturity.

Some pupils may require a systematic, step-by-step approach, and to this end a number of levels of improvisation can be identified that can be used to guide the planning of programmes of study. Perhaps the most straightforward is rhythmic improvising (which takes no account of pitch). While savants may find this musically very simple, it may be appropriate for them in terms of learning to *create* music: taking a step backwards, as it were, to enable them to move ahead. This can be undertaken in a group, for example, individuals taking it in turns to make up rhythmic patterns that are subsequently imitated by the other participants. The improvised material may well make use of musical ideas from the piece being extemporized or others that are familiar. A regular beat would ensure an underlying musical coherence (level P.5).

Melodic improvisation can be approached by encouraging pupils and students to ornament given material using extra notes, initially taken from the scale of the tune in question. Inevitably, this will involve rhythmic embellishment too. See, for example, Ex. 10.6.

Ex. 10.6 Simple melodic ornamentation

A further stage is for students to improvise new melodies using a given set of pitches (such as the pentatonic scale, for example), in the first instance utilizing the phrase structure or rhythm of a familiar piece. For instance, *It's me, O Lord* may be transformed along the lines shown in Ex. 10.7.

Ex. 10.7 Improvising using a given rhythm and set of pitches

The concept of improvising a line against a harmonic background can be introduced by isolating the constituent pitches of the chords concerned, and using these as building blocks to create new tunes. Again, this can be set up as a group activity (Fig. 10.5).

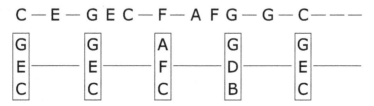

Fig. 10.5 Improvising a melody over given diatonic chords

The incorporation of notes that do not derive directly from underlying harmonies (such as passing notes and auxiliary notes) is an aspect of melody that varies widely from one style to another, and is therefore particularly dependent on exposure to the appropriate repertoire, attentive listening, and careful emulation of what is heard. One way of tackling the issue is to take a simple melody such as that outlined above, and experiment by filling in the gaps between successive notes, in terms of both pitch and rhythm (cf. the improvisation on *It's me, O Lord*, in Ex. 10.6).

At any stage in learning to improvise—and compose—pupils and students may enjoy experimenting with more original groups of pitches, rhythms, and harmonic sonorities.

Although savants are typically self-taught, they may well need a high level of support between lessons for them to get the most from programmes of learning. Effective communication between the specialist music teacher and those who are supporting is essential. To this end, it may be advantageous for parents and others to attend lessons, at least in part. As well as using those that are commercially available, teachers can make their own recordings for pupils, comprising simplified or modified versions of pieces. The right-hand and left-hand parts of keyboard music can be recorded separately, for example, played slowly, and broken down into sections to make learning easier (see Ockelford 1996*b*: 37). Verbal instructions may be included too (see p. 153). Pupils (and their helpers) will probably need to be taught how to derive the greatest benefit from resources such as these. Managing items of music technology, assembling and disassembling instruments where necessary, and ensuring that all equipment is properly maintained and is available when required, are likely to be among the key functions of supporting staff and carers. Deciding how much practice is appropriate each day may be an issue with some children whose interest in music is felt to be obsessive. Clearly, it is a question of balance: if a child's playing takes up so much time that many other forms of purposeful activity are excluded, this may reasonably be deemed excessive; conversely, to deny a child his or her principal source of pleasure and achievement would appear to be nothing less than abusive.

Savants can perform with others more or less successfully, according to their levels of musical, cognitive, and social development. They may show varying degrees of sensitivity to the fluctuating dynamics of a performing group. Some may be able to conceptualize and assume distinct roles; at different times consciously accompanying, for example, or taking the lead. The individuality of other savants may mean that they will always be more suited to solo performance. Where synchronization would normally rely on visual cueing, alternative strategies will need to be developed: discreet counting or the use of touch, for example; and changes in tempo may have to be rehearsed with particular care. But the greatest challenge may be working together and making decisions using little or no language. Even relatively straightforward instructions such as 'play the final chorus twice' may have to be conveyed in purely musical terms. For example, an additional dominant seventh harmony may indicate that more is to come, whereas a slight slowing may show that the end is approaching.

Working with a large group of children who couldn't see, many of whom had complex needs, presented a number of challenges for teacher and pupils alike. Clearly, conducting was out of the question, so starting and stopping, slowing down and speeding up, and making expressive changes or effects such as getting louder or softer had to be coordinated non-visually: through sound, using speech or musical cues. As I soon discovered, calling out what was required was disruptive, and in any case spoken instructions meant little to several of the children, including Derek, on account of their learning difficulties. So, during a performance, the direction of the group had to come solely through inflections in the piano part, to which the children learnt to listen very attentively. For example, if a verse were to be sung sadly, then the accompaniment might reflect this through a reduction in tempo and dynamics and, perhaps, by moving to the 'minor' key. Conversely, the return to a happy state could be conveyed through an increase in movement, loudness and the use of 'major' chords. It was even possible to communicate a sense of irony, which could be appreciated by some of the older and more able pupils, by juxtaposing different pieces with contrasting connotations together—for example, by playing fragments of *Day oh!* while the children were singing *Morning has broken*.

The accompaniment could relay simpler messages too. For instance, if a chorus were to be repeated at the end, this could be signalled through particular chords that suggested there was more to come. From time to time I would link songs together by improvising a 'bridge' between them. Musically, this would borrow material from the first piece and incrementally transform it into the introduction to the second, so it gradually became apparent what this was to be. Sometimes the children would compete to see who could name the upcoming tune first. If things were becoming too straight-forward, I would tease them by appearing to set off in a certain direction only to change course at the last moment. Increasingly, I was able to hold their attention by linking a whole sequence of pieces in this way. Indeed, I came to the conclusion that the most effective lessons were those in which there was little or no talking, and that the more one could teach music *through* music the better. (Ockelford 2007*a*: 134–6)

Savants may play in public—just like any other musicians—enjoying a rapport with their audience and relishing the acclaim their performances bring. There should be no ethical difficulty here, provided the person concerned is aware of what is happening, consents to it, and is not being exploited. Indeed, some savants revel in the excitement of performing to a large group of people, and it would be unethical to deny them that opportunity. However, where individuals have only limited awareness of a situation, an informed decision may have to be made by those closest to them. A number of factors will have to be weighed up. For example, while there may appear to be little short-term advantage, it could be that playing in concerts, experiencing the special atmosphere they generate, and conforming to the patterns of behaviour they require, benefit a pupil's social development over a longer period. Repertoire and context are important considerations too. While it may be desirable, in the course of lessons, for pupils to attempt pieces in a wide range of styles, it may be inappropriate for them to perform a similar variety in public. For instance, a savant whose speciality is jazz may be demeaned by unexpectedly improvising on a Beethoven sonata in the course of a formal concert of classical music. In other circumstances, however, such an exploit may be admired for its telling musicality and pungent wit.

For those supporting savants, playing in concerts is likely to raise a number of practical questions, such as attendance at rehearsals, setting up instruments, and getting about on stage. It is essential that these areas of potential concern are acknowledged in good time and adequately addressed. Other issues, such as facing the audience, learning not to move excessively while playing, and receiving applause appropriately may need special consideration—and rehearsal—too. A savant may find it far more difficult to raise or lower the piano stool than to play the instrument once seated! Here is an account of Derek's first public performance, aged 8.

He was rocking slowly on the piano stool, his fingers fidgeting in readiness for their forthcoming workout. He smiled when he heard his name, and sat still for a moment to give his full attention to what Miss Lingard was saying.
'. . . and now he's going to play the *Streets of London*.'

Derek's smile widened into a broad beam that stretched right across his face. This was the moment that he'd been waiting for.

I decided to assert my authority straight away—and to keep Derek on his toes—by beginning in E flat major, a key in which he had not, as far as I could remember, ever played the song. I couldn't think of another child (except, perhaps, Philip) for whom such an act wouldn't have had disastrous consequences. But for Derek, the unusual was commonplace, and I had complete faith in his ability to follow me. My confidence was well-founded, and before the opening chord had faded away he was there alongside me, as though it were the most natural thing in the world to play a piece in an unfamiliar key before his first ever public audience. The hundreds of hours that we had spent practising all conceivable scales and arpeggios had refined his raw capacity to realise his entire repertoire starting on any note, and he was now equally at home playing pieces in any key—rather like being able to speak twelve languages with native fluency.

I led Derek resolutely through the first verse and chorus of the *Streets of London* and he obediently followed. I was longing to let him go in order to see just where his musical imagination, fired up by the excitement of the occasion, would take us, and as soon as I judged it was prudent to do so—towards the end of verse two—I gradually retreated into the background with a series of *sotto voce* chords. The instant that he sensed my musical grip was released, Derek was off, scampering up the octave with a series of broken chords. Up and up he took the music, ascending into higher and higher realms of musical invention. Just when it seemed as though he was going to run out of notes at the end of the keyboard, he came scurrying down in a series of tumbling scales and rejoined me in the middle register. Seizing my opportunity, I took the lead again and introduced a new syncopated rhythm in the bass. Without a moment's hesitation, his left hand too started skipping along to the new beat before he broke free once more, dancing out of my reach.

And so our pas de deux continued for a few minutes, until it felt appropriate to draw matters to a close, before Derek ran out of steam and his perambulations became repetitive. An almost imperceptible reduction in the pace of my accompaniment signalled that it was time to wind things up, and he fell back into step with a series of expansive chords that served as an effective climax to the piece. He held on to the last *fortissimo* cluster of notes waiting for me to lift my hands up first, and then he couldn't resist his trademark final plonk low down in the left hand.

The audience burst into rapturous applause—this was quite unlike anything they'd ever seen or heard before. There were shouts of 'Well done, Derek!' He was quivering with excitement, his face radiant, his hands alternately clapping and flapping energetically at his sides. I looked across at Nanny. She too was applauding vigorously, her eyes shining with pride. I felt relieved, delighted and (I had to admit) vindicated. From somewhere, Derek seemed to have acquired the instincts of a natural performer: a sense of occasion and the capacity to rise to it, the ability to communicate with an audience and a feeling of exhilaration when his playing was acknowledged. These were things that could not be taught, but with them, Derek's playing had the potential to reach heights that were as yet unexplored. (Ockelford 2007a: 134–6)

Conclusion

In this chapter we have considered the musical abilities and needs of an exceptional group of young people, who have advanced skills in the context of severe learning difficulties—so-called 'savants'. While those with levels of talent that would be regarded as outstanding in any circumstances (that is, disregarding their disabilities) are extremely rare, uneven profiles of development—where musical attainment outstrips progress in other areas—are, as the PROMISE research reported in Chapter 1 suggests, encountered rather more frequently. Indeed, it is quite likely that, within a class of pupils with complex needs, teachers will come across musical abilities that merit particular attention.

While there is no one such thing as a 'savant', and no one educational approach that would suit all savants, it is possible to identify approaches and strategies that have met with a broad range of success in relation to this group as a whole. The key point to bear in mind is that *all* savants, no matter how talented or disabled, or how extreme the disparity between the two, will benefit from systematic and sustained educational input. But teachers should not be surprised if work that lies even a little way outside a savant's intuitively acquired domain of expertise or just beyond their preferred style of learning will need to be tackled primarily in the context of their cognitive impairment. Equally, it may be a considerable challenge to have the encapsulated skills associated with music-making accrue to wider learning and development.

Overall, the most important thing for those responsible for the education of children and young people with learning difficulties who are (or may be) functioning at levels 5 or 6 of the Sounds of Intent framework, is to ensure that specialist provision is put in place as early as possible, with the aim, always, of minimizing the impact of disability through maximizing musical potential.

Conclusion

The beginning of wisdom, it is said, is to call things by their right names, and, hopefully, this book, the first to be dedicated purely to the music education of children and young people with complex needs, has been successful in identifying and defining some of the key concepts that pertain to this emerging sphere of activity—of laying the groundwork upon which a relatively new discipline will be able to evolve coherently over the coming years. Throughout, the aim has been to provide a solid theoretical base—a synthesis of ideas from music theory, psychology, and education—which can account systematically for the music-developmental observations of pupils with SLD and PMLD made to date, and to ground practical suggestions for future pedagogical approaches. The key findings are as follows.

Chapter 1 reports on research suggesting that the potential importance of music in the lives of pupils with complex needs is widely recognized in schools, both as an area of learning and leisure in its own right, and as a tool to promote wider development. However, while some schools offer structured music provision, which is integrated coherently across the wider curriculum, differentiated across the age phases, provided by a music education specialist working alongside a music therapy colleague, and judiciously linked to the wider musical community, these are the exception rather than the rule. The overriding impression is of practitioners having adopted an essentially pragmatic and eclectic approach to music provision in the absence of a cogent and nationally agreed framework of musical development in children and young people with SLD or PMLD.

Chapter 2 investigates one issue in more detail: the apparent lack of clarity as to what constitutes music education and music therapy for pupils and clients with learning difficulties. It seems that the conceptual confusion that exists may well be detrimental to children and young people who, in the course of a school day, may be engaging in very similar activities with quite different sets of expectations being placed upon them by staff. A model is set out that seeks to clarify the distinction between the two disciplines and which could be used by practitioners to ensure that their work is complementary rather than conflicting.

Chapter 3 interrogates the 'P-Levels' for music, as published by the QCA, and finds serious shortcomings. Although its formulation has never been made explicit, the P-level appears to have been founded on social constructs rather than what is known of early musical development, and, just as seriously, conflates musical and extra-musical attainment. Hence, the national framework that teachers are currently using to guide their efforts in planning and providing music education for children and young people with complex needs is conceptually flawed. This manifests itself in inconsistencies and gaps in the statements that are made and the examples that are used.

Chapter 4 takes the first step to addressing this problem by setting out a new theory of how music 'makes sense'—of how it is able to convey thoughts and feelings—even where listeners have little or no formal music education. Two main sources of musical meaning are discussed. First, and most importantly, are the sounds of music themselves, which, it is asserted, relate to each other through a sense of derivation. This mechanism enables series of notes to form metaphorical narratives, which unfold over time to create meaning. The implication of this hypothesis is that the cognition of repetition and regularity must lie at the heart of the musical experience and must, therefore, be central to musical development. Evidence of this is presented from the psychological literature. Second, musical sounds may refer directly to *extra*-musical experiences with which they have become connected—thereby functioning as symbols of activities, places or people, and of the emotions associated with them. These two forms of musical meaning often work together within the context of the prevailing social, physical, attitudinal, and emotional environments of listeners, to create complex and idiosyncratic patterns of response. Nonetheless, commonalities do exist, and so it is that music is above all a shared experience.

Chapter 5 builds on these findings to create, for the first time, a model of musical development in children and young people with SLD or PMLD. Its main source of evidence is observations of the pupils themselves, made by practitioners from the 'Sounds of Intent' research team. These are blended with the musicological theory and mainstream developmental findings set out in Chapter 4 to create a tripartite framework—'reactive', 'proactive', and 'interactive'—distributed over six levels. The 18 segments that are formed are further divided into four 'elements'—each a short statement of attainment. It is suggested that this model has the potential to provide practitioners with both a curriculum framework and a tool for assessment, which could be accessed via tablet PCs. This technology would also enable profiles on individual pupils to be built up over time, using written, audio, and video records.

Chapter 6 takes the Sounds of Intent framework, as it is known, and shows how this can profitably be linked to other areas of school-based activity: in particular, movement, learning, communication, and socialization. Hence musical and extra-musical patterns of development are united within a common pedagogical scheme, which demonstrates how music can be used as a tool to assist teaching and promote learning across the curriculum—but without conflating the two.

Chapter 7 considers how children and young people with complex needs can be supported to reflect on music and communicate about it, using symbols in a range of media, from objects of reference to 'talking scores' and formal music notation in Braille and print. Despite the emphasis placed on 'metamusical' skills such as these in traditional curricular, often, the educational benefits for those with SLD or PMLD will, again, be *extra*-musical.

Chapter 8 moves on to examine special musical *abilities*, and finds, through parental surveys and direct observational research, that a number of factors play a part in exceptional musical development in young people with learning difficulties. An important element in the equation appears to be the level of vision of the child concerned. For example, among those who are born blind (or who lose their sight shortly after birth), the incidence of AP is markedly higher than in those who are partially sighted or who have no visual impairment at all. But the situation is by no means straightforward, since not all blind children with SLD (for example) develop AP. Moreover, the incidence appears to vary from one syndrome to another. Hence a number of complex and interrelated factors may well affect the development of early musicality, and parents, teachers, and therapists need to be alert to the possibilities, to ensure that musical potential—perhaps not readily visible beneath challenging patterns of behaviour—is not missed.

Chapter 9 investigates how *musical* interactions between teachers and pupils, therapists and clients, can be assessed *musically*, rather than through the proxy measures that have typically been used to date. A case study is used of a young pupil with exceptional musical potential, though the analytical principles are equally valid whatever the level of attainment. When a teacher or therapist works with a child, who is in charge (musically speaking)? Who is influencing whom? The musicological system of analysis set out in Chapter 4 presents a new way forward.

Chapter 10, finally, considers exceptional musical potential and ability among those with learning difficulties in some depth, through a series of case studies. The musical exploits of one young man in particular—Derek Paravicini—with whom the author has worked for many years, are described and analysed in detail, above all for the insights they provide of an intriguing musical mind in action. Are people like Derek quite different from the rest of us, or is their musicality essentially the same, but further along the same continuum? The answer to this question is sought by referring back to the Sounds of Intent framework, where it becomes clear that 'savants' like Derek are at once both typical and exceptional. The key thing is the lessons that teachers can learn from his example, not only to inform the teaching of other savants, but pupils with learning difficulties too—and children more widely.

In conclusion, then, *Music for Children and Young People with Complex Needs* aims to provide a fresh perspective in what is a young and diverse field, hopefully bringing a theoretical (and, in time, practical) coherence to what is currently a rich though highly idiosyncratic sphere of endeavour. It is hoped that the models and frameworks that are presented will be of value to policymakers, planners, and practitioners alike, in both mainstream and special education—wherever pupils with complex needs are to be found. It is hoped that the thinking that is set out will bring a new clarity to the role of therapists and educators as they work side by side in schools. It is hoped that there are ideas that will be of value to parents, as they seek out appropriate leisure activities for their children. Above all, it is hoped that the book will be of interest to *everyone* engaged in music education since, although an understanding of those with special needs should be informed by the way that the majority of young people develop, it is equally clear that we all have a great deal to learn from those whose abilities and disabilities lie at the extremes. Ultimately, we should remember that the value of a young person's musicality resides not in where it stands in relation to that of others, but in the extent to which it is harnessed to enhance the quality of life of the individual concerned and the wider circle with which he or she may be engaged.

Appendix: Further information and assessment protocols at level 1 of the Sounds of Intent framework

Reactive, level 1

R.1
Encounters sounds

General Observation

Children and young people appear to pay no attention to sounds to which they are exposed and no consistent responses can be observed other than reflex reactions.

Interpretation

Sound is not being processed as a distinct or meaningful sensory experience.

Element R.1.A
Is exposed to a rich variety of sounds

Approaches

Offer children a rich and stimulating range of auditory experiences, including music. The key is to be *imaginative* but *systematic*: imaginative in introducing young people to a wide range of sounds in a variety of contexts; systematic in observing and noting any reactions they make (that may be taken as potentially positive or negative responses) to inform the planning of future experiences. To children's ears there is often nothing more stimulating than the human voice and the sounds associated with it: talking, humming, singing, whooping, or just whispering. Other body sounds, including clapping, clicking, tapping, slapping, scratching, and stamping may excite attention too. The sounds available from musical instruments—acoustic or electronic—may be no more potentially engaging than those that can be made using everyday objects, such as rustly paper, rattly containers, saucepan lids, chains, pieces of wood, and plastic pipes. Suspending some objects will enable them to resonate, enhancing their sound-making properties. Hence, through very simple means, young people may be exposed to sounds of all kinds: high and low; short and long; quiet and loud. They may be rich in harmonics or pure; they may be bright or dull. They may emanate from any position: in front of a child or behind,

Continued

Element R.1.A Cont.

from the left side or the right, above or below. Sounds may be stationary or moving. They may occur in isolation or together, forming homogeneous blends or contrasting clusters. Streams of sound may be quickly moving or ponderous, describing flowing lines or jagged contours.

Summary and examples

Sources of sound	Basic qualities of sound	Nature of combination of sounds
Vocal	High . . . low	Isolated
Other 'body sounds'	Short . . . long	Smoothly flowing streams
Everyday objects that make sounds	Quiet . . . loud	Sequences of detached sounds
Musical instruments	Strident . . . mellow	Contrasting clusters
Electronically generated sounds	Quickly moving . . . slowly moving	Homogeneous blends

Evidence

Despite the rich variety of sounds, children and young people make, at most, reflex reactions—startling at sudden loud noises, for example.

Gauging co-worker input	Score
Is systematically exposed to at least one source of sound, with variation in respect of at least one basic quality, and combined in at least one way	1
Is systematically exposed to at least two sources of sound, with variation in respect of at least two basic qualities, and combined in at least two ways	2
Is systematically exposed to at least three sources of sound, with variation in respect of at least three basic qualities, and combined in at least three ways	3
Is systematically exposed to at least four sources of sound, with variation in respect of at least four basic qualities, and combined in at least four ways	4
Is systematically exposed to at least five sources of sound, with variation in respect of at least five basic qualities, and combined in at least five ways	5

Element R.1.B

Is exposed to a wide range of music

Approaches

Nothing offers a richer auditory experience than *music*, and nowhere are the qualities of sound organized with such precision and mapped out with such perceptual clarity. Sounds with different qualities that are structured in different ways result in differing musical styles and genres, each of which offers a distinct type of auditory experience to children and young people in the early stages of development. Hence effective music programmes for those with complex needs in the early stages of development are likely to include exposure to a wide range of music. There are, of course, a huge number of possibilities: from ragtime to reggae, folksongs to fugues, and from symphonies to spirituals, for example; using instruments ranging from the piano to the panpipes, the drum kit to the didgeridoo, and the gamelan to the electric guitar.

Summary and examples

Vocalists/ instrumentalists	Styles	Genres
Solo vocal	Bebop	Folksong
Koto	Bhangra	Dance music
Gamelan	Rock and roll	Military march
Brass band	Baroque	Symphonic overture
Jazz trio	Flamenco	Motet

Evidence

Despite the wide range of music, children and young people make, at most, reflex reactions to 'surface' features of the music, sudden loud chords causing a 'startle' reflex, for example.

Gauging co-worker input	Score
Is systematically exposed to at least one vocal/instrumental combination, performing music in at least one style, and in at least one genre	1
Is systematically exposed to at least two vocal/instrumental combinations, performing music in at least two styles, and in at least two genres	2
Is systematically exposed to at least three vocal/instrumental combinations, performing music in at least three styles, and in at least three genres	3
Is systematically exposed to at least four vocal/instrumental combinations, performing music in at least four styles, and in at least four genres	4
Is systematically exposed to at least five vocal/instrumental combinations, performing music in at least five styles, and in at least five genres	5

Element R.1.C
Is exposed to music in different contexts

Approaches

It is essential to consider carefully the environments in which listening takes place. For at least some of the time, children and young people should have the opportunity to work in an otherwise quiet area with the minimum of distractions. In small, enclosed spaces, such as Lilli Nielsen's 'Little Room' (see p. 276), the effects of sounds are enhanced, and auditory clutter—the background noise of the classroom, for example—may be reduced or eliminated. In this way, any attention that young people are striving to bring to bear will be guided to a single, relevant stimulus, rather than them having to figure out what to listen to among the 'great blooming, buzzing confusion' (as William James described it) that would otherwise assail them. Of course, other listening environments are potentially valuable too: consider, for example, the differing qualities of one-to-one teaching/therapy spaces, classrooms, corridors, large, resonant indoor spaces such as the school hall, and different locations outside.

The *social* contexts in which listening occurs are also important. For example, the experience of listening alone, with a co-worker, with classmates, at a whole school assembly, and as a member of a large (unfamiliar) audience are all quite different, and it is worth considering what each has to offer the child or young person concerned.

Auditory input may be augmented with vibration by using a 'resonance board': a hollow wooden platform that amplifies any sounds that are made on it or passed through it (using loudspeakers, for example). A number of vibroacoustic boards, beds, and chairs are commercially available, through which young people can bring a large body area into contact with musical vibration. Other sensory stimulation such as touch, movement, light, or scent may be combined with music too, and it may be that some children come to respond first to an integrated approach. In fact, complex multisensory experiences are typical of everyday life; it is the precise control of their individual elements that can be difficult to achieve. However, multi-sensory environments can be constructed that allow the input to different sensory modalities to be managed with a high level of precision. Here, visual stimuli, such as the colour and intensity of lighting, can be made to vary in response to changes in sound, for instance (Heyes 1997: 28 and 29).

Co-workers and carers should bear in mind that perception may be affected by a range of extraneous factors. The time of day may be an important variable, for example, and internal influences may also be significant: a child's capacity or willingness to make the effort to attend to sounds may be subject to a fluctuating medical condition, for instance, or simply a change of mood.

Continued

Element R.1.C Cont.

Summary and examples

Acoustic environment	Social	Mode of transmission
Small, specially designed environment with minimum of auditory clutter	Alone	Direct (live performance)
One-to-one teaching/therapy space	With co-worker	Standard loudspeakers (potentially in different positions relative to listener)
Classroom	With classmates	Headphones
Large, resonant, indoor space	As whole-school activity	Resonance board
Outside	As part of large (unfamiliar) audience	Acoustic chair

Evidence

Despite the range of contexts in which children and young people are exposed to musical and other sounds, they make, at most, reflex reactions.

Gauging co-worker input	Score
Is systematically exposed to music in at least one acoustic environment, in at least one distinct social context, and through at least one mode of transmission	1
Is systematically exposed to music in at least two different acoustic environments, in at least two distinct social contexts, and through at least two modes of transmission	2
Is systematically exposed to music in at least three different acoustic environments, in at least three distinct social contexts, and through at least three modes of transmission	3
Is systematically exposed to music in at least four different acoustic environments, in at least four distinct social contexts, and through at least four modes of transmission	4
Is systematically exposed to music in at least five different acoustic environments, in at least five distinct social contexts, and through at least five modes of transmission	5

Element R.1.D

Is exposed to particular musical and other sounds being linked to key people, places, and/or activities

Approaches

One of the most basic ways in which people respond to music is through association: music once heard in combination with a particular person, place, or activity may become cognitively linked to it, whereby rehearing the piece concerned brings to mind the related experience and its emotional connotations (Davies 1978: 69). Co-workers and carers may consciously seek to introduce this notion to children and young people with complex needs by consistently connecting particular musical and other sounds with significant people, locations, and activities. Such connections have the added advantage of promoting early communication. For example, key figures in a young person's life may wear sound-making accessories—necklaces, bracelets, or badges, for example—that can be used to augment the experience of meeting and greeting, of reinforcing a person's presence. Similarly, locations and activities may have sounds associated with them, which may be integral (for example, a tambourine used to represent music) or additional (for instance, windchimes meaning 'classroom').

Summary and examples

People	Places	Activities
Jangly bangles (music teacher)	Windchimes (classroom)	Tambourine (music)
Bell necklace (nurse)	Distinctive piece of recorded music (multisensory room)	Tin of jingly coins (shopping)
Squeaky badge (class teacher)	Suspended metal chains (one-to-one room)	Homemade shaker with dried pulses (cooking)
Rattly wooden beads (carer)	Bamboo mobile (art room)	Bird whistle (walk in the park)
Crinkly paper wristbands (physiotherapist)	Two-tone doorbell (home)	Clinking bunch of keys (ride in the car)

Evidence

Despite the connections between sounds and people, places and activities that are made, children and young people do not pick up on them, making, at most, reflex reactions to the multisensory experiences to which they are exposed.

Continued

Element R.1.D Cont.

Gauging co-worker input	Score
Is systematically exposed to sounds being linked to at least one person, one place, and one activity	1
Is systematically exposed to sounds being linked to at least two people, two places, and two activities	2
Is systematically exposed to sounds being linked to at least three people, three places, and three activities	3
Is systematically exposed to sounds being linked to at least four people, four places, and four activities	4
Is systematically exposed to sounds being linked to at least five people, five places, and five activities	5

Gauging consistency (R.1)

Co-worker input	Score
Music and other auditory stimulation is *rarely* integrated into day-to-day programmes of living and learning, and/or there are sessions devoted to sound and music around once a fortnight or less	1
Music and other auditory stimulation is *occasionally* integrated into day-to-day programmes of living and learning, and/or there are sessions devoted to sound and music around once a week	2
Music and other auditory stimulation is *regularly* integrated into day-to-day programmes of living and learning, and these programmes are coherently related to sessions devoted to sound and music which occur around twice a week	3
Music and other auditory stimulation is *frequently* integrated into day-to-day programmes of living and learning, and these programmes are coherently related to sessions devoted to sound and music which occur around three or four times a week	4
Music and other auditory stimulation is *consistently* integrated into day-to-day programmes of living and learning, and these programmes are coherently related to sessions devoted to sound and music which occur every day	5

Scoring

Add the four 'element' scores and multiply by the 'consistency' score. Change in co-worker activity—and therefore change in the systematic exposure of a child or young person to sound—can be measured by comparing scores over a period or periods. The minimum score is 0 (where there is no available evidence) and the maximum is 100.

Proactive, level 1

P.1
Makes sounds unknowingly

General Observation

Children and young people make sounds apparently inadvertently: as a consequence of certain life-processes such as breathing, for example, or through haphazard movements of the limbs, head, or trunk. Sounds may be made *directly* (for example, by knocking against something) or *indirectly* (for instance, through accidentally tapping a switching device). Having made a sound, children appear to make no response (except, perhaps, a reflex reaction—see R.1). They do not try to repeat the movement to make the sound again.

Interpretation

Children and young people are unable to act on their environment, or are unaware of their capacity to do so—having no sense of *agency*.

Element P.1.A
The sounds made by life-processes are enhanced

Approaches

It may be possible to support the development of an awareness of the sounds made through life-processes through amplifying, enhancing, or otherwise modifying the children and young people's self-made sounds: intensifying the auditory feedback they would in any case receive. This may be achieved electronically, picking the sounds up using a microphone or specialist devices such as an electronic stethoscope, and then, for example, increasing the volume, altering tone colours, incorporating frequency modulation (where the pitch of one input is controlled by that of another), adding various types of reverberation, or repeating what is heard (through 'looping'). All these effects are relatively easy to achieve using commercially available equipment. As ever, teachers, therapists, and carers should note carefully anything to which the child or young person concerned may be starting to react.

Continued

Element P.1.A Cont.

Summary and examples

Life-processes	Simultaneous effects	Delayed effects
Breathing	Amplification	Reverberation
Vocal tract sounds	Pitch change	Echo
Heartbeat	Tone-colour change	Looping

Evidence

Children's and young people's self-made sounds do not change when enhanced feedback is provided.

Gauging co-worker input	Score
One sound made by life-processes is amplified	1
One or two sounds made by life-processes are amplified and modified in at least one way	2
Two or three sounds made by life-processes are amplified and modified in at least two ways	3
Two or three sounds made by life-processes are amplified and modified in at least three or four ways	4
Three sounds made by life-processes are amplified and modified in at least five ways	5

Element P.1.B

Involuntary movements are used to control or cause sounds

Approaches

It is possible to use the small movements associated with life that a young person may make without being aware of them (such as the rise and fall of the chest in breathing, blinking, or the twitches caused by muscle spasms) to cause or control sounds by proxy. The necessary interface may take the form of a sensitive electro-mechanical switch or pressure switch, or sounds may be triggered with no direct physical contact at all through an ultrasonic beam linked to a MIDI device (as in the 'Soundbeam'®). Using such equipment, even the most minimal of movement can be made to cause or control *any* sound (Ellis 2004).

Summary and Examples

Movement	Sensor	Output
Rise and fall of the chest	Ultrasonic beam	Single sounds are initiated by movement
Blinking	Pressure switch	Sound(s) are initiated and terminated by movements
Other involuntary movements	Movement switch	Variations in sounds are linked to the nature of movement

Evidence

No change in involuntary movements can be discerned when feedback is supplied (nor reactions to the sounds produced beyond reflex reactions).

Gauging co-worker input	Score
One involuntary movement is used to cause or control one type of sound in one way	1
One involuntary movement or more is used to cause or control two types of sound in one way	2
One involuntary movement or more is used to cause or control three types of sound in two ways	3
One involuntary movement or more is used to cause or control four types of sound in two ways	4
One involuntary movement or more is used to cause or control five types of sound or more in three ways	5

Element P.1.C
Sounds are made through co-active movements

Approaches

A widely held view (or at least, a widely observed approach!) is that children can be supported to develop an understanding of cause and effect through *co-activity*: that is, through assisting them to make the movements necessary to effect change in the environment (including creating or controlling sounds). For example, a co-worker's hand may be placed *under* a child's, so that he or she can potentially sense what is going on proprioceptively,[1] and a cognitive map of the necessary movements built up. A further (or alternative) approach is 'hand-over-hand'. Here, children and young people are guided to make the movements that are required.

Summary and examples

Means of sensing co-worker's movement	Means of being assisted to move	Means of making sound
'Hand-under-hand'	'Hand-over-hand'	Range of hand-held percussion
Fingers tapping with the child's fingers placed over them	Child is assisted to make tapping movements	Keyboard
Leg shaking next to child's leg	Child's leg is shaken	Drum machine
Swaying movement in contact with child	Child is swayed	Ankle bells
Head moving from side to side adjacent to child's head	Child's head is moved from side to side	Ultrasonic beam linked via MIDI

Evidence

Sounds are produced co-actively, but with no evidence of independent volition, and no reaction beyond reflexes to the sounds that are made.

Gauging co-worker input	Score
One type of sound is created, caused, or controlled through a co-active movement	1
Two types of sound or more are created, caused, or controlled through two co-active movements	2

Continued

[1] In relation to the child's sense of movement and position.

Element P.1.C Cont.

Gauging co-worker input	Score
Three types of sound or more are created, caused, or controlled through three co-active movements	3
Four types of sound or more are created, caused, or controlled through four co-active movements	4
Five types of sound or more are created, caused, or controlled through five co-active movements or more	5

Element P.1.D

Sounds are made accidentally through voluntary movements

Approaches

There are contrasting approaches that derive from competing philosophies of how a child who can make voluntary movements can best be supported to develop a sense of agency. It is possible to set up environments that are particularly conducive to sensorimotor interaction and allow children to discover for themselves how they can affect the world around them—at first wholly by chance, then through an iterative process of trial and improvement. This is the principle behind the 'Little Room' devised by the Danish teacher and psychologist Lilli Nielsen, who refers to her approach as 'active learning'. The Little Room is a plastic cuboid, open at the base and on one side, large enough for a small child to lie in completely or to accommodate the head and trunk of a teenager. A number of sound-makers are suspended from the top of the box and others are secured to the sides—all within reach of the supine user (Nielsen 1992). Any gross motor movement is almost guaranteed to make a sound, whose impact will be maximized by the high level of acoustic feedback that the confined environment offers. At the same time, the potential distractions of extraneous sounds are minimized. It is also possible to use switches and beams (as in R.1.B above).

Summary and examples

Movement	Means of making sound	Type of sound
Hand flaps	Small gong	Resonant metallic
Forearm moves to and fro	Suspended beads	Percussive wooden
Head moves from side to side	Bells on ankle/wrist	Jingling
Foot twitches	Ultrasonic beam	Single sound via switch and MIDI
Lower leg moves up and down	Switch	Series of sounds via switches and MIDI

Continued

Element P.1.D Cont.

Evidence

Sounds are made through voluntary movements, but there is no apparent reaction nor attempt to repeat them—hence a movement may continue in the same way regardless of whether it causes a sound or not, or if the sound is changed.

Gauging attainment and co-worker input	Score
One type of sound is created, caused, or controlled utilizing voluntary movement in at least one way	1
Two types of sound or more are created, caused, or controlled utilizing voluntary movement in two ways	2
Three types of sound or more are created, caused, or controlled utilizing voluntary movement in three ways	3
Four types of sound or more are created, caused, or controlled utilizing voluntary movement in four ways	4
Five types of sound or more are created, caused, or controlled utilizing voluntary movement in at least five ways	5

Gauging consistency (P.1)

Co-worker input	Score
The circumstances in which children and young people can create, cause, or control sound are *rarely* integrated into day-to-day programmes of living and learning, and/or there are sessions devoted to sound- and music-making around once a fortnight or less	1
The circumstances in which children and young people can create, cause, or control sound are *occasionally* integrated into day-to-day programmes of living and learning, and/or there are sessions devoted to sound- and music-making around once a week	2
The circumstances in which children and young people can create, cause, or control sound are *regularly* integrated into day-to-day programmes of living and learning, and these programmes are coherently related to sessions devoted to sound- and music-making which occur around twice a week	3
The circumstances in which children and young people can create, cause, or control sound are *frequently* integrated into day-to-day programmes of living and learning, and these programmes are related to sessions devoted to sound- and music-making which occur around three or four times a week	4

Continued

Gauging consistency (P.1) Cont.

Co-worker input	Score
The circumstances in which children and young people can create, cause, or control sound are *consistently* integrated into day-to-day programmes of living and learning, and these programmes are coherently related to sessions devoted to sound- and music-making which occur every day	5

Scoring

Add the four 'element' scores and multiply by the 'consistency' score. Change in co-worker activity—and therefore change in the systematic exposure of a child or young person to sound-making opportunities, and support and encouragement in making sounds—can be measured by comparing scores over a period or periods. The minimum score is 0 (where there is no available evidence) and the maximum is 100.

Interactive, level 1

I.1
Relates unwittingly through sound

General observation

Attempting to interact with children and young people through sound, either by responding to any sounds that they may produce or through offering them sounds in an effort to stimulate a response, has no apparent effect.

Interpretation

Children and young people have no sense of agency between 'self' and 'other' in the domain of sound.

Element I.1.A

Co-workers make sounds in an effort to stimulate responses

Approaches

Co-workers should follow their instincts, since (as we have seen, p. 67) humans intuitively know how to communicate with young children, simplifying what they do while exaggerating the salient features of their vocal efforts, using a sing-song quality in their voices, and employing a good deal of repetition—using sound as one element in a broader pattern of multisensory contact. Those seeking to interact can try different approaches, ranging from the gentle and the subtle to the loud and the brash, bearing in mind that a young person's threshold of arousal may vary from one occasion to another. In any case, co-workers need to be sensitive to any responses that may appear to be evoked, however idiosyncratic, all the while seeking to interpret a child's personal sounds and other reactions as attempts to communicate, reacting in turn to what he or she does (see I.1.B).

Summary and examples

Type of sound	Disposition of sounds	Other, simultaneous sensory input
Female voice(s)	Single sounds, surrounded by silence	Touch
Male voice(s)	Series of sounds the same	Movement
Non-pitched, percussive sounds	Simple patterns of sounds rising and/or falling in pitch	Visual
Pitched sounds	Simple patterns of other sounds changing in intensity and/or timbre	Scent
Clusters of sounds	Short chants or songs	Combinations

Continued

Element I.1.A Cont.

Evidence

Children and young people do not respond to co-workers' efforts to interact through making sounds.

Gauging attainment and co-worker input	Score
Co-worker uses one type of sound of a particular disposition with other simultaneous sensory input in efforts to stimulate a response	1
Co-worker uses sounds of two types or dispositions with other simultaneous sensory input in efforts to stimulate a response	2
Co-worker uses sounds of three types or dispositions with other simultaneous sensory input in efforts to stimulate a response	3
Co-worker uses sounds of four types or dispositions with other simultaneous sensory input in efforts to stimulate a response	4
Co-worker uses sounds of five types or dispositions with other simultaneous sensory input in efforts to stimulate a response	5

Element I.1.B

Co-workers respond empathetically through sound to any sounds (or other gestures) that are made

Approaches

Effective working at this level is all about keen observation and empathy. Necessarily, teachers, therapists and carers must start 'where the child is at'. It may well be necessary to wait, allowing time and space for the young person to act, while constantly being prepared to interpret any sound or other gesture that she or he may make as a signal in the context of early communication (Ockelford 2002a). As soon as anything happens, offer an appropriate response, remembering that the purpose is to support the child in developing a sense of agency in the context of another person. Intuition may suggest repeating (or varying) the sound that the child has made—though reactions should also be of a kind that co-workers consider the young person may find stimulating, enjoy, and so wish to experience again. It may be important to balance consistency in responses with one's intuitions as an interactive human being, in which variety is important too. Sound may be reinforced with other sensory input, including touch, movement, scent, and visual stimulation. As ever, it is a question of being imaginative but systematic.

Continued

Element I.1.B Cont.

Summary and examples

Influence of child's sounds on co-worker's	Variety of sounds used by co-worker	other simultaneous sensory input
Straightforward imitation of sound that is produced	Vocal	Touch
Exaggeration of features (such as contour)	Instrumental	Movement
Pitch change	Sounds amplified	Visual
Change of tone colour	Sounds played through resonance board	Scent
Multiple repetitions and/or variations	Electronically synthesized sounds	Combinations

Evidence

Empathetic co-worker responses produce no discernible reaction

Gauging attainment and co-worker input	Score
Co-worker responds to child or young person using one approach (for example, repetition)	1
Co-worker responds to child or young person using two approaches (for example, repetition and amplification)	2
Co-worker responds to child or young person using three approaches	3
Co-worker responds to child or young person using four approaches	4
Co-worker responds to child or young person using five approaches or more	5

Element I.1.C

Early interactive work is undertaken in a variety of contexts

Approaches

For young people in the very early stages of development, it may well be most appropriate for proto-interactive work to be undertaken on a one-to-one basis, with the young person and 'familiar' adult in close proximity, with the minimum of external distractions, and where sound features as one element in a broader pattern of multisensory contact. However, attempts to 'kick-start' interaction should rule nothing out, and different contexts—acoustic and social—should be tried systematically (see R.1.C).

Summary and examples

Acoustic environment	Social	Mode of transmission
'Familiar' one-to-one teaching/therapy space	With 'familiar' co-worker	Direct
Classroom	With other co-workers	Amplified/modified acoustically
Music room	With co-workers and classmates	Supplemented with vibration

Evidence

Notwithstanding the variety of contexts, at most only reflex responses and 'accidental' interactions occur.

Gauging attainment and co-worker input	Score
Interaction through sound is attempted in one social/acoustic context	1
Interaction through sound is attempted in two social/acoustic contexts	2
Interaction through sound is attempted in three social/acoustic contexts	3
Interaction through sound is attempted in four social/acoustic contexts	4
Interaction through sound is attempted in at least five social/acoustic contexts	5

Element I.1.D

Co-workers model interaction through sound

Approaches

Co-workers model simple interaction for the child or young person concerned—possibly as equal partners in a 'give and take' scenario, or with one taking the part of the child in a simulated teacher-pupil/therapist-client exchange. The modelling may start very simply with the first party producing a single sound followed immediately by the second party repeating it. From this most straightforward of situations, more extended and complex sequences of events may follow, involving turn-taking with a range of different sounds and modes of imitation.

Summary and examples

Nature of initial sound(s) in exchange	Nature of response	Pattern of interaction
Single consonant-vowel combination	No imitation	Single exchange
Repetition of single sound	Repetition	Two exchanges (the same)
Pattern formed by regular change	Variation	Three exchanges or more (the same)
Group formed by internal similarity	Transformation	Evolving exchanges

Evidence

Children and young people show no signs of recognizing the interactions that are modelled.

Gauging attainment and co-worker input	Score
Co-workers model one form of interaction	1
Co-workers model two forms of interaction	2
Co-workers model three forms of interaction	3
Co-workers model four forms of interaction	4
Co-workers model five forms of interaction or more	5

Gauging consistency (I.1)

Co-worker input	Score
The circumstances in which children and young people can potentially interact through sound or experience interaction are *rarely* integrated into day-to-day programmes of living and learning, and/or there are sessions devoted to sound- and music-making, which promote interaction, around once a fortnight or less	1
The circumstances in which children and young people can potentially interact through sound or experience interaction are *occasionally* integrated into day-to-day programmes of living and learning, and/or there are sessions devoted to sound- and music-making, which promote interaction, around once a week	2
The circumstances in which children and young people can potentially interact through sound or experience interaction are *regularly* integrated into day-to-day programmes of living and learning, and these programmes are coherently related to sessions devoted to sound- and music-making, which promote interaction, and occur around twice a week	3
The circumstances in which children and young people can potentially interact through sound or experience interaction are *frequently* integrated into day-to-day programmes of living and learning, and these programmes are related to sessions devoted to sound- and music-making, which promote interaction, and occur around three or four times a week	4
The circumstances in which children and young people can potentially interact through sound or experience interaction are *consistently* integrated into day-to-day programmes of living and learning, and these programmes are coherently related to sessions devoted to sound- and music-making, which promote interaction, and occur every day	5

Scoring

Add the four 'element' scores and multiply by the 'consistency' score. Change in co-worker activity—and therefore change in the systematic exposure of a child or young person to interaction through sound—can be measured by comparing scores over a period or periods. The minimum score is 0 (where there is no available evidence) and the maximum is 100.

References

Adamek, M., and Darrow, A.-A. (2005). *Music in Special Education*. Silver Spring, Md.: The American Music Therapy Association.

Aldridge, V. (1989). 'Moon and Music Notation', *British Journal of Visual Impairment* 7: 30.

Anastasi, A., and Levee, R. F. (1960). 'Intellectual Deficit and Musical Talent: A Case Report', *American Journal of Mental Deficiency* 64: 695–703.

Andersen, E., Dunlea, A., and Kekelis, L. (1984). 'Blind Children's Language: Resolving Some Differences', *Journal of Child Language* 11: 645–64.

Association of Professional Music Therapists (1992). *Music Therapy in the Education Service,* (2nd edn.) Cambridge: APMT.

Baharloo, S., Johnston, P. A., Service, A. K., Gitschier, J., and Fremier, N. B. (1998). 'Absolute Pitch: An Approach for Identification of Genetic and Nongenetic Components', *American Journal of Human Genetics* 62: 224–31.

Bailey, P. (1973). *They Can Make Music.* Oxford: Oxford University Press.

Balkwill, L. L., and Thompson, W. F. (1999). 'A Cross-cultural Investigation of the Perception of Emotion in Music: Psychophysical and Cultural Cues', *Music Perception* 17: 43–64.

Barrett, M. (2003). 'Meme Engineers: Children as Producers of Musical Culture', *International Journal of Early Years Education* 11(3): 195–212.

—— (2006). 'Inventing Songs, Inventing Worlds: The "Genesis" of Creative Thought and Activity in Young Children's Lives', *International Journal of Early Years Education* 14/3: 201–20.

Bashour, M., and Menassa, J. (2006). 'Retinopathy of Prematurity', <http://www.emedicine.com/oph/topic413.htm>.

Berliner, P. F. (1994). *Thinking in Jazz. The Infinite Art of Improvisation.* Chicago: The University of Chicago Press.

Berlioz, H. (1855/1858). *A Treatise upon Modern Instrumentation and Orchestration,* 2nd edn, trans. M. C. Clarke. London: Novello.

Boden, M. (2004). *The Creative Mind: Myths and Mechanisms,* 2nd edn. London: Routledge.

British Society for Music Therapy (1998). *Information Booklet.* East Barnet: BSMT.

Bruhn, H. (2000). *Musiktherapie: Geschichte, Theorien, Grundlagen.* Göttingen: Hogrefe.

Bruscia, K. E. (1987). *Improvisational Models of Music Therapy.* Springfield, Ill. Charles C. Thomas.

Bunt, L. (1994). *Music Therapy: An Art Beyond Words.* London: Routledge.

Byers, R. (2003). Editorial, *British Journal of Special Education* 30/4: 174.

Chávez, C. (1961). *Musical Thought.* Cambridge, Mass.: Harvard University Press.

Childs, J. (1996). *Making Music: Special Practical Ways to Create Music*. London: David Fulton.

Clayton, M., Sager, R., and Will, U. (2004). 'In Time with the Music: The Concept of Entrainment and its Significance for Ethnomusicology', *ESEM CounterPoint*, 1: 1–45.

Cohen, J. E. (1962). 'Information Theory and Music', *Behavioural Science* 7: 137–63.

Corke, M. (2002). *Approaches to Communication through Music*. London: David Fulton.

Crowder, R. G. (1985). 'Perception of the Major/Minor Distinction: III. Hedonic, Musical, and Affective Discriminations', *Bulletin of the Psychonomic Society* 23: 314–16.

Davidson, R. (1994). 'On Emotion, Mood, and Related Affective Constructs', in Paul Ekman and Richard Davidson (eds), *The Nature of Emotion: Fundamental Questions*. Oxford: Oxford University Press.

Davies, J. B. (1978). *The Psychology of Music*. London: Hutchinson.

Deutsch, D. (1999). 'Grouping Mechanisms in Music', in D. Deutsch (ed.), *The Psychology of Music*, 2nd edn. New York: Academic Press, pp. 299–348.

Dickinson, P. (1978). *Music with E.S.N. Children*. London: NFER.

Dobbs, J. P. B. (1966). *The Slow Learner and Music: A Handbook for Teachers*. London: Oxford University Press.

Dowling, W. J. (1982). 'Melodic Information Processing and its Development', in D. Deutsch (ed.), *The Psychology of Music*. New York: Academic Press, pp. 413–29.

Eliot, T. S. (1920/1997). *The Sacred Wood: Essays on Poetry and Criticism*. London: Faber and Faber.

—— (1933). *The Use of Poetry and the Use of Criticism*. London: Faber and Faber.

Ellis, P. (1996). *Sound Therapy: The Music of Sound*. Bristol: The Soundbeam Project.

—— (2004). 'Moving Sound', in M. MacLachlan and P. Gallagher (eds), *Enabling Technologies—Body Image and Body Function*. London: Churchill Livingstone, pp. 59–75.

Eschman, K. (1945/1968). *Changing Forms in Modern Music*, 2nd edn. Boston, Mass.: E. C. Schirmer Music Company.

Fassbender, C. (1996). 'Infants' Auditory Sensitivity towards Acoustic Parameters of Speech and Music', in I. Deliège and J. A. Sloboda, *Musical Beginnings*. Oxford: Oxford University Press, pp. 56–87.

Forte, A. (1973). *The Structure of Atonal Music*. New Haven: Yale University Press.

Gaab, N., Schulze, K., Ozdemir, E., and Schlaug, G. (2006). 'Neural Correlates of Absolute Pitch Differ between Blind and Sighted Musicians', *NeuroReport* 17/18: 1853–7.

Gabrielsson, A., and Lindström, E. (2001). 'The Influence of Musical Structure on Emotional Expression', in P. N. Juslin and J. A. Sloboda, *Music and Emotion: Theory and Research*. Oxford: Oxford University Press, pp. 223–48.

Gaver, W. (1993). 'What in the World do we Hear? An Ecological Approach to Auditory Event Perception', *Ecological Psychology* 5: 1–29.

Gundlach, R. H. (1935). 'Factors Determining the Characterization of Musical Phrases', *American Journal of Psychology* 47: 624–44.

Hamilton, R. H., Pascual-Leone, A., and Schlaug, G. (2004). 'Absolute Pitch in Blind Musicians', *NeuroReport* 15/5: 803–6.

Hargreaves, D. J. (1986). *The Developmental Psychology of Music*. Cambridge: Cambridge University Press.

—— and North, A. C. (1997). *The Social Psychology of Music*. Oxford: Oxford University Press.

Heaton, P. (2003). 'Pitch Memory, Labelling and Disembedding in Autism', *Journal of Child Psychology and Psychiatry* 44/4: 543–51.

Hevner, K. (1936). 'Experimental Studies of the Elements of Expression in Music', *Amercian Journal of Psychology* 48: 246–68.

Heyes, T. (1997). 'The Musical Journey', in I. Rødbroe and T. Heyes, *Communication through Active Music* (video and booklet). London: Royal National Institute for Deaf People.

Hill, A. L. (1974). 'Idiots Savants: Rates of Incidence', *Perceptual and Motor Skills* 44: 12–13.

Huron, D. (2001). 'Tone and Voice: A Derivation of the Rules of Voice-Leading from Perceptual Principles', *Music Perception* 19/1: 1–64.

—— and Fantini, D. (1989). 'The Avoidance of Inner-Voice Entries: Perceptual Evidence and Musical Practice', *Music Perception* 7/1: 43–7.

Jackson, M. (1987). 'The Moon System Adapted for Musical Notation', *British Journal of Visual Impairment* 5: 93–7.

James, W. (1890). *The Principles of Psychology*. Available on the internet at <http://psychclassics.yorku.ca/James/Principles/index.htm>.

Jaquiss, V., and Paterson, D. (2005). *Meeting SEN in the Curriculum: Music*. London: David Fulton.

Jariazbhoy, N. (1971). *The Ragas of North Indian Music*. Middletown: Wesleyan University Press.

Johnson-Laird, P. N., and Oatley, K. (1992). 'Basic Emotions, Rationality, and Folk Theory', *Cognition and Emotion* 6/3: 201–23.

Judd, T. (1988). 'The Varieties of Musical Talent', in L. K. Obler and D. Fein, *The Exceptional Brain: Neuropsychology of Talent and Special Abilities*, pp. 127–55. New York: The Guilford Press.

Juslin, P. N. (1997). 'Perceived Emotional Expression in Synthesized Performances of a Short Melody: Capturing the Listener's Judgement Policy', *Musicae Scientiae* 1: 225–56.

—— Friberg, A., and Bresin, R. (2001–2). 'Toward a Computational Model of Expression in Music Performance: The GERM Model', *Musicae Scientiae, Special Issue: Current Trends in the Study of Music and Emotion*, 63–122.

—— and Sloboda, J. A. (2001). *Music and Emotion: Theory and Research*. Oxford: Oxford University Press.

Kessen, W., Levine, J., and Wendrich, K. (1979). 'The Imitation of Pitch in Infants', *Infant Behavior and Development* 2: 93–100.

Krumhansl, C. (1990). *Cognitive Foundations of Musical Pitch*. Oxford: Oxford University Press.

—— (1997). 'An Exploratory Study of Musical Emotions and Psychophysiology, *Canadian Journal of Experimental Psychology* 51: 336–52.

Kuhl, P. K., and Meltzoff, A. N. (1982). 'The Bimodal Perception of Speech in Infancy', *Science* 218: 1138–41.

Kumar, H., and Singha, U. (1997). 'Retinopathy of Prematurity: Clinical Aspects', *Community Eye Health Journal* 10/22: 19–22.

Lauchlan, F., and Boyle, C. (2007). 'Is the Use of Labels in Special Education Helpful?', *British Journal of Learning Support* 22/1: 36–42.

Lecanuet, J.-P. (1996). 'Prenatal Auditory Experience', in I. Deliège and J. A. Sloboda, *Musical Beginnings*. Oxford: Oxford University Press, pp. 3–34.

Lee, M., and MacWilliam, L. (2002). *Learning Together*. London: Royal National Institute of the Blind.

Legerstee, M. (1990). 'Infants Use Multimodal Information to Imitate Speech Sounds', *Infant Behavior and Development* 13: 343–54.

Lenhoff, H. M. (2006). 'Absolute Pitch and Neuroplasticity in Williams-Beuren Syndrome', in C. A. Morris, H. M. Lenhoff and P. P. Wang, *Williams-Beuren Syndrome: Research, Evaluation, and Treatment*. Baltimore, Maryland: The John Hopkins University Press, pp. 325–42.

—— Perales, O., and Hickok, G. (2001). 'Absolute Pitch in Williams Syndrome', *Music Perception* 18: 491–503.

Lerdahl, F., and Jackendoff, R. (1983). *A Generative Theory of Tonal Music*. Cambridge, Mass.: MIT Press.

Levitin, D. J., Cole. K., Chiles, M., Lai, Z., Lincoln, A., and Bellugi, U. (2006). 'Characterizing the Musical Phenotype in Individuals with Williams Syndrome', *Child Neuropsychology (Neuropsychology, Development and Cognition: Section C)* 10/4: 223–47.

—— and Zatorre, R. J. (2003). 'On the Nature of Early Music Training and Absolute Pitch', *Music Perception* 21/1: 105–10.

Lewin, D. (1987). *Generalized Musical Intervals and Transformations*. New Haven: Yale University Press.

London, J. (2001–2). 'Some Theories of Emotion in Music and their Implications for Research in Music Psychology', *Musicae Scientiae, Special Issue: Current Trends in the Study of Music and Emotion*, 23–35.

Longhorn, F. (1988). *A Sensory Curriculum for Very Special People*. London: Souvenir Press.

Lowes, J. L. (1927). *The Road to Xanadu: A Study in the Ways of the Imagination*. Boston: Houghton Mifflin.

Maess, B., Koelsch, S., Gunter, T. C., and Friederici, A. D. (2001). 'Musical Syntax is Processed in Broca's Area: An MEG Study', *Nature Neuroscience* 4: 540–5.

Malloch, S. N. (1999–2000). 'Mothers and Infants and Communicative Musicality', *Musicae Scientiae, Special Issue: Rhythm, Musical Narrative and Origins and Human Communication*, 29–57.

Mang, E. (2005). 'The Referent of Early Children's Songs', *Music Education Research* 7/1: 3–20.

Marshall, N., and Hargreaves, D. J. (2005). 'Musical Style Discrimination in the Early Years', *Journal of Early Childhood Research* 5/1: 32–46.

Mehta, A., and Dattani, M. (2004). 'Clinical Aspects of Septo-optic Dysplasia'. *Eye Contact* 38: 5–7.

Meltzoff, A., and Prinz, W. (2002). *The Imitative Mind: Development, Evolution and Brain Bases*. Cambridge: Cambridge University Press.

Merton, R. K. (1968). *Social Theory and Social Structure*. New York: Free Press.

Mervis, C. A., Yeargin-Allsopp, M., Winter, S., and Boyle, C. (2000). 'Aetiology of childhood vision impairment, metropolitan Atlanta, 1991–1993', *Paediatric and Perinatal Epidemiology* 14: 70–7.

Meyer, L. B. (1956). *Emotion and Meaning in Music*. Chicago: The University of Chicago Press.

—— (1967). *Music, the Arts, and Ideas.* Chicago: The University of Chicago Press.

—— (1973). *Explaining Music.* Chicago: The University of Chicago Press.

—— (1989). *Style and Music: Theory, History, and Ideology.* Philadelphia: University of Philadelphia Press.

—— (2001). 'Music and Emotion: Distinctions and Uncertainties', in P. N. Juslin and J. A. Sloboda, *Music and Emotion: Theory and Research.* Oxford: Oxford University Press, pp. 341–60.

Miller, L. (1989). *Musical Savants; Exceptional Skill in the Mentally Retarded.* Hillsdale, NJ: Lawrence Erlbaum Associates.

Miller, O., and Ockelford, A. (2005). *Visual Needs.* London: Continuum.

Moog, H. (1968/1976). *The Musical Experiences of the Pre-school Child,* trans. C. Clarke. London: Schott.

Morris, R. D. (1995). 'Equivalence and Similarity in Pitch and their Interaction with pcset Theory', *Journal of Music Theory* 39: 207–43.

Narmour, E. (2000). 'Music Expectations by Cognitive Rule-Mapping', *Music Perception* 17: 329–98.

Nattiez, J.-J. (1990). *Music and Discourse: Toward a Semiology of Music,* trans. C. Abbate. Princeton: Princeton University Press.

Nettelbeck, T., and Young, R. (1996). 'Intelligence and Savant Syndrome: Is the Whole Greater than the Sum of the Fragments?', *Intelligence* 22: 49–68.

Nielsen, L. (1992). *Space and Self.* Copenhagen: Sikon Press.

Nielzén, S., and Cesarec, Z. (1982). 'Emotional Experience of Music as a Function of Musical Structure', *Psychology of Music* 10: 7–17.

Nordoff, P., and Robbins, C. (1971). *Therapy in Music for Handicapped Children.* London: Victor Gollancz.

Ockelford, A. (1988). 'Some Observations Concerning the Musical Education of Blind Children and those with Additional Handicaps', paper presented at the 32nd Conference of the *Society for Research in Psychology of Music and Music Education* (now *SEMPRE*) at the University of Reading.

—— (1991) 'The Role of Repetition in Perceived Musical Structures', in P. Howell, R. West, and I. Cross (eds), *Representing Musical Structure.* London: Academic Press, pp. 129–60.

—— (1993). 'A Theory Concerning the Cognition of Order in Music', Ph.D. diss., University of London.

—— (1994). *Objects of Reference: Promoting Communication Skills and Concept Development with Visually Impaired Children who have Other Disabilities.* London: Royal National Institute of the Blind.

—— (1996a). *All join in! A Framework for Making Music with Children and Young People who are Visually Impaired and have Learning Disabilities* (CD, 24 songs and teaching materials). London: Royal National Institute of the Blind.

—— (1996b). *Music Matters: Factors in the Music Education of Children and Young People who are Visually Impaired.* London: Royal National Institute of the Blind.

—— (1996c). *Points of Contact: A Braille Approach to Alphabetic Music Notation.* London: Braille Authority of the United Kingdom.

—— (1998a). *Sound Moves: Making Music with Children who have Severe or Profound and Multiple Learning Disabilities* (video). London: Royal National Institute of the Blind.

—— (1998b). *Music Moves: Music in the Education of Children and Young People who are Visually Impaired and have Learning Disabilities.* London: Royal National Institute of the Blind.

—— (1999). *The Cognition of Order in Music: A Metacognitive Study.* London: Roehampton Institute.

—— (2000). 'Music in the Education of Children with Severe or Profound Learning Difficulties: Issues in Current UK Provision, a New Conceptual Framework, and Proposals for Research', *Psychology of Music* 28/2: 197–217.

—— (2002*a*). *Objects of Reference: Promoting Early Symbolic Communication,* 3rd edn. London: Royal National Institute of the Blind.

—— (2002*b*). 'The Magical Number Two, Plus or Minus One: Some Limitations on our Capacity for Processing Musical Information', *Musicae Scientiae* 6: 177–215.

—— (2003). 'Focus on Music', *Focal Points* 2/3, available at <www.wisconsinmedicalsociety.org/savant/sodarticle.pdf>.

—— (2004). 'On Similarity, Derivation and the Cognition of Musical Structure', *Psychology of Music* 32/1: 23–74.

—— (2005*a*). *Repetition in Music: Theoretical and Metatheoretical Perspectives.* London: Ashgate.

—— (2005*b*). 'Sound Track', in O. Miller and A. Ockelford, *Visual Needs.* London: Continuum, pp. 49–72.

—— (2005*c*). *Making Sense of Music Making Sense.* Unpublished Music Education Research Seminar held at Institute of Education, University of London on 18th May, (PowerPoint available from the author).

—— (2005*d*). 'Musical Structure, Content and Aesthetic Response: Beethoven's Op. 110', *Journal of the Royal Musical Association* 129/2: 74–118.

—— (2006*a*). 'Implication and Expectation in Music: A Zygonic Model', *Psychology of Music* 34/1: 81–142.

—— (2006*b*). 'Using a Music-Theoretical Approach to Interrogate Musical Development and Social Interaction', in N. Lerner and J. Straus (eds), *Sounding Off: Theorizing Disability in Music.* New York: Routledge, pp. 137–55.

—— (2007*a*). *In the Key of Genius: The Extraordinary Life of Derek Paravicini.* London: Hutchinson.

—— (2007*b*). 'Exploring Musical Interaction Between a Teacher and Pupil, and her Evolving Musicality, Using a Music-Theoretical Approach', *Research Studies in Music Education* 28: 3–23.

—— and Pring, L. (2005). 'Learning and Creativity in a Prodigious Musical Savant', *International Congress Series* 1282: 903–7.

—— Pring, L., Welch, G. F., and Treffert, D. A. (2006). *Focus on Music: Exploring the Musical Interests and Abilities of Blind and Partially-Sighted Children with Septo-Optic Dysplasia.* London: Institute of Education.

—— Welch, G. F., and Pring, L. (2005). 'Musical Interests and Abilities of Children with Septo-optic Dysplasia', *International Congress Series* 1282: 894–7.

—— Welch, G. F., and Zimmermann, S. (2002). 'Music Education for Pupils with Severe or Profound and Multiple Difficulties', *British Journal of Special Education* 29/4: 178–82.

O'Connor, N., Cowan, R., and Samella, K. (2000). 'Calendric Calculation and Intelligence', *Intelligence* 28: 31–48.

Ofsted (2004). *Provision of Music Services in 15 Local Education Authorities. (HHI 2296).* London: Ofsted.

O'Neill, S. A., and Boulton, M. J. (1996). 'Males' and Females' Preferences for Musical Instruments: A Function of Gender?', *Psychology of Music* 24: 171–83.

Overy, K. (1998). Discussion Note: 'Can Music really "Improve" the Mind?', *Psychology of Music* 25: 97–9.

Papoušek, H. (1996). 'Musicality in Infancy Research: Biological and Cultural Origins of Early Musicality', in I. Deliège and J. A. Sloboda, *Musical Beginnings*. Oxford: Oxford University Press, pp. 37–55.

Papoušek, M. (1996). 'Intuitive Parenting: A Hidden Source of Musical Stimulation in Infancy', in I. Deliège and J. A. Sloboda, *Musical Beginnings*. Oxford: Oxford University Press, pp. 88–112.

Peretz, I. Gagnon, L., and Bouchard, B. (1998). 'Music and Emotion: Perceptual Determinants, Immediacy, and Isolation after Brain Damage', *Cognition* 68: 111–41.

Peters, M., and Wills, P. (1995). *Music for All*. London: David Fulton.

Petran, L. A. (1932). 'An Experimental Study of Pitch Recognition', *Psychological Monographs* 42: 1–124.

Postacchini, P. L., Borghesi, M., Flucher, B., Guida, L., Mancini, M., Nocentini, P., Rubin, L., and Santoni, S. (1993). 'A Case of Severe Infantile Regression Treated by Music Therapy and Explored in Group Supervision', in M. Heal and T. Wigram (eds), *Music Therapy in Health and Education*. London: Jessica Kingsley, pp. 26–31.

Pring, L. (2005) (ed.). *Autism and Blindness: Current Research and Reflections*. London: Wharr Publishers.

—— and Ockelford, A. (2005). 'Children with Septo-optic Dysplasia—Musical Interests, Abilities and Provision: The Results of a Parental Survey', *British Journal of Visual Impairment* 23/2: 58–66.

Qualifications and Curriculum Authority (2001). *Plannning, Teaching and Assessing the Curriculum for Pupils with Learning Difficulties*. London: QCA.

Rahi, J. S., and Cable, N. (2003). 'Severe Visual Impairment and Blindness in Children in the UK', *Lancet* 362: 1359–65.

Rahn, Jay (1983). *A Theory for all Music: Problems and Solutions in the Analysis of Non-Western Forms*. Toronto: University of Toronto Press.

Rahn, John (1980). *Basic Atonal Theory*. New York: Schirmer Music Books.

Réti, R. (1951). *The Thematic Process in Music*. Westport, Conn.: Greenwood Press.

Rimland, B. (1978). *Infantile Autism: The Syndrome and its Implications for a Neural Theory of Behavior*. New York: Appleton-Century-Crofts.

Rimland, B., and Fein, D. (1988). 'Special Talents of Autistic Savants', in L. K. Obler and D. Fein, *The Exceptional Brain: Neuropsychology of Talent and Special Abilities*. New York: The Guilford Press, pp. 474–92.

Robertson, J. (2000). 'An Educational Model for Music Therapy: The Case for a Continuum', *British Journal of Music Therapy* 14/1: 41–6.

Rødbroe, I. (1997). 'The Changing Focus in Developing Communication with Congenitally Deafblind People', in I. Rødbroe and T. Heyes, *Communication through Active Music* (video and booklet). London: Royal National Institute for Deaf People.

Ruwet, N. (1966/87). 'Methods of Analysis in Musicology', trans. M. Everist, *Music Analysis* 6: 3–36.

Scherer, K. R. (1991). 'Emotion Expression in Speech and Music', in J. Sundberg, L. Nord and R. Carlson (eds), *Music, Language, Speech and Brain*. London: Macmillan, pp. 146–56.

—— Banse, R., and Wallbott, H. G. (2001). 'Emotion Inferences from Vocal Expression

Correlate across Languages and Cultures', *Journal of Cross-Cultural Psychology* 32/1: 76–92.

—— and Oshinsky, J. (1977) 'Cue Utilization in Emotion Attribution from Auditory Stimuli', *Motivation and Emotion* 1: 336–46.

—— and Zentner, M. R. (2001). 'Emotion Effects of Music: Production Rules', in P. N. Juslin and J. A. Sloboda, *Music and Emotion: Theory and Research*. Oxford: Oxford University Press, pp. 361–92.

Schwalkwijk, F. W. (1994). *Music and People with Developmental Disabilities*. London: Jessica Kingsley.

Selincourt, B. de (1920). 'Music and Duration', *Music and Letters* 1: 286–93. In S. K. Langer (ed.) (1958). *Reflections on Art*. Oxford: Oxford University Press, pp. 152–60.

Sergeant, D. (1969). 'Experimental Investigation of Absolute Pitch', *Journal of Research in Music Education* 17: 135–43.

Sloboda, J. A. (1985/2005). 'Immediate Recall of Melodies', in J. A. Sloboda, *Exploring the Musical Mind: Cognition, Emotion, Ability, Function*. Oxford: Oxford University Press, pp. 71–96.

—— (1996/2005). 'The Acquisition of Performance Expertise: Deconstructing the "Talent" Account of Individual Differences in Musical Expressivity', in J. A. Sloboda, *Exploring the Musical Mind: Cognition, Emotion, Ability, Function*. Oxford: Oxford University Press, pp. 275–96.

—— O'Neill, S. A., and Ivaldi, A. (2001). 'Functions of Music in Everyday Life: An Exploratory Study Using the Experience Sampling Methodology', *Musicae Scientiae* 5/1: 9–32.

Snyder, B. (2000). *Music and Memory: An Introduction*. Cambridge, Mass.: MIT Press.

Sparshott, F. (1994). 'Music and Feeling', *Journal of Aesthetics and Art Criticism* 52/1: 23–35.

Streeter, E. (1993/2001). *Making Music with the Young Child with Special Needs*. London: Jessica Kingsley.

Swanwick, K. (1991). 'Further Research on the Developmental Spiral', *Psychology of Music* 19: 22–32.

—— and Tillman, J. (1986). 'The Sequence of Musical Development: A Study of Children's Composition', *British Journal of Music Education* 16/1: 5–19.

Takeuchi, A. H., and Hulse, S. H. (1993). 'Absolute Pitch', *Psychological Bulletin* 113/2: 345–61.

Tarrant, M., Hargreaves, D. J., and North, A. C. (2002). 'Youth Identity and Music', in R. A. R. MacDonald, D. J. Hargreaves and D. E. Miell (eds), *Musical Identities*. Oxford: Oxford University Press.

Thompson, W. F., and Robitaille, B. (1992). 'Can Composers Express Emotions through Music?', *Empirical Studies of the Arts* 10: 79–89.

Treffert, D. A. (1989/2000). *Extraordinary People: Understanding Savant Syndrome*. Lincoln, Nebr.: iUniverse.com (originally published 1989 in New York by Harper and Row).

Trehub, S. E. (1990). 'The Perception of Musical Patterns by Human Infants: The Provision of Similar Patterns by their Parents', in M. A. Berkley and W. C. Stebbins (eds), *Comparative Perception*, Vol. 1: *Mechanisms*. New York: Wiley, pp. 429–59.

—— and Nakata, T. (2001–2). 'Emotion and Music in Infancy', *Musicae Scientiae Musicae Scientiae, Special Issue: Current Trends in the Study of Music and Emotion*, 37–61.

Trevarthen, C. (2002). 'Origins of Musical Identity: Evidence from Infancy for Musical Social Awareness', in R. A. R. Macdonald, D. J. Hargreaves and D. E. Miell (eds), *Musical Identities*. Oxford: Oxford University Press, pp. 21–38.

Vraka, M. (2008). *The Cultural Influence on the Development of Absolute Pitch*, Ph.D. thesis in progress, University of London, Institute of Education.

Watson, K. B. (1942). 'The Nature and Measurement of Musical Meanings', *Psychological Monographs* 54: 1–43.

Webster, A., and Roe, J. (1998). *Children with Visual Impairments: Social Interaction, Language and Learning*. London: Routledge.

Welch, G. F. (1988). 'Observations on the Incidence of Absolute Pitch (AP) in the early blind', *Psychology of Music* 16/1: 77–80.

—— (1991). 'Visual Metaphors for Sound: A Study of Mental Imagery, Language and Pitch Perception in the Congenitally Blind', *Canadian Journal of Research in Music Education* 33, Special ISME Research Edition.

—— (2001). *The Misunderstanding of Music*. London: Institute of Education, University of London.

—— (2006). 'The Musical Development and Education of Young Children', in B. Spodek and O. Saracho (eds), *Handbook of Research on the Education of Young Children*. Mahwah, NJ: Lawrence Erlbaum Associates, pp. 251–67.

—— Ockelford, A., and Zimmermann, S. (2001). *Provision of Music in Special Education ('PROMISE')*. London: Institute of Education and Royal National Institute of the Blind

Wood, M. (1983/1993). *Music for People with Learning Disabilities*. Guernsey: Guernsey Press.

Zbikowski, L. (2002). *Conceptualizing Music: Cognitive Structure, Theory, and Analysis*. New York: Oxford University Press.

Zuckerkandl, V. (1956). *Sound and Symbol: Music and the External World*. New York: Pantheon Books.

Index